Romania Revisited

On the Trail of English Travellers, 1602-1941

Alan Ogden

Romania Revisited

On the Trail of English Travellers, 1602-1941

The Center for Romanian Studies
Las Vegas ◊ Oxford ◊ Palm Beach

Published in the United States of America by
Histria Books, a division of Histria LLC
7181 N. Hualapai Way, Ste. 130-86
Las Vegas, NV 89166 USA
HistriaBooks.com

The Center for Romanian Studies is an imprint of Histria Books. Titles published under the imprints of Histria Books are distributed worldwide.

Second Printing, 2021

Library of Congress Control Number: 2020951022

ISBN 978-973-9432-05-4 (hardcover)
ISBN 978-1-59211-104-6 (paperback)

Table of Contents

Appendices

Introduction

Romania Revisited is a light-hearted account of two journeys I made to Romania in the summer and winter of 1998. In it, I draw on the experiences of previous travellers, up to 1941, to contrast what I found in comparison to them. Inevitably, this has introduced an element of nostalgia for the onward march of the twentieth century in Romania did not discriminate between the good and the bad, the beautiful and the ugly.

Since the fall of the Ceauşescus in 1989, much of the news coming out of Romania has been grim, of Aids-infected children left to rot in appalling conditions in under-funded orphanages, and of abandoned teenagers living in subways under the streets of Bucharest. All of it is true. Yet, this sort of coverage distorts the real picture of the country, its history and culture. In this book, I have tried to give a very general background, enlarging the canvas for the reader through the perspective of history and focusing on the extraordinarily rich and diverse cultural heritage of the country.

I have used as my starting point the accounts of previous travellers from before the Second World War since their accounts make a benchmark on which to calibrate today's Romania. Their style is generally admirable since it is not restricted to "this-is-what-I-did," which may or not be of interest; it extends to include those critical dimensions of historical perspective and cultural observation in the broadest sense — painting, poetry, architecture, fashion, religion, ethnology and genealogy, to name a few. Since their names often crop up more than once, I have used the device of putting the date of their travels or publication as a footnote to help the reader keep chronological track.

Some of the travellers like Patrick Leigh Fermor, Stephen Runciman and Ivor Porter published their accounts of Romania long after 1941 but their testimony was pre-war and it is essential to my theme. Their dates are shown in the text as the year of their travels. Although I have used 'English travellers' in the title, several were American and Canadian, some were French and German, a few Romanian and poor Ovid, that most reluctant of travellers, was Roman. What they all have in common is that their work has been published in the English language.

In the course of my research, every time I thought I had exhausted the list of travellers, I came across yet another one, often on the way back from Russia or the Caucasus. My final tally thus remains about 90% complete and given that my starting point was Sitwell's claim that "English literature is nearly silent where that country (Romania) is concerned," some very real progress has been made.

A few travellers like William Wilkinson (1820) are disappointingly judgmental in their views; fortunately the majority follow Charles Boner's dictum of 1858: "We in England are far too much accustomed to judge other countries and their institutions by an English standard, and to condemn arrangements unlike our own, without considering their origin or fittingness for certain conditions of a land and people". Without such an approach, the history and behaviour of Romanians is more often than not quite baffling. Cultural relativism may be today's 'contemporary cant'[1] and excuse travellers from making any moral judgements, but its validity in recognising others' values and experiences is, for me, unquestionable.

Why stop in 1941? Quite simply, after that date, the eclectic style and expressionism which, together, were the driving forces behind Romania's reputation for the exotic were shunted off into a siding of history where they were left to languish. They were replaced by an ideology that in public denied creativity and individuality and in private aped the worst excesses of philistinism and vulgarity. For forty long years, that crazy mélange of cultures, which had fascinated travellers for over three hundred years, was stifled; the Romanian genius for creating its own identity was suffocated. Only in the first days of 1990 did the oxygen of freedom return and begin to restore that priceless pride of being "Romanian."

My intention is certainly not to glamorise epochs when the vast majority of people received scant education and lacked most other forms of social support, which are fundamental to a modern society. But I sense there is now a will to recall the esprit and élan that once characterised Ro-

---

[1] Robert Carver: *The Accursed Mountains,* 1998.

mania, that alluring combination of panache and eccentricity which a rather staid world found endearing, if at times rather shocking.

Throughout my travels, the friendship and hospitality of the Romanian people were unstinting and tremendously warm. In spite of the horrors they have endured in the twentieth century — the ruthless suppression of a peasants' revolt in 1907, the heaviest per capita losses of the First World War[2], the scourge of fascism in the Second, followed by Stalinist terror and then rule by the invidious security apparatus of a megalomaniac — the Romanian people have emerged with their individual values of tolerance and decency intact. Above all, they are warm and fun which is what I have tried to convey in this book.

I would like to thank all those who have given me their time, advice, and support. My wife Jose for her uncomplaining stint as a literary 'grass widow'; Norina Constantinescu for her support and encouragement in Romania; Aida Ionescu for her courage in joining up as an interpreter on both journeys; Lindsey Gulley for acting as unpaid typist and IT wizard in London; Sarah Whitebloom for her constructive criticism and eagle-eyed proof reading skills; Şerban Cantacuzino for his advice on the history and architecture of Romania; the dedicated staff of the British Library for their courteous and efficient service; and to my publisher, Kurt W Treptow, who, from the beginning, believed in the project far more than I did myself.

Alan Ogden
London, March 1999

[2] Romania's military losses were 4.8% of her pre-war population, compared to France 3.5%, Germany 3.25% and Great Britain 1.6%

Map Symbols

At various points throughout the book, the text is accompanied by hand drawn maps, outlining the route followed by the author in his travels throughout Romania. Below is a key to the map symbols.

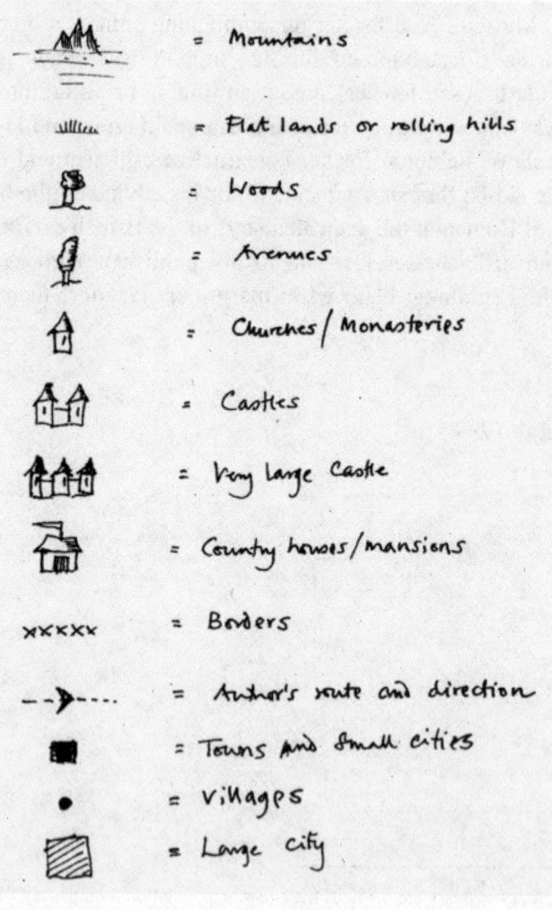

The Photographs

Whenever possible, I tried to use the same vistas as Kurt Hielscher did in 1931. His book, *Roumanie,* is by far the best photographic record ever assembled of pre-war Romania. He spent very nearly two years travelling around the country, covering over 25,000 kilometers and taking over 5,000 photographs. "To his regret," he was only able to publish 304. But what photographs they are — of the churches and princely courts, of peasants and their countryside. Hielscher knew that he was witnessing the end to an age-old style of life and wrote:

> At the same time as enjoying compiling my book, I also felt a sadness of seeing all this national culture of Roumania threatened by an implacable enemy which comes from the West: the civilization which snuffs out everything which is primesautier. More than one village had already been contaminated. The colours of the furniture and of the costumes had been replaced by the grey uniformity of current fashion.

Thanks to the Romanian government of the time who sponsored him and to Hielscher himself, one of the great ethnographic photographers of this century, we have a unique record of old Romania against which to measure the present. And, looking through my lens, what did I find? Costumes had changed nearly everywhere and the old peasant clothes consigned to folk museums or festivals. Yet, in much of the country, the way of life remained the same, based on self-sufficiency and centuries-old traditions of subsistence farming. The landscape too had survived in those areas not subjected to collectivisation. And, miraculously, so had the fortified churches of the Saxons — but for how long, now that their congregations have departed?

Compared to Hielscher's day, some towns like Mangalia and Constanţa were unrecognisable; others like Iaşi, barely. Occasionally, as in the case of Sibiu and Mediaş, they were virtually identical. The greatest contrast between Hielscher's record of 1931 and today was undoubtedly the post-war industrialisation that has left permanent scars on the landscape. No more fitting example than Hunedoara illustrates this tragedy, with its thirteenth century castle clamped on either side by iron and steel works. Of course, this spoilage is not limited to Romania but somehow, in its soft and sensual landscape, the impact is more devastating.

Romania Revisited

On the Trail of English Travellers, 1602-1941

Summer

The road down to the Moldovița Monastery

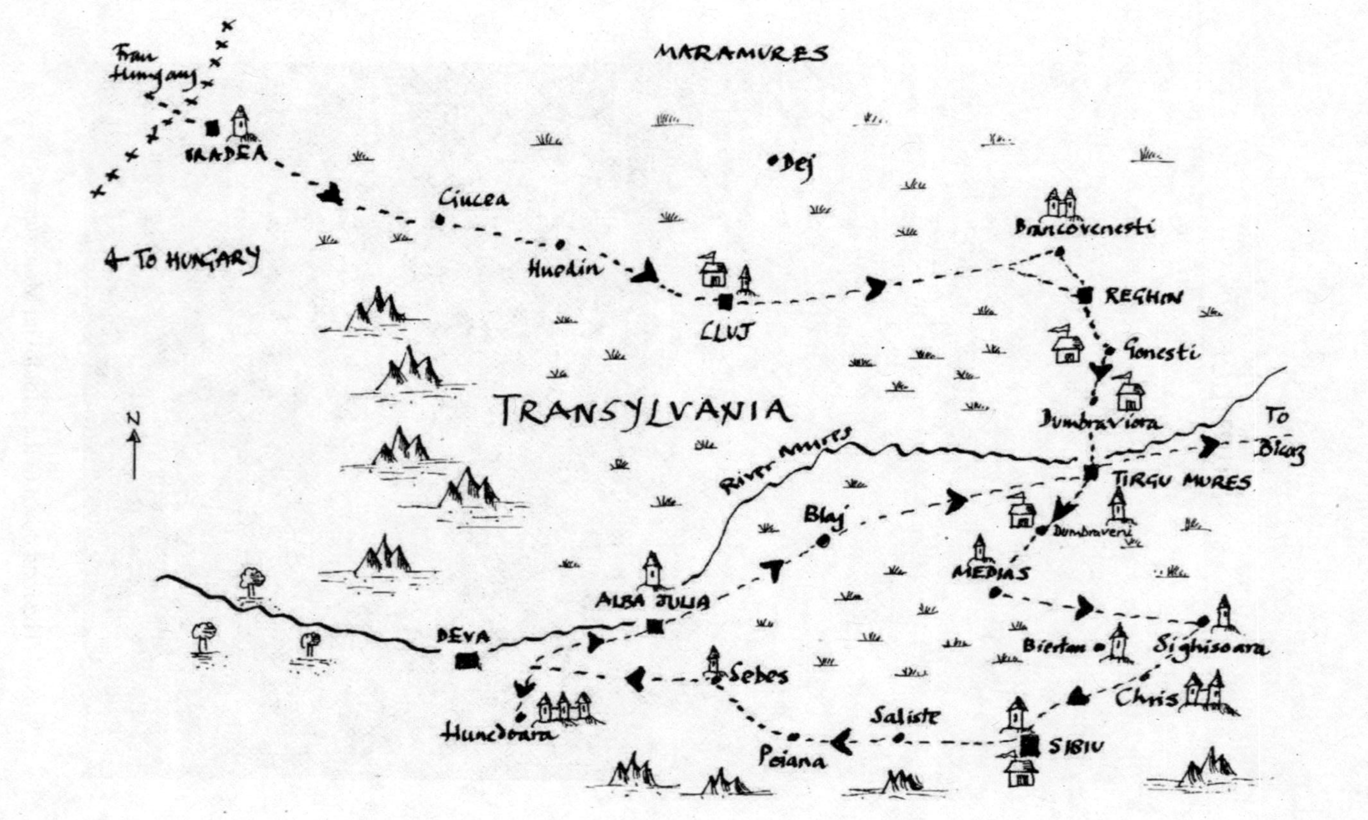
MARAMURES
From Hungary
ORADEA
Ciucea
Dej
Huedin
To HUNGARY
CLUJ
Brancovenesti
REGHIN
Gonesti
TRANSYLVANIA
N
Dumbraviora
To Bicaz
River Mures
TIRGU MURES
Blaj
Dumbraveni
MEDIAS
ALBA JULIA
DEVA
Biertan
Sighisoara
Sebes
Chris
Saliste
SIBIU
Hunedoara
Poiana

Chapter One

Cluj, a City of Contradictions

Weary of chasing the endless dusty horizon of the great Hungarian Plain, I was relieved, once past the busy border town of Oradea, to see the distant rim of low blue hills which marked the edge of Transylvania, that mysterious land the Romans called 'beyond the forest.' Flocks of grazing geese and sheep mingled on the pastures between fields of ripening maize and fading sunflowers, which had tired of raising their heavy heads to the blazing summer sun. Along the roadside, village women presided over shaded trestle tables, heavy with elaborate displays of red ripe peaches supporting luscious bunches of grapes, piled high like an eighteenth century Flemish still-life oil painting.

For Robert Townson,[1] a young man from Yorkshire, who passed through Oradea in 1797, there was a pleasant surprise in store for him. Visiting the hot baths, he witnessed:

> For here alone, and only under the grey canopy of heaven, "whilst evening drew her crimson curtain round," and the serenity of the air and the melody of the neighbouring woods awakened sweet sensibility, friend to our pleasure, but often enemy, alas! To our peace; separate from the vulgar throng and all alone, as if conscious of her superior beauty, the loveliest girl Nature ever

[1] *Travels in Hungary,* 1797.

formed lay quite exposed, reclining in a shallow bath in the very attitude of desire.

Before Ciucea, fifty miles to the cast of Oradea, the road rose into a land of wooded hills, their leafy green blankets punctured with small hay meadows dotted with stooks of drying winter fodder. In Ciucea town, it was market day where plump summer vegetables, garish gladioli, and small pigs changed hands in a vivacious melee of villagers and chattering Gypsies. The latter were just like South American parrots, with red and green kerchiefs, gold earrings, and vivid floral patterned skirts. Ten miles further on, towards Huedin, I passed little convoys of Gypsy wagons, hooped with canvas roofs, heading towards the Munţii Gilău plateau of wide, open grasslands.

Little had changed here since William Lithgow,[2] a prodigious early seventeenth century traveller, arrived.

> I stepped into Transilvania... for on the incircled plaine, there groweth nothing but Wheate, Rye, Barley, Pease, and Beanes: and on the halfe, or lower parts of the Hills about, nothing but Wines, and infinite villages: and towards the extreame circulary heights, only Pastorage for Kine, Sheepe, Goates, and Horses, and thickets of woods.

Cluj was my first port of call in this sea of wheat fields intersected by timbered spurs like the peaks of waves in a slow Atlantic swell. It had taken four days to get here, through Belgium, Germany, Austria, and Hungary, the last two once former owners of Transylvania. There is a plaintive little song or 'doina' about Cluj that goes:

> The way to the city of Cluj is long,
> But longer is the way of longing.
> The road to Cluj ends,
> But the way of longing is endless.

For a city to have four names is unusual but then Cluj is not a common place. It was known to the Romans as Napoca, when it was one of seven cities in Transylvania to have had the status of a *colonia.* In the Middle Ages it was called Culus; at the beginning of the fifteenth century, Cluj, probably from Castrum Clus, a small fortification dating from 1213; to the Saxons, who in all respects refounded it in the twelfth century, its

---

[2] *Rare Adventures and Painefull Peregrinations,* 1632.

name was Klausenburg, and to the Hungarians, Kolozsvar. To emphasise its Dacian pedigree, Ceauşescu rechristened it Cluj-Napoca in 1974.

Not surprisingly, Cluj has a muddled persona. It witnessed the first peasants' revolt in 1437, then went about its business as an outpost of the Hapsburg Empire until the tumultuous year of 1848 when the Hungarian Diet was held there, making it the centre of Hungarian nationalist aspirations. These were bitter and divided times. Andrew Paton in *The Goth and the Hun* in 1851 tells a typically tragic story:

> Pastor Roth[3] was condemned to death for anti-Magyar activities. As he was led to the ramparts (of Cluj) — being the month of May, the foliage had just come out — he said: "The world is beautiful," as he looked around the valley; "but let my humanity stand confused — how much more beautiful when one sees it for the last time." A few minutes later he was shot.

In 1894, the trial of the 'memorandists' of the Romanian National Party was staged in the city, an event which marked the end of a hundred years of political dialogue between the Romanian majority in Transylvania and the Imperial court at Vienna. Their 'memorandum' to the Emperor on the subject of national rights had been returned, unread, to the Hungarian, government in Budapest, who forwarded it by mail to its senders. It was unopened.

At the end of the nineteenth century, the Hungarian Count Apponyi declared "inside the Hungarian state there must not exist any nationalities or national rights... in any event we shall not recognise them." Yet how quickly history can prove such statements untenable in this part of the world. Sixty years later Transylvania united with Romania at the end of the Great War and Romanian it has been in title ever since.

Such nationalistic tugs of war have given the city a strange look. From the top of the steps on Cetăţuia hill, by the neo-modernist monument to the martyrs of the 1848 rebellion, one can discern a ring, almost a concrete fence of 1970s tower blocks encircling the walls of the old Magyar town. It must remind the ethnic Hungarians that Cluj is today a Romanian settlement, and that its old defences are truly redundant. Paradoxically; in the main Liberty Square, Matthias Corvinus, the Hungarian King from 1458 to 1490, sits clad in armour astride his battle-horse, conveniently claimed by the Romanians as the scion of a noble Romanian family from

[3] Roth was the schoolmaster at Mediaş and was opposed to the introduction of Hungarian as the official school language.

Huncdoara.[4] His birthplace lies a hundred yards away, a traditional medieval townhouse with a long sloping roof and mullioned windows set in old stone jambes. Now, a gallery of mundane modern art is 'in residence.'

Behind this statue stands St Michael's Cathedral, a Gothic Catholic church begun in 1350 and taking two centuries to complete. With slender perpendicular columns and vaulted ceilings, it boasts some original frescoes but sadly they are in poor condition, a shadow of their former luminosity. The size of St Michael's gives an indication of the scale of Cluj for it is small and insignificant as cathedrals go. The site today is a traffic island with jerky jalopies and belching buses hurtling round it from six different directions, leaving a greasy film of black smelly powder in their polluted wake. Not a place to sit and watch the world pass by.

I went in search of my hotel and found an ornate late nineteenth century edifice on the southwest corner of the square. Now dubbed the Hotel Continental, in its heyday it was the Hotel New York, famed for its cocktail. In 1938, Patrick Leigh Fermor[5] and his friends made a bee-line for it:

> The Hotel New York — a great meeting place in the winter season — drew my companions like a magnet. Istvan said the barman had invented an amazing cocktail... which it would be criminal to miss. He stalked in and we settled in a strategic corner while the demon-barman went mad with his shaker.

Somehow, the hotel had managed to divide itself unhelpfully into two: the restaurant *cum* café and the bedrooms. After a while, I discovered the secret to admission was to enter by a separate door in Napoca Street. The manager, who had been watching my inept entry, grinned politely from behind a glass screen like a bank clerk waiting to inform me that my account was overdrawn.

"You have my reservation?" I inquired with the experience that even an empty hotel could be awkward without such preliminary pleasantries.

"There are no problems"

"I am thirsty after my journey. Is there a bar?"

"Bar is closed."

"But what about the cocktail for which you are world famous?"

---

[4] The statue, sculpted by Fadrusz, was actually erected by the Austro-Hungarians in 1902.

[5] *Between the Woods and the Water,* 1986.

"Sadly, recipe is lost." Such regret was academic in the absence of an open bar but nevertheless sincere.

"But is there anybody left alive who may know it?" I pleaded.

There was a pause whilst both parties assessed independently that further progress was impossible.

"Since cocktail, there have been many changes. First, hotel becomes Nazi Headquarters. Then part of university. Then a casino. Now hotel again." I nodded sympathetically for how can a recipe survive such discontinuity. Our dialogue ended with the offer of a historical tit-bit.

"Outside door, you can see iron ring in wall. That is where my grandfather used to tie his horse."

I left to explore the town, passing the University 'librărie' which seemed adept at cultural compromises, one window devoted to Hungarian titles, the other to Romanian and a third to foreign languages. An American visitor[6] before the Second World War went to the cinema:

> At the Urania... I saw a Wallace Beery picture, shown in the original English version. Subtitles were flashed on the screen simultaneously in Rumanian, Hungarian and German, which pretty well disposed of space.

He concluded that Cluj was 'a curious mishmash of a town.'

The University was 'down', so the city was relatively deserted. In his *Impressions of a Balkan Journey,* William Wedgwood Benn had found here "troops of theological students soberly garbed in cassocks and bowler hats... with bands of girls in white berets," welcoming a Uniate bishop at the railway station early one morning in 1935.

The style of houses in the square was similar to the hotel, late nineteenth century, probably from French pattern books for their neo-Renaissance floridity would be at home in any French provincial town. Aida, who had joined me as an interpreter for the trip, excitedly pointed out a house with Diesel painted in large letters on the wall. This, she assured me, was one of Romania's most famous nightclubs and was the sole reason why anyone under the age of thirty in Bucharest had heard of this city.

Down the Boulevardul Eroilor lies Victory Square, an empty oblong space dominated at one end by the gloomy Orthodox cathedral of 1924, a grey vaulted symbol of yet another round of tit-for-tat colonisation. Inside,

---

[6] John McCulloch, *Drums in the Balkan Night,* 1936.

its poorly painted modern frescoes confirmed my impression that it had been hastily erected to counter the fervour of the indigenous Roman Catholic Hungarians. The square is redeemed by a pretty neo-Baroque opera house at the south end.

Andrew Crosse[7] went to a performance there in 1878.

> There is a good theatre in Klausenberg. I found the acting decidedly above the average of the provincial stage generally. I saw a piece of Molière given, and though I could only understand the Hungarian imperfectly, I was enabled to follow it well enough to judge the acting.

His critical powers in assessing French translated into Hungarian must have been formidable.

Having been denied my cocktail at the Hotel Continental, I dived into a noisy grădină, or garden restaurant, off Iuliu Maniu Street. Tall poplar trees sprung through the open courtyard, competing with the steeples and spires of the city. The blasting pop music killed all possibility of charm and I quickly left. Walking down towards the Someş River, I was overwhelmed by the multiplicity of stunning colours of Gh. Doja Street — primrose yellow, yellow ochre, pink, cobalt blue, sky blue, aquamarine, off-white, jade green, lilac. They had that wonderful Mediterranean luminosity and vibrancy of Matisse's Moroccan triptych in the Pushkin Museum in Moscow, quite out of place in this inland city.

Walter Starkie, a wonderfully eccentric Irish professor of Spanish and a great scholar on Gypsies and their music, arrived here in 1929 with his violin and rucksack to lead the life of a vagabond. His best friend described him thus:

> A small, stocky man, broad-shouldered, and thick about the girth; complexion fresh and hair fair; jaw strong but his face chubby and double-chinned; eyes blue and in the opinion of senoritas Nordic; eyebrows short and one twists up diabolically; walks with ambling gait, gets easily out of breath, rests often, laughs immoderately, drinks moderately, but prefers red to white; has fits of melancholy, is superstitious, and remembers his dreams; is quick to observe a rolling and romping eye, but prefers an eye of gentle salutations; is never merry when listening to sweet music, and when playing a fiddle feels like Don Quixote or Rozinante. In fact the fiddle is as

---

[7] *Round about the Carpathians,* 1878.

> Sterne would say, his hobby-horse, his sporting little filly-folly carrying him cantering away from the cares of life."

> In his hilarious and engaging book, *Raggle Taggle,* he noted that

> in this city we may study the clash of nationalities which gives to the province its characteristic appearance. Here are Hungarians, Roumanians, Saxons, Szekels, Jews, and Gypsies all of them conscious of their individual qualities but living at peace with one another. The atmosphere of the city is calm and serene: nobody hurries for life has not yet been modernised in the American fashion."

That doyenne of Irish travel writers, Devla Murphy, quotes this passage of her fellow countryman in her book *Transylvania and Beyond* when she visited Cluj in 1991 but concludes that "there was too much agonised resentment on the Magyar side, and too much understandable insecurity and regrettable vengefulness on the Romanian side, for the atmosphere to remain 'calm and serene.'"

The term "Szekels" or "Szecklers," which Starkie refers to, needs an explanation. When the semi-nomadic tribes, who lived in the vast spaces between the Caucasian and Ural mountains, moved West in the eighth and ninth centuries, a small group of them, after crossing the Eastern Carpathians, found themselves on the rich fertile plain of Eastern Transylvania. There they stayed. Later when the greater body of Hungarians settled in the area, the two peoples fraternised as kinsfolk, indeed they were descended from a common family tree. Yet there remains a separation; as the Szecklers put it, the difference between a Szeckler and a Hungarian is the same as that of a man and his grandson.

The cultural pride of Cluj is the Banffy Palace Museum, a late Baroque townhouse built between 1774 and 1785 as the home of a Hungarian Count, Gheorghe Banffy. Entering through wrought iron gates on the west side of Liberty Square, I passed through a columned vaulted hall into a courtyard of arcades surmounted by balconies with balustrades of oval and Doric designs. The graceful proportions and balance of light and shade produce an elegant harmony whilst the downward slope of the red tiled roof gives a feeling of intimacy. Despite the unkempt garden, I could imagine the ghostly hubbub of long gone servants, the clatter of horse's hooves, and the clash of metalled carriage wheels on stone as visitors arrived to be entertained in this grandest of Cluj town houses. Inside, rooms of white and gold cornices glide into each other along polished parquet floors. Now the palace is an art gallery with a collection from the seventeenth century to the present day. Nothing leaps out of its frame nor jumps off its pedestal to surprise and delight the visitor with a "discovery" with the exception of two marvellous Grigorescus[8] (1838-1907), 'The fair at Sinaia' and 'Turkish Prisoners,' the latter brilliantly encapsulating the abject misery and demoralised faces of captured soldiers. The paintings of Josef Iser (1881-1958), in a distinct dark and colourful style, of languid Harlequins and sultry Spanish women, hauntingly combine the mystery of mime with an intense Iberian passion.

That evening I dined in the faded, marble-floored dining room of the Continental Hotel, with its red walls bordered with a dado of square bevelled glass panels. Light bulbs protruded rudely out of art deco proboscis-shaped opaque lamps, some alight, some inert. It was a room full of ghosts, yet I sensed they weren't there that night; after all, this was harvest time and everyone would have been on their estates in the countryside. At least the décor had survived if not the cocktail, for as Patrick Leigh Fermor meticulously observed in 1938:[9]

> We sipped with misgiving and delight among a Regency neo-Roman décor of cream and ox-blood and gilding; Corinthian capitals spread their acanthus leaves and trophies of quivers, and hunting-horns, lyres and violins were caught up with festoons between the pilasters.

Dinner consisted of a piece of white fish, proudly brought to my table for inspection in its deep-frozen state, then removed and re-presented, covered in a layer of heavy batter. It was still cold. Nothing much had changed in the culinary realm since Charles Boner has passed through in the mid-nineteenth century. On eating in a tavern in Cluj, he jokingly recalled[10] that a knowledge of our peculiar taste in cookery had penetrated even hither. When the meat was very underdone it was said to be 'Englisch.'" As far as I was concerned, when fish is half-frozen, it can be said to be Romanian.

Walter Starkie had been invited by a flower seller in the main square to a Gypsy wedding. He set out for the Street of Spoons and found it

---

[8] See short biography in Chapter 4.

[9] *Between the Woods and the Water,* 1986.

[10] *Transylvania: its Products and its People,* 1865.

"straggling up a hill in a zigzag as though it was firmly determined not to fit into any orderly mosaic of town streets." He came across Rosa

> stirring a huge cauldron of steaming tomato soup... in the light of the fire she looked like a priestess of some oriental rite; she was wearing an astrakhan cap which was shaped like a wizard's conical hat. Her complexion was olive and her eyes had the glint of opals; her black hair was tousled and the rebellious tresses seemed to writhe like the serpent locks of a Medusa.

At the wedding, Walter inquired of 'an old hag' the secrets of marital bliss.

> The most important thing of all is to see to it that the marriage will be a sweet. Thar is why we Gypsies spare no money in buying sweetmeats for the feast, ay, and a girl when she is going before the priest with her bridegroom must put a lump of sugar under her armpit to ensure the sweetness of her wedding... she must burn flowers gathered on St John's Eve as a protection against sickness and she must hang up branches of garlic in her house for luck and against evil, for the garlic turns black after attracting all the evil into itself and so protects her.

Her advice for the groom sounded more familiar to Western readers for she urged the young man "the week before the marriage to go around the town drinking with his friends in every tavern, for water is the one drink he must avoid."

In 1935 Bernard Newman[11] had a rather different experience at a Gypsy wedding:

I didn't like the bridegroom and he didn't like me. I was unconsciously stealing some of his thunder; few, if any, of the party had ever seen an Englishman before, and for the moment I attracted more attention than the groom. He was a vicious-looking brute, dark almost as an Indian, with thick, sensuous lips; the way he looked at his bride disgusted me; and when he lifted the poor girl's ragged skirt to display her attractions to the whole company, I could have hit him... it would have given me a great deal of pleasure to have given him a damned good hiding

---

[11] *The Blue Danube*, 1935.

Chapter Two

The Medieval World of Sighişoara

Leaving the centre of Cluj behind, covered in its fin-de-siècle architectural icing like a giant birthday cake, I passed by soft valleys, folding into each other over crests of maize and sunflower fields, through the villages of Căianu, Mociu, Cămăraşu, Crăieşti, and Fărăgău, nestling in the hillside troughs. For those who work this land, it is a life of toil and sweat, if not blood and tears; for every tractor, there were a thousand carts pulled by an assortment of hardy horses, donkeys and docile oxen. The harvest was scythed with nothing more than a sharp blade and muscle power; no one from the youngest to the eldest was exempt. There was a sense of cheerful purposefulness in the haymaking whilst the proverbial sun shone down. Winters here are cruel and with a multitude of mouths to feed through the long, dark days ahead, there was no time for frolicsome diversions. All the farms had to lay in food to husband the geese, pigs, and cows on which they will subsist.

The heat of summer shrouded everything in a lazy haze, creating an eerie silence that pervaded the landscape and masked the frenetic activity of the harvest. This false quietness was a phenomenon of the long distances, which lay between the small groups of people thrashing at the standing hay, all out of earshot of each other on this great expanse of yellow and green. Fields planted in long, skinny strips gave the hillsides subtle patterns of line and colour. This was a journey across a vanished world of non-mechanised farming, the long-forgotten English village world of Flora Thompson.[1]

By midday I had reached Reghin, a pretty county town of pastel coloured houses. To the north lay Brâncoveneşti, advertised as a "magnificent building with four towers," built in 1557-1558. Perched on a small hill on the west bank of the Mureş River, the castle was difficult to spot, for thick trees had been allowed to obscure its once commanding view. After climbing forever up a narrow flight of stone steps from the valley floor, I was stopped at a small "sentry box" beside a high wire fence.

"Bună ziua, I would like to look at the castle," I announced breathlessly.

The sentry, for that was the role he assumed, replied: "Have you permission from the director?"

"No."

"Then you can't come in."

"Perhaps I could speak with the director?" I optimistically suggested.

"Director is away," he bluntly replied. Then, in the manner of delivering the coup de grace to a dying man, he triumphantly added: "In fact, he is not in country."

I sensed that something was amiss for a director who could travel abroad was obviously a figure of some import and unlikely to be a mere curator. Aida intervened with some well-chosen words that resulted in the "sentry" leaving his post to search for a higher authority. We slipped through the gate in his absence and found a community of mentally handicapped adults, all effusively friendly. So all was explained: the director was a doctor. After much handshaking with the inmates, I deduced there would be little to see inside now that the castle had become a medical institution and bade my farewells.

Following the Mureş Valley south, back through Reghin, I searched for Gorneşti Castle, a Baroque house of 1770 placed in the middle of "a beautiful dendrological park."[2]

I eventually found a children's home with a sprawling playground, albeit with the famous 52 rooms and 365 windows of Gorneşti, and once again defeated by institutionalisation, I moved on to a third house, Dumbrăvioara. There was little sign of it when I came to a village of the same

[1] *Larkrise to Candleford.*

[2] *The Travel Guide to Romania.*

name, so Aida asked an old man for directions. They were both equally baffled at the outcome of their conversation since he only spoke Hungarian and Aida Romanian. It turned out that the yellow ochre manor house in the centre of Dumbrăvioara was indeed the castle. Now it stood semi-derelict with the once-tended courtyard garden overgrown with rank weeds, the broken window panes of the elegant façade unreplaced. A passer-by told me that it was a school with little enough money for books, let alone paint. Once, it must have been the splendid home of a prosperous Magyar nobleman, a picture of 'an admirably found estate'[3] with children and dogs at play on the gravel drive that swept up to the graceful stone steps of the oak-panelled entrance.

Soon I arrived at Târgu Mureş, a big bustling market town or Târgu where Hungarian was the everyday lingua franca: it was known as Maros Vasarhely to most of its inhabitants. Dark skinned Gypsy men stood on the corners in the shade of floppy leafed poplar trees, engaged in heated and, judging by their laughs, amusing conversations which were conducted in a cloistered moustachioed space beneath the broad brims of their black trilbys. The town of Târgu started around 1300 as Novum Forum Syculorum, the new 'burgh' of the Szecklers. As the Protestant work ethic gathered momentum in the fifteenth century, it became a hive of crafts and in 1616, with its sister cities, Sibiu and Sighişoara, Târgu was granted the status of a "royal free town," a status it was to hold onto for the next three hundred years.

As in Cluj, a twentieth century Orthodox church has been erected at one end of the main square, a lumpen design clumsily contrasting with the Gothic elegance and simplicity of line of its next door neighbour, the Reformed Church of 1316-1442. The Medieval fortress lies just to the East of the main square and contains a simple Franciscan church in the centre. The walls were well preserved as were its towers which, by custom, were allocated to various guilds to defend; in this instance, the cobblers, butchers, furriers and coopers, who were numerous enough to provide round the clock guards and rich enough to maintain the fabric of the towers of Târgu Mureş and provide the necessary arms and munitions to defend them.

Twenty miles to the south of Târgu Mureş lies the fabled Saxon town of Schassburg, styled in Romanian Sighişoara. Once Castrum Sex — Fortress Number Six — Schassburg was one of the siebenburgen[4] of

[3] Charles Boner in 1865.

the Saxon settlers of the twelfth century. Patrick Leigh Fermor succinctly summarised[5] their early history:

> What happened was this. When the early kings of Hungary, notably Geza the Second in the twelfth century, found this region — according to the Hungarian chroniclers — deserted, they summoned colonies of 'Saxon' settlers from the Middle and Lower Rhine, some from Flanders, and others, it is said, from the Mosel, and even a few Walloons. They tilled the land and built the towns, often, as here, on ancient Dacian sites; these are the Bergen in question, and in time the growing constellations of their farms and villages dovetailed with the regions of the Szecklers and Hungarians and Roumanians... Their spoken dialect strayed a little from that of their countrymen in the West but no further than a regional dialect should; and later, when the Reformation found its way to the Carpathians, feelings of tribal solidarity prompted them to adopt Luther's teaching. To a remarkable degree, these settlements followed the line of evolution of the German towns and villages in the west; the same burgher and artisan way of life prevailed, very different in style from Magyar dash and vainglory and the self-sufficient stubbornness of the Szecklers and smouldering pastoral diligence of the Roumanians.

Up the narrow cobbled street, under the fairy tale clock tower with its green and gold tiled roof and elaborate Swiss-engineered clock, I entered the world of Medieval Germany. Arriving on a market day where 'numerous white-horned oxen lying unyoked before their carts of corn and vegetables, formed pretty and picturesque groups,' Charles Boner could scarcely believe his eyes in 1865:[6]

> 'Are you sure,' you ask yourself, 'that this really is the nineteenth and not the sixteenth century?'

Surrounded by three walls and fourteen towers, named as in Târgu Mureş after their patron guilds, tanners, tinkers, goldsmiths, ropers, butchers, furriers, tailors, cobblers and ironsmiths, Sighişoara was wrapped in a time warp save for the inevitable bands of tourists who roamed its narrow streets.

---

[4] The Seven Saxon forts: Bistriţa (Bistritz), Braşov (Kronstadt), Cluj (Klausenburg), Mediaş (Mediasch), Sebeş (Muhlbach), Sibiu (Hermannstadt), Sighişoara (Schassburg).

[5] *Between the Winds and the Water,* 1986

[6] *Transylvania: its Products and its People.*

I found lodgings by the Roman Catholic Church with Madame Maria Drăgan, which approximately translates into Darling.[7] Aged 91, she was delighted to put us up and made a great fuss over Aida, treating her as a surrogate granddaughter. Maria had memory lapses of fairly monumental proportions; in making up the beds, she discovered a trove of objects she was convinced she had long ago lost, not to mention a library of unpaid bills secreted under cushions and behind chairs. There was neither running water nor lavatory; she suggested we followed her routine and used the communal 'bath' in the platz in the lower town. Since it was a warm summer's evening, no one demurred from this but on a freezing winter's night, it would have been a dire trip.

Her house was over an old apothecary's shop, which once would have dispensed some strange prescriptions. For *Schweins-fieber,* or swine fever, when a fever occurred every three days, the victim was advised to eat with the pigs out of their trough and to lie down on the threshold of the pigsty. For the ague, the Saxons advised one to cover the patient with nine layers of different clothing or to go into the garden, shake a tree, and thereby transfer the fever to it. To improve one's love life, the advice was to take the two hind legs of a green tree frog, bury them in an anthill until all the flesh was removed, then securely tie the bones in a linen cloth and make sure it touched the object of your desire.

On the highest ground above the town, yet still within the walls, is the *Biserică din deal,* or Church from the Hill, reached through a long wooden-covered stairway dating from 1662. I arrived to find a funeral in progress; in front of the bier, mourners were carrying simple wreaths of pine branches. As the procession silently shuffled into the graveyard, the churchwarden announced that the *Biserică* was closed for the day. He relented when I begged for five minutes grace, mildly protesting that I had come all the way from London to see it. The Church itself was being restored but it was possible to go inside and view the stark, simple interior, no wall or facing given to decoration or ornateness.

The setting sun cast long shadows across the steep streets of stone timber-framed houses, their colours of pink, blues, greens, and ochre, slowly stolen by the approaching night. I roamed the town for Leigh Fermor's) "inn with gabled and leaded windows in a square lifted high above the roofs and triple cincture of the town wall... and the heavy oak table in the Gastzimmer[8] but to no avail.

---

[7] Drăgan the surname is akin to *dragă* or 'darling.'

Aida meanwhile had discovered the story of Ali Pasha and recited it as we sat over glasses of cool white wine at a cafe in the Town Square:

By Schassburg, on the mountain
A turret grey doth stand,
And from the heights it gazes
Down on the Kokel land.
And ne'er a passing wand'rer
This turret who doth see,
But pauses to enquire here
What may its meaning be.

It is a proud remembrance
Of doughty deeds and bold.
Still faithfully the people
Relate this legend old:
In bygone days of trouble
Went forth, with sword and brand,
A mighty Turkish Pasha,
To devastate the land.

Thus also would he conquer
This ancient Saxon town;
But here each man was ready
To die for its renown.
And there upon the mountain
The Pasha took his stand,
An elephant bestriding,
A scimitar in hand.

The mighty Ali Pasha,
He swears with curses wild,
That by his beard will he destroy
The Saxon, chick and child.
Then struck the haughty Moslem
Full in the breast a ball;
With curses yet upon the lip,
A death-prey he must fall.

The leaden ball came flying,
Full thousand paces two,
From out a fortress turret,

---

[8] *Between the Woods and the Water,* 1986

I. Sighişoara: Village Street

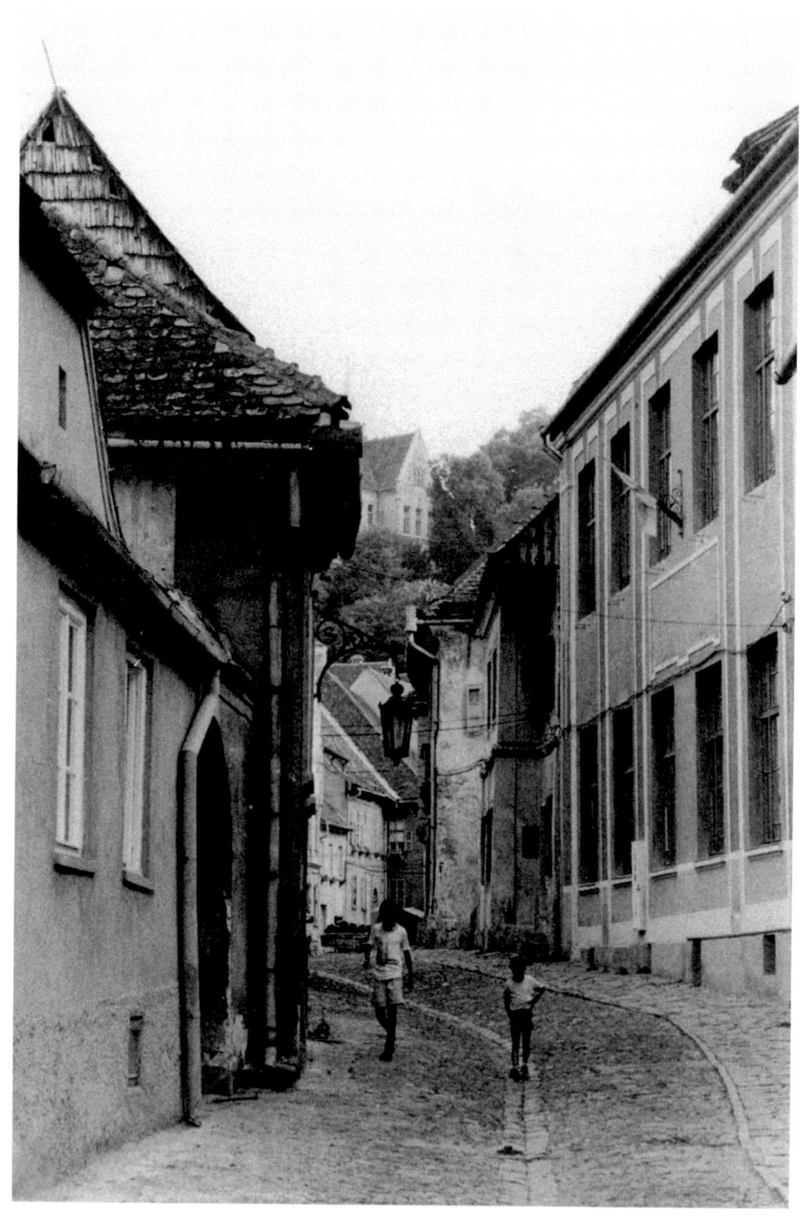

II. Sighişoara

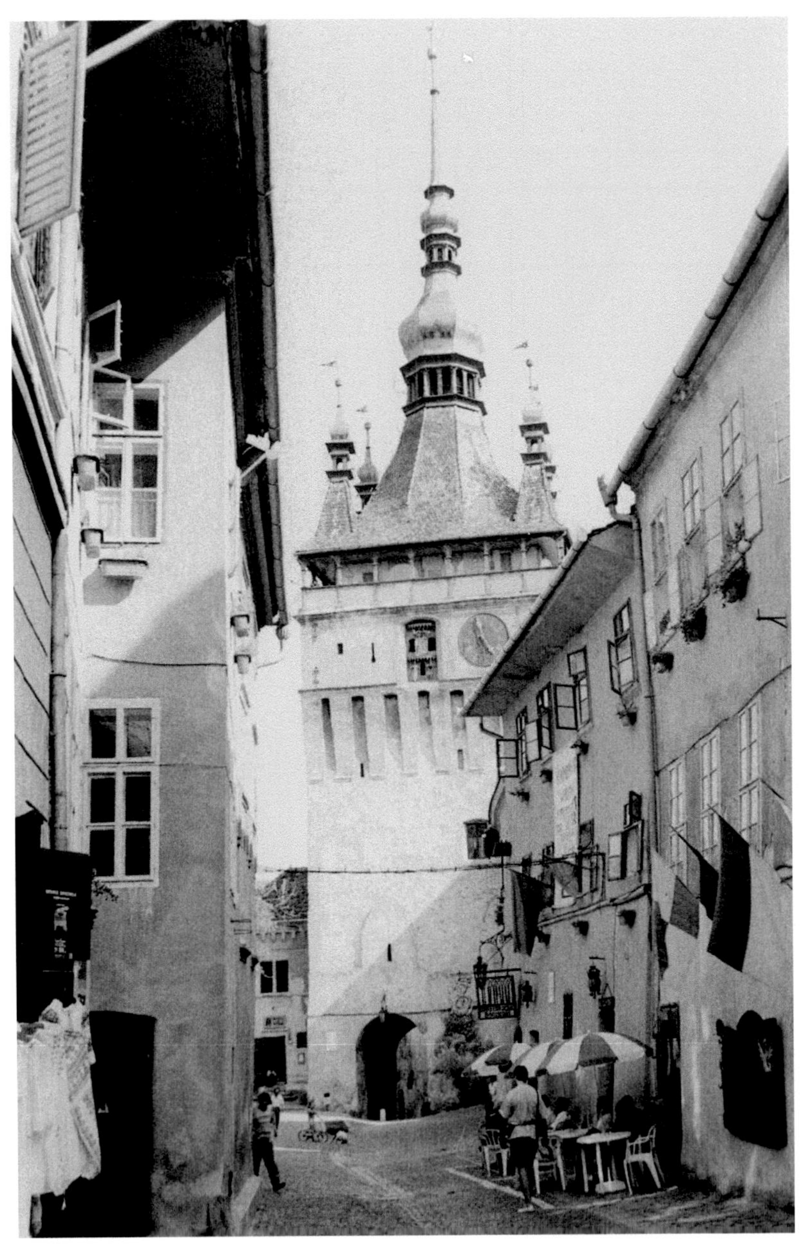

III. Sighişoara: The Clock Tower

IV. Sighişoara: Village Children

V. Criş: Fortified Tower

VI. Savoş pe Târnava: The Kirchen-

VII. Biertan: The Kirchenburg

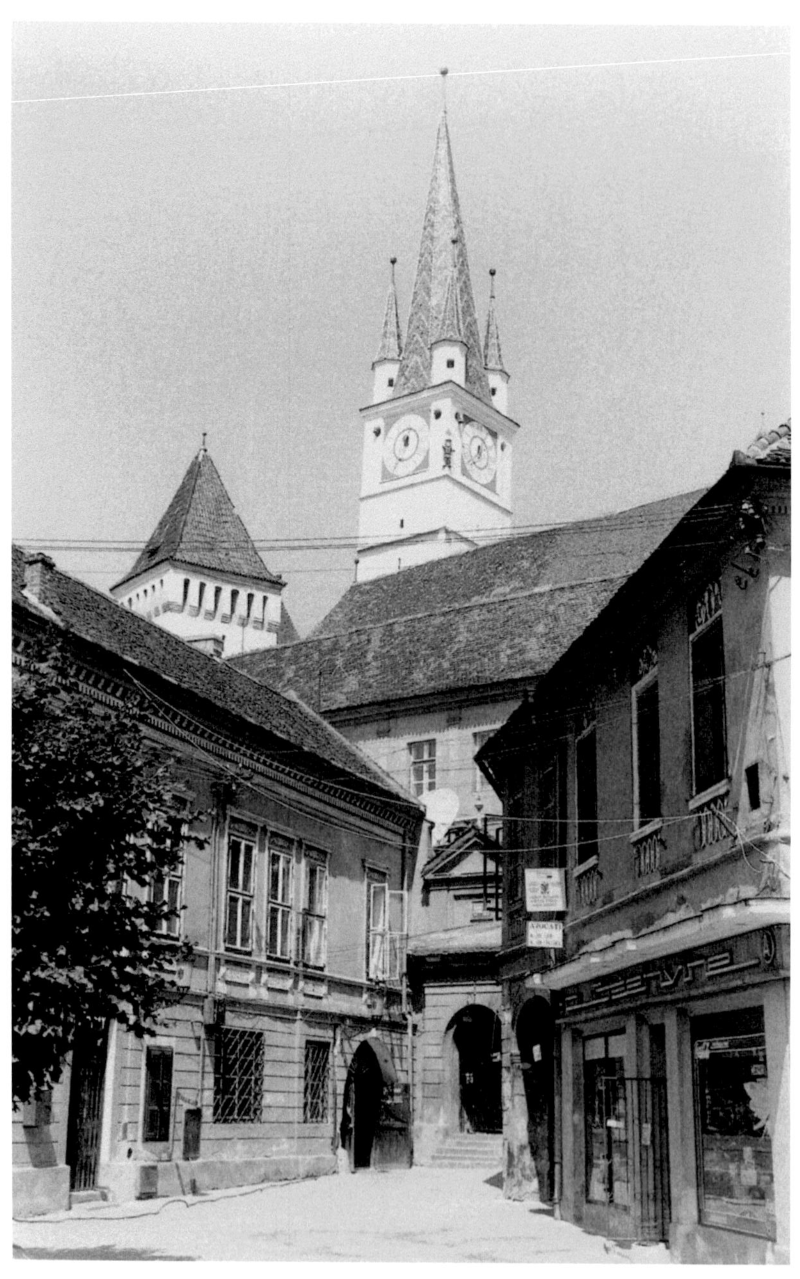

VIII. Mediaş: The Church

IX. Sibiu: Entrance to the Fingerling Staircase

X. Sibiu: The Old Walls

XI. Sebeş: The Church

XII. Eastern Carpathians

XIII. Bucovina: Sucevița Monastery

XIV. Bucovina: Suceviţa Monastery

XV. Maramureş: New Gate

XVI. Maramureş: Maria the Poetess

With deadly aim and true.
A sturdy goldsmith was it
Who fired this famous shot;
The Turkish horde, which seeing,
Their courage all forgot.

And panic-struck escaping,
Their Pasha left to die,
The elephant still bestriding.
With fixed and glassy eye.
Then sallied forth the Saxons
As thus the Moslems fled.
And gazed on the dead Pasha
With joy and yet with dread.

They built up Ali Pasha
Within that turret grey,
From head to foot still armed
In battle-field array;
His elephant beside him
Was buried here as well,
And outside an inscription
Their history doth tell.

By times a plaintive wailing
May here be heard at night;
Or chance you to see flitting
A phantom figure white,
The pasha 'tis, who cannot
Find lasting rest, they say,
Because 'mid heavy curses
His spirit passed away

That night in the Town Hall, there was a *concertul absolvenţilor* or graduation concert for young musicians from all over Romania. Held in the Festival Hall, a late nineteenth century room of gilded mirrors and silver-painted panels, lit with candle-filled chandeliers, the music of flute, piano, and oboe wafted across the ancient roofs, seeping into garret and cellar alike. With the support from proud parents tangible in the excitement of the evening, each student rose to the occasion without a false note, not a sign of nerves at any time. The partisan applause was rapturous and fully deserved.

As I walked back to my lodgings in the moonlight now flooding the little town and bouncing in luminous glints off the wet cobblestones, the old Romanian incantation came to mind, in which the moon is a beautiful maiden and the sun her brother:

> O luminous moon, luminous moon, come and take away the spell and the desolation, and the hatred from the world, and from my house, and from my table, and from my garden, and from my vineyard, and from my craft, and from my trade, and from my purse, and drive it away to wild mountains and forests; and us and our children and those who shall be born unto us hereafter, leave us clean and pure like refined gold and like the sun that shines brilliantly in the skies.

I sensed that Sighişoara was teetering on the cusp between its old way of life and the demands of modern tourism. My visit had been just in time. It would be inappropriate for mass tourism to come here for, as Sacherverell Sitwell[1] observed in 1938, it was "a small town which is picturesque but has little, beyond that, to detain the attention" and therein lay its charm. Unfortunately, 'little' includes the house where Dracula was supposedly born and this is the monetary magnet for the tourist industry.

The myth of Bram Stoker's Count Dracula, in many cases the sum total of people's knowledge about Romania, is as preposterous as it is fanciful. The real Dracula was called Vlad "Dracula," that is son of "Dracul," a word meaning both the 'devil' and 'dragon' in Romanian and used here in the context of his father's right to wear the dragon insignia of a Knight of the Crusader Order of the Dragon. Dracula earned another nickname, "Tepeş" or the Impaler, his favourite method of execution, used extensively by the Persians hundreds of years before. It was the Persians, too, who began the practice of crucifixion.

Dracula lived between 1431 and 1476, ruling the lawless principality of Wallachia no less than three times. These were troubled times — in the north, his lands marched with the Hungarian Kingdom, ruled by the formidable Matthias Corvinus, and to the south, the Ottomans were the new regional superpower after the fall of Constantinople in 1453. Although a skilled diplomat, Dracula tended to resort to the sword with alacritous enthusiasm and earned the undying hate of the Saxons whom he impaled with gusto. Yet his raids against the Ottomans along the banks of the Dan-

[1] Sitwell, one of the famous Sitwell trio, poet, art historian, and connoisseur, wrote one of the best-loved books about Romania, *Roumanian Journey,* published in 1938.

ube, ferocious in their intensity, protected Christendom from the onward march of Islam.

The powers of the Ottoman Sultan were absolute and, over life and death, utter and arbitrary. It was he, who on finding one of his prize cucumbers missing, had ripped open the stomachs of his gardeners to discover which one of them had eaten it. Dracula understood this blood-thirsty tendency better than most since, at the age of twelve, he had been given as a hostage to the Sultan and held in the fortress of Egrigoz in Western Anatolia in bond for his father's future good conduct. He was released at the age of seventeen, after his father had been murdered by Hunyadi boyars and his elder brother hideously tortured, then buried alive. When Mehmed the Second, the conqueror of Constantinople and a man well versed in the use of mass terror himself, approached Dracula's headquarters at Târgovişte in 1462, a Turkish chronicler of the time noted down the blood curdling sight that greeted him.

> In front of the wooden fortress where he (Dracula) had his residence he set up at a distance of six leagues two rows of fences with impaled Hungarians, Moldavians and Wallachians (and Turks). In addition since the neighbouring area was forested, innumerable people were hanging from each tree branch.

His reaction, recounted a Greek chronicler, was that of an emperor "overcome by amazement, admitting that he could not win land from a man who does such great things and above all knows how to exploit his rule and that over his subjects in this way."

Three hundred and fifty years later on Dracula's old Danubian battlefields the Ottomans were still using mass murder as an instrument of rule; the grisly pyramid at Nish contained the skulls of over 16,000 Bulgarian Christians executed after the rebellion of 1816. Mercia MacDermott in her portrait[2] of the Bulgarian patriot, Vasil Levsky, writes:

> Whitened by rain and sun, these grisly relics gleamed like polished marble, and, at first sight, may have seemed a fitting portal to the birthplace of Constantine the Great. Only when the approaching traveller reached the shadow of the edifice itself was its ghastly secret revealed Hair still clung to some of the skulls, floating in the air like hideous lichens, while the mountain breezes rushed through the empty eve-sockets and open jaws, so that the skulls seemed to

---

[2] *The Apostle of Freedom.*

> wail and sigh, as those they were still alive and suffering. To the faint-hearted, these ghostly voices spoke a warning which sent them fleeing to their homes, with their bodies drained of manhood, and their right hands numbed with fear.

Vlad was a man of his times, undoubtedly misguided "in his attempts to legislate virtue and morality through the use of terror,[3] but an inspired strategist in the containment of Ottoman power and thus the defence of Christianity. His obsession with gory statistics in his reports to King Matthias, '840 killed at Vectrem; 630 at Turtucaia; 210 at Marotim...,' accompanied by two bags of heads, noses, and ears as physical evidence seems obscene, even by the standards of contemporary Europe. Yet five years after Vlad's death, whilst in Italy Bellini and Boticelli may have been at their most prolific under the patronage of the Medicis, *the* Spanish inquisition began its proceedings, initiating a wave of terror that shook Spain to its foundations and led to the expulsion of Jews eleven years later.

My favourite story of Vlad is told by James Skene in his *Frontier Lands of the Christian and the Turk.*[4] The Sultan had sent a party of officers to parley with Vlad. When they appeared before him, he bade them salute him by taking off their turbans. So far, so good. Alas, they refused to do so, and he retorted that if they wished to keep them on, they should be fully satisfied; and he had them nailed into their heads.

Maria was waiting up anxiously to warn me about a complaint from across the street. Apparently the unintentional slamming of my defective car door had incensed the elderly inhabitants of the house opposite; threats had been traded and recourse to the police mooted. Maria put it down to commercial jealousy — "they have no lodgers" — but their vengeance was truly Machiavellian in its design. They shut their pampered dog out for the night and sleep was near impossible in the unending cacophony of yelps and miserable howls.

---

[3] Florescu and McNally, *In Search of Dracula.*

[4] 1850-1851.

Chapter Three

In Saxon Transylvania

The river which Sighişoara overlooked, the Târnava Mare, flowed west, gradually running into a wide plain of fertile fields. I was looking for the village of Criş to find the Castle of Bethun and, after following a long winding valley enclosed by tonsured hills of beech woods, I passed through the village of Stejărenii only to find that, a mile beyond, having successfully negotiated my way across a broken, rickety wooden bridge, the road petered out into oblivion, half way up a hillside. It would have only been possible to continue by a tractor, or, more fittingly, by horse.

Coming back through the village, Aida asked direction at the tiny shop or *magazin* where we were offered delicious coffee in steaming tin mugs. This was a traditional Saxon farming village with a long dirt street of low, blue and pink-washed houses with gate lintels high enough for full haywains to cross under. A motley gang of ducks, geese, and chickens controlled the muddy road like gangsters, extracting their "cut" by making all wait until they had decided on when and where to disperse to. There was a poignant inscription on the wall of an empty house:

> Raum ist in der kleinsten Hutte fur ein glucklich liebend Paar.
> There is space in the smallest hut to contain a happy loving couple.

The story of Stejărenii was typical of this area. Where once had lived over 150 Saxon families, there were now five. Encouraged to emigrate by Ceauşescu, openly welcomed by Kohl in his post-1989 embrace of all the German peoples, the Franconians of Stejărenii returned from whence they had come eight hundred years before. The effect on the economy of the village was visible; where once there had been neatly cultivated fields, there was now untended fallow land. The *Bruderschaft* or the brotherhood had departed and with them their self-imposed mutual controls like the *clacă* system of farming in which the labour force voluntarily congregated to work on one piece of land, irrespective of ownership. Without the requisite numbers, the system cannot absorb the abandoned acres; likewise, the system also extended to housework and this was the same story. Many of the empty houses, although cared for by neighbours, had been occupied by itinerant Gypsy families. I didn't detect any resentment about this: just a forlorn sense of resignation. The village school, a large, imposing building falling into disrepair, had just seven Hungarian and fifteen Romanian families to educate, in addition to the five surviving Saxon families.

The heyday of Saxon Transylvania was witnessed by Emily Gerard, a Scot who had been educated at a convent in the Tyrol and then, when she was twenty, married a dashing officer of the Austrian Hungarian army, the Chevalier Miecislas de Laszowski. She accompanied him on a posting to Sibiu where he was sent to command a cavalry brigade in 1883. Her book, *The Land beyond the Forests,* published in 1888, is a unique account of its time. She started by writing about the Saxons who arrived between 1141 and 1161, and revealed a robust judgmental style.

> From an artistic point of view, these Saxons are decidedly an unlovely race — the women may usually be described as having rather good hair, indifferent complexions, narrow shoulders, flat busts, and gigantic feet.

She correctly noted that "The Saxon dialect — totally different from Modern German — has, I am told, most resemblance to the patois spoken by the peasants near Luxembourg."[1] Emily's own sons had to speak Polish, English, German, French, Greek, Latin, and Hungarian. She considered they had got off lightly by not having to learn Bohemian, Slavonian, Ruthenian, and Italian.

Her observations of country life were astute and concise: the sheep in the villages belong to the Romanians, the pigs to the Saxons. She spotted an inscription inside a straw thatched cottage:

> Till money I get from my father-in-law
> My roof, it, alas, must be covered with straw.

[1] The City of Luxembourg has since developed close links with Sibiu.

She was also very funny: “An underdone potato may prove so very indigestible as to sever the conjugal links.” She discovered some strict dress regulations of 1651:

> in church, the men shall wear neither red, blue nor yellow boots nor shall women venture to approach the Holy sacrament or baptismal font in red shoes.

Her obvious affection for the Saxons did not wholeheartedly extend to the Romanians who were reviewed in a separate section “The Roumanian is a very obstinate character and does not let himself be easily persuaded.” Furthermore, “revenge is cultivated as a virtue.”

Long before Emily, Edmund Chishull had passed through Transylvania on his way back to England with Lord Paget’s embassy. In 1702 he wrote:[2]

> As to the temper of disposition of the inhabitants, they appear cordial and hospitable, drink almost continually, and eat plentifully, are unpolite but importunate in their civility and even the vulgar sort usually speak Latin.

However, as a clergyman, he was perturbed about their morals:

> With regard to matrons, their law formerly admitted no proof of adultery, unless under the eve witness of twenty four persons at least, which in a virtuous age was an egregious testimony to the chastity of their women, but in a vitious one must needs prove too great an encouragement to that heinous sin.

Fifty years before Emily, John Paget[3] was stronger in his views:

> The Wallach is generally considered treacherous, revengeful, and entirely deficient in gratitude.... that the Wallach is idle and drunken, it would be very difficult to deny.

The attitude of James Noyes,[4] an American surgeon serving with the Ottoman army in the 1850s, was similar to Paget’s but leaves me confused:

> The men are indolent and cowardly, except when it comes to smuggling, plundering, horse-stealing or attacking a bear.

---

[2] *Travels in Turkey and Back 1698-1703.* His manuscript remained unpublished until discovered by his son after his death. It was published in 1747.

[3] *Hungary and Transylvania,* 1839.

[4] *Roumania: the Borderland of the Christian and the Turk,* 1858.

To which he added that they were:

> remarkably superstitious. They believe in fairies, monsters, both horrid and picturesque, strolling vampires, sorceries, and the blighting charms of the evil eye.

I don't know how English villagers conducted themselves during a total eclipse of the sun in the eighteenth century but Captain Socivizca[5] strikes me as being unduly harsh on the Vlachs:

> Any phaenomenon, or Effect of unknown Causes, is considered by them as a Miracle. They look upon a solar Eclipse as a Fray of the Infernal Dragon with the Sun: for that Reason, during an Eclipse, they keep a constant firing of guns to frighten away the Dragon, who otherwise would conquer and devour the Sun, and plunge the World into Eternal darkness.

Nearly eighty years later, Bernard Newman[6] found evidence to support this spooky reputation:

> There was an old woman in a Carpathian village who was accused of being a witch and suspected of being a vampire. Not surprisingly, she threatened to return and haunt the village after her demise. When she died, the peasants cut off her head and stuffed her mouth with garlic; drove a stake through her heart in the approved style; and finally nailed horses shoes to her feet so that, should she return, they would hear her coming. All this in 1923.

Emily did however approve of the Romanian dancing, instructing us that 'you dance a girl, not dance with her.' Her knowledge of local folklore was encyclopedic. My short selection of the many proverbs she listed is:

> It is easier to keep guard over a bush full of live hares than over one woman.
>
> A wise enemy is better than a foolish friend.
>
> No one throws a stone at a fruitless tree.
>
> You cannot carry two melons in one hand.
>
> Wealth is only a hurdle: poverty is a stone wall.

Marcu Beza,[7] in his little book of proverbs, came up with these:

---

[5] *The Life and Adventures of Captain Socivizca,* 1778.

[6] *The Blue Danube,* 1935.

[7] *Roumanian Proverbs,* 1925.

Woe to the house where the hen crows and the cock keeps silent.

When three women meet, it is worse than a hundred ducks quacking.

The Transylvanian tales Emily recounted were all wonderful material for the writer of fairy tales. Bram Stoker, the author of *Dracula,* supposedly lifted pages of her book and, with minor additions, printed them verbatim For instance, she identified five strange people to watch out for when walking in the forests of Transylvania. First, she warned of the *Oameni micuţi* or the small men, grey-bearded dwarfs who, attired like miners with axe and lantern, haunted the gold and silver mines. They gave warning to a miner's wife by three knocks on the door when her husband has perished. Although in principle well-disposed towards human beings, they were very quarrelsome amongst themselves and were often heard hitting at each other with their sharp axes or blowing their horns as signals of battle. Next came the *Om ren* or wildman of winter, the terror of all hunters and shepherds. He was followed by the mountain monk, a malevolent spirit, who specialised in breaking tools. Then there was Panusch who lay in forest glades, waiting for helpless maidens; this, of course, was the pagan Pan who had been up to his philandering tricks for thousands of years. And, lastly, Gana, a beautiful but malicious witch, was out to 'doom' any man weak-willed enough to succumb to her charms.

In the next valley, I finally found the castle of Bethune on a hillside overlooking the village of Criş, its towers and covered battlements shrouded in thick mid-summer foliage. It was a splendid example of a defensive manor house, where a nobleman had his residence with all the attendant administrative and military offices he needed to control the villages, fish ponds, woods, vineyards, and mills of his estate. The compound of these manors enclosed not only the living quarters and formal rooms of the nobleman and his family but would have also been a home to scholars and chroniclers using the library, a refuge where travellers, both laic and cleric, could find shelter and hospitality. It must have been an exciting place to be, a crossroads where tradition met with innovation.

Built between 1559 and 1589, Castle Bethune is a hybrid of traditional designs, with the added influence of the Hapsburg and Polish Renaissance, epitomising the development of a once solely defensive castle. The tall walls and fortified towers would have indicated the castle from afar, a signal intended to deter passing Tartars and itinerant bands of brigands. But once the gates had opened, a visitor would have been pleasantly surprised by the qualities of the architecture of the two houses on either side of the courtyard. To the right, there is a long loggia or belvedere, supported by an arcade of slim stone columns. Here the nobleman would have met his visitor at the foot of the stairs and taken him up to the shade where he would have sat and entertained him whilst overseeing, out of the corner of his eye, the running of the estate. Beneath the stairs are vaulted cellars, a space of beautiful proportions, suggesting that they may have had some additional role besides the storage of wine.

In the far right corner stands the square watchtower, a much older edifice than the house, which would have been manned day and night to espy marauders, whom James Skene[8] described as those 'lawless ancestors of those rude Cossacks.' Below the roof of the watchtower are four bas relief figures of soldiers, giving it an unmistakable martial look. To the left, a three-storied house, similar to the great Năsturel house at Herăşti,[9] was constructed with elegant stone profiles emphasising the doors and windows. Around the main yard, there would have been stabling for horses and carriages and a servants' yard at the rear for farriers, cutters, tailors, laundry women and all the other Gypsy trades. A nineteenth century traveller[10] found on a visit to a country house,

> the long passages, broad staircases and great ill-furnished antechambers thronged by crowds of serfs and Gypsies, lying on the stone floors, as they had no other sleeping-place.

Bethune was in the midst of restoration and, not unusual in matters of restitution, its future was in doubt. The project, financed by the government with the aim of creating a museum, is being contested by the dispossessed owners, a Hungarian family, who seek its return and, if successful, plan a hotel. It is to be hoped that whatever the outcome, the superb standard of restoration can be maintained and completed, for this is an exceptional Transylvanian architectural treasure.

It was an extraordinary coincidence on my return to England to discover that Charles Boner[11] had stumbled across this very castle in 1865, even getting stuck in the same place — "none but horses of the country would have dragged a waggon up such steeps, and through hollow ways so narrow that our vehicle was always tilted to one side." He too found the

---

[8] *The Frontier Lands of the Christian and the Turk,* 1858.

[9] To the southeast of Bucharest, the house was built in 1641-1643 by Udrişte Năsturel, a great scholar of his day.

[10] James Samuelson, *Roumania, Past and Present,* 1882

[11] *Transylvania: its Products and its People,* 1865.

castle is disrepair, 'this old place, so historically interesting, so picturesque beautiful, moulders year by year into decay.' But he had better luck than I in the condition of the interior:

> One inscription says, 'This old castle was repaired A.D. 1557.' Thus three hundred years ago it was thought ancient. The oldest date to be found is 1340, with the initials M. B(ethlen). An old-fashioned bedstead has the name Clara Karoli, 1578: it is little better than a trough, but must then have been looked upon as something out of the common way, for the circumstance 'this bedstead renovated 1678' is recorded on the side.

The fortified manor house had its equal and opposite in the fortified church or kirchenburg,[12] a separate site in Transylvania unlike in the great courts of Wallachia. The enemy was the same: Turkish raiders and Tartars, whose last incursion took place in the mid-eighteenth century. Who exactly were the latter? After the death of Genghis Khan in 1227, the decision was taken to expand his empire to the West, to include Russia and Hungary. In 1241 Mongol scouts crossed the frozen rivers of Russia into Eastern Europe, the spearhead of an army of 60,000 men. Covering forty miles a day in the snow, the Mongol columns joined up outside Budapest and defeated their European enemy decisively at the battle of Leignitz ; no less than nine sacks of ears were sent to Batu to exultantly show the extent of this victory. This was followed by an even more disastrous encounter on the plain at Mohacs where a Hungarian army of 65,000 men was annihilated. Then, suddenly, without warning, the Mongols pulled out, ostensibly to choose another Khan after the death of Occodai in Karakoram, thousands of miles to the East. It is rare in the annals of civilisations for one party to be awarded such an unexpected breathing space: a weak and divided Europe was let off the Mongol hook.

For the next two hundred years the Mongol khanates battled it out with the Russians and remained a potent irritation to Eastern Europe. Indeed in 1490 it was the threat of the Crimean Tartars which prompted the Poles to form a costly standing army. And on went the raids — in 1667 the Crimean Tartars destroyed 300 villages and rustled 50,000 cattle from the estates of Jan Sobieski, the Polish king. Five years later he attacked them and found over 44,000 of his countrymen as captives, ready to be sold as slaves into the Turkish empire and their women sorted by age and size to

---

[12] There are over 30 main kirchenburgs to see, including Cisnădie, Viseri. Richis, Dealu Frumos, and Homorod.

be shipped to Indian harems. Only when Catherine the Great's General Potemkin marched decisively into the Crimea in 1771 did the era of the steppe warriors come to an end.

A raid would have begun with the Tartars swiftly approaching on horse, using surprise to position four groups around a village to prevent the villagers from reaching the fortified church. Those villagers fortunate enough to have scented the approach of danger — 'the first glimpse of the turban on the mountain-top was sufficient to ring the bell'[13] — would have headed for the church where vital supplies had been stockpiled to survive a siege. Once ensconced behind the thick walls, the danger for them was far from over; no one was ever safe from these ferocious warriors and on more than one occasion, the men were saved by the ingenuity of their women-folk. At the siege of Holzmengen, the defenders were in desperate shape, having run out of ammunition of all sorts, and it was only the quick wits of little Lieschen, who seizing the village beehives in both her hands, lobbed them down one after another on top of the Tartar attackers, that saved the day.

Elizabeth Kyle[14] remembered meeting a young Saxon girl on her way to church who showed her to a 'family room' in the outer fortified wall. Each family had the right to store food in such a room, a legacy from the days of sieges. In it, she found hams the colour of bright green and stinking to high heaven. The girl told her they had been there for 'about two hundred years'.

> "But why?" I could only repeat weakly.
>
> "Because, Gott sei Dank, they were not required. There was no siege."

A few miles on from Criş, at Saroş pe Târnava, there is a stark and simple Lutheran church on a small hillock, surrounded by thick, tall walls. The verger was surprised to see me for her life these days was that of a custodian. She explained that her congregation "had gone" and that in the last four years there had only been one service, sad evidence of the Saxon diaspora. No longer did the strains of 'Ein feste Burg ist unser Gott' echo round the nave. She urged me to take the valley road to the south to see a 'bigger and better church.' This led me to Bierton, a magnificent fortified

---

[13] James Skene, *The Frontier Lands of the Christian and the Turk,* 1858.

[14] *Mirrors of Versailles.* 1939.

Evangelical Gothic church of 1522, situated in the centre of a small farming town.

From a distance, the church had an almost theatrical quality, its three lofty wooden bell and watchtowers clustered within high stone walls reached through a long wooden covered staircase like at Sighişoara. Charles Boner generically described these Saxon churches as 'a sort of Kremlin in miniature.' This was a place of quite extraordinary beauty where decoration to the glory of God had such an urge as to overcome the strictures of the Puritan ethic. In the nave, the long wooden benches without backrests, incidentally not designed to save the rich embroidery on the women's blouses as some would have it but more for Puritan discomfort, stood in bleak ranks: opposite the entrance were the boxed pews of the wealthy with enchanting rustic paintings of cornflowers and wheat sheaves. The vaulted roof of the nave was a seventeenth century improvement, leading the eye to the altar roof, rebelliously decorated with bold strokes of red reeds. The breathtaking altar-piece in the shape of a cross had in its fifteen panels exquisitely painted figures in the costumes of the sixteenth century. This design could well be related to Byzantium, for the cross was the emblem of Constantinople for over seventeen generations. To the left of the altar was a beautifully crafted marquetry door of 1550, a treasure which travelled to Paris for the Great Exhibition of 1900.

Anyone who fell asleep in this church would have been fined eight farthings by the Broderschaft or possibly drinks all round might have sufficed.

On one of her visits, Elizabeth Kyle[15] was lucky enough to watch the procession of villagers attending Matins one Sunday.

> Old women with wrinkled. Durer faces, in the dress which German masters of the time had often painted; with the horned head dress of the 14th and 15th centuries, the full, stately skirts, velvet or brocade, beetle-wing green or dark red, the fine lace aprons, the jewels which, brass and silver gilt they might be instead of gold, and with set paste rather than the baroque diamonds, the square rubies and emeralds of the richer townswomen citizens, glittered massively enough.... young women with pasty, moonlike faces and whitish eyelashes in the high, round hats of maidenhood, each clasping her Bible, velvet-bound with hinges of worked brass.... young men in

[15] *Mirrors of Versailles,* 1939.

dull black and white, and a few old ones in the three cornered hats, the long green surtouts silver-buttoned of the past.

Rejoining the road to Sibiu, I stopped at Dumbrăveni, the old Elizabethstadt which Andrew Patton[16] had found in 1851 'very neatly built, and having a pompous church with almost the appearance of a cathedral, inhabited almost entirely by Armenians.' There were two large town houses of note; one, the family home of the Transylvanian Prince Michael Apafi, was a Renaissance building of 1552-1553 and now a school; the other, a hospital for the deaf. Both were closed to the public but such disappointments were more than compensated by the next medieval town of Mediaş and its fortified church with a tower nearly three hundred foot high, similar in form to the Clock Tower of Sighişoara, with the same green and gold tiles. Emil Hoppe,[17] author of *In Gypsy Camp and Royal Palace,* found himself in 1924 "standing in the midst of a cluster of odd steep-gabled houses, the fifteenth century church looked exactly like an old German engraving." For a time, the church was the prison of Vlad Dracula in 1476 after he had fallen out with Matthias Corvinus.

When I arrived, there was a wedding service in progress, spoken sequentially in Romanian and German. It was clear from the uniforms of the bridegroom's attendants that he was a German student marrying a Mediaş girl; she lived in Germany as well and had come home to be married before leaving forever. If a Saxon marriage hit the rocks a hundred and fifty years ago, Charles Boner[18] came across a splendid list of matrimonial grievances that constituted grounds for divorce:

Compulsion;
Offensive breath in either party;
Antipathy;
Drunkenness;
Insuperable disgust;
Ill-treatment;
Staying out at night;
Groundless complaining;
Wife's stubborn ways;
Niggling;

---

[16] *The Goth and the Hun.*

[17] Hoppe was mainly known as a photographer.

[18] *Transylvania: its Products and its People.*

(And my favourite) *Augenverdrehen* — either party 'rolling about their eyes.'

In her simple long white dress, the bride was totally eclipsed by the maid of honour. Dressed in a cling-film red satin ankle-length dress, her Hollywood hourglass figure brought the lunchtime traffic to a standstill. Long curling auburn hair, red lipstick, red shoes and a bunch of red gladioli in her hand, the "maid" swept past the star-struck onlookers and slid into the back of a car, a matching red BMW.

I was certainly not the first to witness such a Romanian femme fatale; many English writers have allowed themselves to be completely carried away by such apparitions. When Emil Hoppe visited a stud farm at nearby Sâmbota in 1924, he discerned that "the finest feature of the stud farm was Mlle. Zoe Drăgănescu, Rumania's first female veterinary surgeon. She was quite alluring." He then headed for Celiste where

> I had been told to see the most lovely girls in the whole country Celiste is celebrated for its dark beauties; and when I looked upon them I agreed that they were veritable houris. The hair is the purple black of the Connemara peasant; their eyes are large, lustrous, and loving, their complexion is like magnolia blossoms, and their mouths are curved bows of red delight. They walked with wonderful grace and again 1 remarked extraordinary beauty of hands and feet.[19]

Henry Baerlein in *And Then to Transylvania* in 1931 argued speciously that this beauty stemmed from the genes of Austrian Grenadiers who were left to their own devices by Marie Theresa with a vague brief to 'repopulate the land."

James Ozanne, who had left London in 1870 on a lengthy journey to Romania, positively swooned over Romanian women:[20]

> Such brilliant eyes, such raven tresses, such dainty hands and feet were never seen anywhere else... the Romanian women are famed for their beauty and they whole existence is devoted to loving and being loved.

Quickly negotiating my way through Copşa Mică, the most polluted site in all Romania where fortunately the demonic chimneys now lay silent after bequeathing a legacy of hideous, cancerous genes, I followed the

[19] *In Gypsy Camp and Royal Palace,* 1924.

[20] *Three Years in Roumania,* 1878.

river to the West and then southwards to Soroştin. Pollution was nothing new in Transylvania for an early nineteenth century traveller[21] had observed:

> Some of them (the villages) were marked with volumes of smoke from the smelting works.... established by the Austrian government for the mines which produced silver in large quantities and some gold.

From here the road climbed out of the valley up to a point where the most spectacular panorama of the central Transylvanian Plain unfolded. Rolling grasslands spanned the horizon, dotted with the occasional copse on a far-off hillock. Even an isolated, scrawny bush assumed the legitimacy of a landmark in these deserted fields of Arcadia. An exhausted army of sunflowers stood at ragged attention on the brow where I halted. All life had stopped under the merciless midday sun, not a birdsong, not a car, not a tractor, only the silent trek of carts, with their horses plodding in slow motion across the distant hillsides.

[21] An anonymous account published by Richard Phillips in 1805.

Chapter Four

Sibiu, the Anatomy of a Lobster

It was long into the afternoon when I reached Sibiu, Hermannstadt to the Saxons, Nagyszeben to the Hungarians. Originally a Roman city, Cibinium, its name is derived from a tributary of the Olt, which rises in the Cibin Mountains to the southwest. The old medieval town is in two parts; the upper town built on a natural terrace and the lower on the banks of the Cibin River, the two connected through a narrow cobbled alley called the Fingerling Staircase. Walter Starkie (1929) was disappointed by Sibiu, "in contrast to the gay atmosphere of Cluj, Hermannstadt is sad and mysterious." Sacherverell Sitwell,[1] usually dismissive of towns, was guardedly enthusiastic:

> Besides the Bruckenthal gallery and the Church, there is not much in Sibiu but the flower market is full of tuberoses, the curiosity shops have something special for sale, in the shape of painted glass icons which are peculiar to the district and the streets are made picturesque by the elaborate black and white costumes of the neighbourhood.

When Emily Gerard[2] accompanied her husband on his posting here, she found a town that

---

[1] *Roumanian Journey,* 1938.

[2] *The Land beyond the Forest,* 1888.

> has been sleeping for a hundred years and is only now slowly and reluctantly waking up to life, yawning and stretching itself and listening with incredulous wonder to the account of all that has happened in the outside world during its slumber.

Charles Boner arrived here in 1865[3] and found his "room was dirty and disorderly, the stove was tumbling to pieces, the lock on the door half off. What a mess, too, the courtyard was in! And the stairs, and the passages, and the places they led to!"

He remonstrated with his chambermaid:

Es ist bei Euch eine Hottentotten Wirthschaft
— it is like being among the Hottentotts here with you.

This had no effect.

Es ist hier bet Euch eine Zigeuner Wirthschaft
— it is like living among the Gypsies to be here.

His room was as neat as a pin in half an hour!

It was late afternoon when I checked in to the elegant Hotel Împăratul Romanilor[4] on Nicolae Bălcescu Street, just off the main square of Piața Mare, I set off immediately to the Bruckenthal Palace, hoping against hope that it was still open. I was in luck. The palace is on a corner of the square, entered through a central gate into the first courtyard, which leads into a second. With the surrounding buildings four stories high, the opportunity of the grandeur of an open space had been sacrificed to an imperious clausure. In this 'well,' one could sense the critical gaze of onlookers, either brazenly leaning, arms folded, on the windowsills above or, more sinisterly, surreptitiously pecking from behind drawn curtains. The palace is mightily grandiose in its design within its context in Sibiu and would be more in place in a fashionable, condensed city like Prague, alongside such peers as Cernin and Kucera, or the Ballhausplatz in Vienna.

The museum in the palace had received mixed reviews from previous travellers. Charles Boner[5] fumed at the collection:

> Unless seen, it is impossible to form any notion of the rubbish here brought together. You go from room to room, the walls of which are filled with paintings which are utterly worthless. Many of them

---

[3] *Transylvania: its Products and its People,* 1865.

[4] Around since 1770 it was known to the Hapsburgs as the 'Romischer Kaiser.'

[5] *Transylvania: its Products and its People,* 1865.

are such wretched daubs that it is quite a marvel to you how they ever got there... Is all this a joke, or is it serious?... it is no joke. Here is a Wouvemans, and here a Titian, and a Rubens or two..."

The first room is daringly flamboyant in taste, hung with a Chinese wallpaper of blue and white giant mysterious flowers à la mode oriental. This theme is continued into the next salon where the flowers gave way to exotic, paradisiac birds on blossom-heavy boughs. Both rooms share a collection of superb pieces of marquetry chests of drawers and cabinets, the best by far being an escritoire with inlay of such intricacy that it must be attributable to the French court 'fournisseurs'. A portrait of Baron Bruckenthal (1721-1803) inspected me with disdain on arrival, his inquiring eyes searching out fools and parvenues. With his long, curved aristocratic nose and semblance of a Hapsburg lower lip, the Baron demanded respect as a collector of impeccable taste, not to mention his formidable reputation as an administrator of ruthless efficiency when he was a reformist governor of Transylvania from 1777 to 1787. He also kept a summer residence at Avrig about twenty miles from the city, a huge Baroque house set in parkland with terraces descending to the Olt River. Today it is listed as a sanatorium which dissuaded me from visiting it.

On the first level of the palace are pictures from the Romanian schools which include an enchanting painting, "Adornment of a Saxon Bride." The voting bride shyly poses in a bright floral jacket with fur trimmed edges; in the background, her trousseau is covered with a patterned Oltenian rug. Then there are some delightful paintings by Nicolae Grigorescu (1838-1907) whose work I first saw in Cluj. Many consider him the greatest of Romanian painters. As a young boy, he began his career by painting icons to support his family. Starting by mixing colours and painting the robes of the saints, it was during a stay at Neamţ that his work was seen by the Abbess of Agapia and she commissioned him to paint her church. The resultant oil paintings in a neo-classical style were considered a triumph and he attracted the attention of the Prime Minister, Mihail Kogălniceanu, who helped him travel to Paris where he settled in Barbizon alongside Corot, Millet, and Courbet. He became moderately successful, selling two of his paintings to Napoleon the Third. Nearly thirty, he returned to Romania after further travels in Italy and Greece and founded the Romanian School of Art. His output was prodigious; his portraits, still lifes, sea scapes and landscapes, together with his work as a war artist in the Russo-Turkish war of 1877, amount to a portfolio of over 4,000 pictures. He brilliantly adapted the techniques he had learnt with the Impressionists to scenes of peasant life in Romania, not I would argue to romanticise it but to give an expression to its timeless soul. His biographer, George Oprescu,[6] stressed that “he liked these brave people who, in their difficult, exhausting pursuits, never despair.” The oil sketch at Bruckenthal Palace of ‘A Peasant Girl with Distaff’ exuded enormous energy, the spring in her step full of youthful life, her head held high with ‘joie.’ It was fitting that Grigorescu’s last wish was that he should be taken to his grave on an ox-cart, as was the custom of the peasants whom he had so often painted.

Another most enjoyable painting is Theodor Pallady’s (1871-1956) ‘Still Life of Flowers.’ The spatial composition and colour contrasts of chrysanthemums, lilacs and peones against a backdrop of red and white stripped wallpaper is masterful.[7] Josef Iser, whom I had so much admired in Cluj, has more pictures here from his Spanish period, dark, colourful compositions of harlequins and dancers. A more difficult artist to appreciate is Nicolae Tonitza (1886-1940) whose style of using dots for eyes in otherwise extremely accomplished portraits is bizarre. The one painting when he eschews this technique, ‘Portrait of a Girl in a Red Dress,’ is a charming head and shoulders study, her bobbed hair typical of the 1920s.

Sitwell[8] noticed “a small portrait by Jan van Eyck; and the rest of the interest is dissipated into obscure and unlikely directions.” Donald Hall[9] had noted the Van Eyck and also Hans Memling’s ‘Woman praying’ — she had a nice little dog who was waiting for her to stop” — but overall, he found it ‘uninteresting.’ This was fair comment on the collection on the second floor where there is a mediocre display of seventeenth and eighteenth century Flemish, Italian, and German painting, including two rather gross and primitive Reubens which once must have adorned a church wall. Emily Gerard[10] said that many of the works of art were purchased from refugees fleeing the French Revolution which would account for the sheer amount of nondescript works. But there was one painting which Sitwell missed. It is a charming portrait of Charles I and his wife, Queen Henrietta, by Anthony Van Dyck. Henrietta, gazing adoringly at her king, hands him a bunch of laurel leaves which, from the expression in his face, he intended to accept gracefully albeit with reluctance, perhaps sensing that their symbolism of

---

[6] *Nicolae Grigorescu,* 1961.

[7] As one would expect from a friend of Matisse; indeed, they shared a studio in Paris.

[8] *Roumanian Journey,* 1938.

[9] *Roumanian Furrow,* 1933.

[10] *The Land beyond the Forest,* 1888.

victory would pass over him to another, namely the unknown Oliver Cromwell.[11]

The person who first drew attention to the existence of this portrait in the Bruckenthal Palace was Lady Craven in 1786. Her story is well worth telling. She was one of those astonishing, larger than life English ladies of the eighteenth century, on par with Mrs. Jordan and Georgiana, Duchess of Devonshire, in the almost heroic scale of her life. Born in 1750, the youngest daughter of the 4th Earl of Berkeley, a general of the '45 rebellion, she was seventeen when she married William Craven, later 6th Earl. She produced six children for him in quick succession and on the death of her father-in-law, she moved to London with her husband where she soon attracted attention to herself, both as a notable beauty and as a playwright, the Whig Club speaking of her "unblushing profligacy."

One of her greatest admirers was Horace Walpole, who wrote about the performance of her comedy in Drury Lane in 1780.

> She went to it herself the second night in form, sat in the middle of the front row of the stage box, much dressed with a profusion of white bugles and plumes, to receive the public homage due to her sex and loveliness.... It was amazing to see so young a woman entirely possess herself; but there is such an integrity and frankness in her consciousness of her own beauty and talents that she speaks of them with a naiveté as if she had no property in them but only wore them as gifts of the gods.

Such was her allure that the great painters of the day, Reynolds, Gainsborough, and Romney, all vied for her sitting. Of the three, Walpole was quite clear which he preferred, the full length 1778 portrait by Romney; he even wrote a poem about it.

> Full many an artist has on canvas fixed
> All charms that Nature's pencil ever mix'd
> The witchery of her eyes, the grace that tips
> The inexpressible douceur on her lips
> Romney alone in this fair image caught
> Each charm's expression, and each feature's thought;
> And shows how in their sweet assembly sit
> Taste, spirit, softness, sentiment and wit.

---

[11] The 1911 Baedeker lists this picture as 'after Van Dyck.' I am not aware of any doubt about its artist.

Walpole bought the picture and hung it in his house at Strawberry Hill. Elisa didn't care for it herself — "the picture of me by Romney... has by no means given a just idea of my face or figure; the former is too severe and the latter much too large."[12] I prefer the sketch by Reynolds in 1781 which shows Elisa with a sharp and intelligent face, her eyes looking at one with mischief and naughtiness. Thomas Beach's 1776 portrait of a 'Lady with a Harp' shows a sensuous full-bodied Elisa with face full of fun and laughter, very different from the other two.

With such good looks and attractive personality, it was perhaps only a matter of time before a scandal involving Elisa surfaced in the libertarian society of eighteenth century London. Her partner in passion was the Duc de Guines, the French ambassador in London. Elisa was caught with him in a private room at a ball in London. Her husband hot on her trail, forced the door and:

> found her ladyship sitting on the ambassador's knee in such a state as clearly proved that a few minutes would have brought on an amorous conflict. When Lord Craven perceived that she had become a democrate in love and had shewn marks of complaisance to the canaille, he was surely and indignant and advised her to take herself off.... The peer settled £1500 a year on his spouse.[13]

In her Memoirs, Elisa blamed the breakup of her marriage entirely on her husband whom, she claimed, had taken a mistress. Walpole was his usual forgiving self, for Elisa could do no wrong in his eyes.

> She has, I fear, been infintamente indiscreet but what is that to you or me? She is very pretty, has parts, and is good-natured to the greatest degree; has not a grain of malice or mischief.

Now separated, Elisa took herself off to France with her youngest son, Richard Keppel Craven, and settled into the Pavillion de la Jouchere at St. Germain en Laye. A frequent visitor there was the Margrave of Brandenburg — his full title was Christian Frederick Charles Alexander, Margrave of Brandenburg, Anspach and Bareith, Duke of Prussia and Count of Sayn — and it was much rumoured that this was the renewal of an old liaison. Eliza herself states that, after her arrival in France,

> it was the Margrave of Anspach who so frequently visited me: that he had known me from my childhood and had conceived for me

---

[12] Lady Craven's letters.

[13] *Jockey Club*, 1792.

> the same partiality that all who had known me from my infancy retained for me.[14]

Since the Margrave had only been to England once in 1763 when Elisa was 13, her story seems unlikely.

On 15 June 1785, frustrated by the formalities of the court at Versailles and 'the impertinent interest' which people took in her life, Elisa set off on "a long and extraordinary" journey to Constantinople via the South of France, Genoa, Florence, Venice, Vienna, Warsaw, St. Petersburg, Sevastopol, Pera, and Bucharest. Accompanied by the "celebrated and veracious" Henry Vernon as a *companion de voyage,* she wrote long letters to her "brother," the Margrave, addressed to him in the spirit of "chaste sisterly intercourse," signing herself "I remain unalterably, your affectionate sister."

Writing letters from far away places was an established way of making a name for oneself in London as Lady Mary Wortley Montagu had proved in 1718. She had embarked on a similar journey with her husband[15] and reached Constantinople via Vienna, Budapest, Belgrade, and Galaţi. Her letters to her sisters and friends were eagerly awaited by London society, especially when they contained such dramatic statements as "I am threatened... with being frozen to death, buried in the snow, and taken by Tartars". She was superb at relating to her friends back home:

> The pleasure of going in a barge in Chelsea is not comparable to that of rowing.... down the Bosphoros, where the most beautiful variety of prospects present themselves.[16]

When Lord Craven died in September 1791, Elisa married the Margrave and, in 1792, she persuaded him to sell up in Germany and come to England where they lived in Brandenburg House in Hammersmith and Benham in Berkshire, ironically the Craven country home. Although she succumbed to another dalliance, this time with Count Alexander de Tilly, it was a happy and successful marriage. The Margrave died in 1806, aged 70, but Elisa went on to write, produce and star in a series of plays — *The Yorkshire Ghost, Princess of Georgia, Puss in Boots* and *Love in a Convent.* In 1819, she was given land by Ferdinand IV to build a villa, the Villa Craven or now Villa Marie, at Posilipo outside Naples, where she lived out the rest of her days with her youngest

---

[14] Lady Craven's memoirs.

[15] The newly-appointed ambassador to the Ottoman Court.

[16] *Letters,* 1763.

son who had never married. She died on 13 January 1828 and lies buried in the Old British cemetery.

Her biographers, Broadley and Melville,[17] were generous to her:

> Gifted with a ready wit and wielding a fluent pen, she was probably more feared than loved. Her beauty was of a very high order until it greatly faded... in her relations with Lord Craven she was possibly more sinned against than sinning and it must not be forgotten that she retained the sympathy and affection of the children of her first marriage... she proved herself worthy of the traditions of the race from which she sprang.

Passing from Wallachia to Transylvania, she found the road torn up and destroyed, the carriage behind her "breaking into a thousand pieces."

She wrote to the Margrave from Sibiu:

> I have been extremely well entertained here by the Governor, who is a sensible old man and the only Governor remaining in Imperial service... He is very fond of pictures and has a collection among which a Charles the First and his wife are extremely fine — and a St. Jerome, by Guido, with a lion, is invaluable — indeed he said he had been offered four thousand pounds for the last.

John Jackson,[18] returning to England from India in 1797, found Sibiu "a tolerably well-built city" and was warmly received by the General Commandant, an effusively friendly old soldier. Observing that Jackson was a bachelor, the General wished

> me much to marry a German, saying they had plenty of very handsome women, and that if I would fix upon any one, he would pledge himself that I should not meet with a refusal in the whole province.

Like other travellers, he mentioned Baron Bruckenthal's 'extensive collection of the most valuable paintings' but also referred to his 'beautiful garden about half a mile out of the city, laid out after the English taste.'

Edward Clarke,[19] who dined with Baron Bruckenthal in 1777, remembered "wines served in porcelain cups" and, to his horror,

---

[17] *The Beautiful Lady Craven,* 1914.

[18] *Journey from India towards England,* 1799.

[19] *Travels in Various Countries,* 1810-1823.

> the ladies... yet held theire forks perpendicularly, grasping the handles as if they were walking canes, in a manner that would be thought singularly uncouth and barbarous in our country.

Bemused at the thought of Elisa in this very palace two hundred years ago, I wandered back into the Piaţa Mare to find the vast Evangelical church, with its multi-coloured tower, well and truly locked. Nearby was the Fingerling Staircase, linking the upper and lower levels of the town, somewhat overrated as an architectural attraction; the streets of Mala Strana cascading down from Hradcany Castle in Prague are much more atmospheric, though on a foggy night, there could be a sense of seventeenth century city life here.

Across the square, at the end of a maze of narrow streets, is Moldoveanu Street where the three surviving watchtowers guard the south-east wall of the city. In 1376, Sibiu boasted nineteen guilds and forty watch-towers; the three survivors belong to the carpenters (octagonal), the potters (square), and the clothmakers (pentagonal), all impressive fortifications which resisted three major Turkish attacks in the fifteenth century.

Returning to the Piaţa Mare, I sat at the terrace of a small café with a fine prospect of the eighteenth century Roman Catholic church and the magnificent Old Town Hall of the second half of fifteenth century which supremely bridges the gap between the Gothic and Renaissance styles. The square was empty, with no sign of Paget's splendid recruiting party:[20]

> Eight to ten smart young fellows, dressed in hussar uniforms, and preceded by a Gypsy band playing the national airs, promenade the town in loose order, talking and laughing with all they meet, and looking so idle and so happy, that it is impossible not to envy them.

The next door table was eyeing me with curiosity, and after a while, unable to restrain themselves, the drinkers sent a middle-aged man over as an emissary.

"English? You like football?"

"Yes, I'm English. No, I don't like football." This seemed polite in order to avoid a post-mortem on England's recent defeat by Romania in the World Cup.

"Not like football? Impossible!"

---

[20] *Hungary and Transylvania,* 1839.

I was then at the receiving end of an increasingly heated lecture on why I should like the game. Suddenly, he stopped in mid-sentence.

"Sorry. I am paranoiac. Look here is my hospital record," and he waved an official looking book in front of me.

His table roared with laughter and called him back. Just then, the door behind the terrace opened and a scowling woman beckoned him inside. She turned and smiled sadly at me.

"My husband is not a paranoiac. He's drunk." And she led him away by his left ear.

Over dinner in the excellent Hotel Împăratul, the roof of the dining drawn open in the summer heat, Aida told me how her grandfather had been imprisoned by the Communists for the "crime" of being the half-brother to King Michael's tutor. On release he died of ulcers, a cruel and untimely end for a man who had only ever aspired to be a village schoolmaster.

I left Sibiu, in broad agreement with Emily Gerard who found:

> Life at Hermanstadt always gave me the impression of living inside one of those exquisitely minute Dutch paintings of still-life, in which the anatomy of a lobster, or the veins on a vine-leaf, are rendered with microscopic fidelity, and where such insignificant objects a half-lemons or mouldy cheese-rinds are exalted to the rank of centre-pieces."[21]

In 1851, when Sibiu had just been made the capital of Transylvania, the town lay covered in deep snow. Andrew Paton,[22] after being shown to his room in an inn by a "plump Amazon with red cheeks," was unimpressed:

> In the society of Hermannstadt I observed nothing worthy of particular remark. Dinners, soiree's, and balls there were, just like dinners, soiree's and balls elsewhere... (although) at one dinner party I noticed Dutch herrings and Russian vodka served as a preliminary whet.

One man who was pleased to see Sibiu was the Rev. Nathaniel Burton.[23] On arrival at Hermannstadt in 1836, after a ten day quarantine on the

---

[21] *The Land beyond the Forest,* 1888.

[22] *The Goth and the Hun,* 1851.

[23] His book had the catchy title: *Pedestrian Journey from Constantinople through Turkey, Wallachia, Hungary, and Prussia to the Town of Hamburg.*

border between Wallachia and Transylvania, he wrote in his diary: “for the first time, I may say, since my departure from home, I saw real, honest butter.” He was greatly relieved to discover that the journey from Hermannstadt to Vienna was only ten days by coach; he hadn’t really enjoyed his travels at all.

Chapter Five

Into the Dacian Heartland

The valley to the west of Sibiu levelled into a great expanse of flat, dull country, which encouraged me to make a detour to the more undulating south. Passing through Sălişte, too early in the morning to spy any of Emil Hoppe's Conemarra beauties, I wove my way up through the beech woods into the spruce covered Cibin Mountains of the Southern Carpathians and on to Poiana Sibului on the slopes of Cindrel. A teeming Sunday market was in full swing. Stalls of onions, cabbages, tomatoes, cloves of garlic, and melons gave the colours of a fairground to the little square. A few basic clothes and ironmongery items were on sale, jumbled between massive displays of wicker and woven baskets of all shapes and sizes.

From there, I drove across country down a long, bare spur, stopping to scan the vast plain to the north. A lone shepherd came over the brow with his flock and guard dogs; these hill pastures are known as the "kingdom" of the Romanian shepherds.

At the next town, Sebeş, the thirteenth century Evangelical Church of St. Maria was remarkable for its exceptional external carvings of stone figurines, a marvellous symbiosis of the Romanesque and Gothic styles. The mason and his sculptors had endowed their stone saints with a serene slenderness to fit their perches on the narrow perpendicular buttresses.

Andrew Crosse[1] was interested in local sporting pursuits in these parts. He noted that Sebeş "has very good snipe in spring and autumn" and

---

[1] *Round about the Carpathians,* 1878.

"there is good coursing in the neighbourhood of Cluj." He also had an eye for the ladies and discovered Morul, another one of those villages "celebrated for the beauty of its women:"

> Several very pretty girls in their picturesque costumes were gathered round the village well, engaged in filling their classical-shaped pitchers. Every movement of their arms was grace itself. The action was not from the elbow, but from the shoulder, whereby one sees the arm extended in the curved line of beauty, instead of sticking out at a sharp angle, as with us western races.

In the Orăştie Mountains, to the southwest of Sebeş, lies the very heart of Dacian Romania. During the great migrations of the third millennium BC, Indo-European groups of warriors and their families had settled in large areas of Europe and in the southeast in what is now Bulgaria. They were known as Thracians and their northern kinsfolk in Romania as Dacians. The culture of these people was far in advance of their fellow European barbarians; towns sprung up around their great defended strongholds such as Blidaru and Costeşti and key trading posts, defended by minor forts, were established. Trade was well organised and encouraged; silver and gold work, pottery, iron implements and weapons, all of extremely high quality, were produced for home consumption and for export to the sophisticated Roman world to the south.

The Romans had been on the Danube since 12 BC, the river forming the northern boundary of their Eastern Empire, and they were well aware of the attractive prize which lay across the river. In 85 AD, Dacian forces attacked the Romans in Moesia, killing the governor. This prompted the Emperor Domitian to take personal charge of the counter attack which succeeded until he handed over command to General Fuscus, whose army was wiped out in the next engagement. Rome regained the initiative at the battle of Tapae in 89 AD when the Dacians were thoroughly beaten and their teenage warrior king, Decebalus, made to pay an annual tribute to Rome and allow Roman armies free passage through his territories. Yet the Emperor did not view these arrangements as conclusive for he refused to adopt the title "Dacicus" at this point.

The Emperor Trajan came to power in 98 AD, at a moment when there were increasing threats to his northern frontier. In the west, the German tribes were getting bolder; in the east, he perceived the Dacians were flexing their muscles. In the winter of 100-101 AD, Trajan massed ten legions, vexillations of other legions, and a huge number of auxiliary troops at Viminacium on the south banks of the Danube (today's Vidin in Bulgaria) and crossed by pontoon bridge the following spring. No opposition was encountered until Tapae when there was an indecisive encounter. The Romans settled into their winter quarters and the next spring launched an attack on Sarmizegetusa through the Red Tower Pass. Decebalus, nervous of the outcome, was trying throughout to get in touch with Trajan. He sent him a giant funghus with a request scratched on it in Latin to the effect: 'Leave me alone.' So great was the dread of the messenger that he fell down dead after delivering it into Trajan's hands. Decebalus finally succeeded in establishing contact when the Emperor received a delegation of prominent Dacian nobles. Unfortunately for them, Trajan's terms were unacceptable and after a further battle Decebalus was forced to surrender and his capital occupied.

By 105 AD, the Dacians had rearmed and took the Roman garrison commander hostage. Once more the legions hurried to Sarmizegetusa, making the journey in remarkable time by using their new bridge over the Danube at Turnu-Severin, described by Cassius Dio as "surpassing all others (of Trajan's constructions) in its magnitude." In the spring of 106 AD, they mounted a two-pronged assault on the town, which they put to a ferocious siege. For the Dacians, all was lost; some nobles took poison; others, including Decebalus, escaped. They were ruthlessly hunted down. A surrounded Decebalus took his own life by cutting his throat; he was just twenty-five. Trajan sent his head to Rome.

The story of these wars is told on the spiral ribbon of reliefs on Trajan's column in Rome, which was dedicated to him in 113 AD. The monument can also be seen in the Victorian and Albert Museum in London where there is a full scale 1861 plaster cast of the 2,500 relief figures, in two sections for ease of viewing. The dominant articles on the pedestal are the dozens of Dacian shields, richly decorated with an array of floriate and planetary designs. Decebalus would have carried just such a shield, probably wearing a Phrygian type helmet and chain mail body armour with a braided tunic and cloak. One relief features the Standard of Decebalus, the body of a dragon surmounted by a wolf's head. An interpretation of this configuration suggests the harnessing of evil, symbolised by the dragon, as a gift to the ancient god Zalmoxis, his totem being the wolf's head — the very name Dacian means 'wolf.'

Yet the Roman occupation was to last but a short time as one barbarian attack followed another; Carps, Goths, Taifali, Bastarns, and Heruli battered at the doors until the Emperor Aurelian ordered the withdrawal from Dacia in 271. By 275, the Romans had gone forever, leaving the country open for the Gepids and the Visigoths. For the next thousand years, it was the prey of one invader after another. William Miller in his *History of the Balkans*[2] eerily described this time:

> The lamp of history sheds but little light upon the gloom of this long period. We can see in the dim distance the figures of the barbarians moving in lengthy processions across the scene but we cannot discern their features or observe their gestures.

Emily Gerard[3] told the story of the treasure of Decebalus. Surrounded by the Roman legions, he diverted the Sargetia, or Strell River, from its course, built strong vaulted cellars on the dry river bed for storing his gold, silver, and precious stones, covered them up with stone and gravel and then had the river brought back to its original course. As an afterthought, he executed the entire workforce in the interests of national security. However, according to James Noyes,[4] Decebalus's secretary, Vicilis, reportedly told Trajan where the treasure was in order to save his own life and that should have been the end of the story. How come, then, that over 40,000 gold pieces were found on the banks of the river by local anglers in 1543?

Never one to pass up the chance to tell a good story, Emily went on to relate the tale of another Romanian hoard, the treasure of the Persian King, Darius.

> To approach the treasure, one must pass through a strong iron door lying towards the west. This door can be opened from the outside but whoever is not in the possession of the secret is sure to fall down through a trapdoor into a terrible abyss where he will be cut to pieces by a thousand swords set in motion by machinery; therefore it is necessary to bridge over the trapdoor with several stout planks before entering. After this a second iron door is reached, in front of which there are lying two life-sized lions of massive silver. This second door leads onto a large hall where round a long table are sitting figures of King Darius and of twelve other kings whom he had

---

[2] 1894.

[3] *The Land beyond the Forest,* 1888.

[4] *The Frontier Lands of the Christian and the Turk,* 1858.

> vanquished in battle. King Darius himself who sits at the head of the table is formed of purest gold whilst the other monarchs, six on either side, are of silver. This hall leads into a cellar where there are ranged twenty four barrels bound with hoops of silver; half contain gold, the other half silver pieces.

From Sebeş, I headed west to Hunedoara, the great thirteenth century castle of the Corvin family. After King Sigismund of Hungary had met with near total disaster against the Turks at Nicopolis in 1396, he was forced to reorganise his army, and it was during this time that John Hunyadi,[5] a Vlach and member of the Romanian elite in Southeastern Transylvania, appeared on the scene. The story of John's origin is woven in the annals of folklore. Donald Hall had one version in his book, *Romania Furrow:*[6]

> Towards the end of the 14th century, Sigismond de Luxembourg, King of Hungary, held his parliament at Hunedoara. One day when he was out hunting, he met a peasant girl, Elisabeta Margineanu, and fell passionately in love with her. Escaping from the hunt he spent days with her in the forest and in the end asked her to marry him. When she refused he left her. But later when she thought she was with child, she went to Sigismond and said she was ready to be his wife. But he had changed his mind, so she returned to her home and married a peasant, Voicu. The child was born and called Ion Huniade. One day when Elisabeta and Voicu and their child were in the forest, Voicu left them to find food. Elisabeta lay down under a tree and fell asleep. The child, playing with his mother's ring, dropped it and a raven swooped down and flew away with it. When Voicu returned, the raven hopped from branch to branch mocking him. So Voicu shot it and recovered the ring. Ion Huniade, when he grew up, took as his arms a raven with a ring in its beak.

Somehow this version struck me as rather flat compared to John Paget's.[7] After days and nights of passion in the forest, the King gave Elisabeta his signet ring and said that if she was ever with child, she should present it to him in Buda where he would treat her and the child with kind-

[5] Also known as John Corvinus and as Johann Corvin von Hunniad, prince of Siebenburgen.

[6] 1933.

[7] *Hungary and Transylvania,* 1839.

ness. She did indeed have a child and it was on her way to Buda with the ring that she fell asleep. It was a jackdaw that stole the ring and her brother who shot it. And when they arrived at Buda, Sigismond was so overjoyed that he presented his son with the town of Hunyed — and sixty villages all round. Szonakos, Elisabeta's birthplace, was declared a tax free zone forever!

Having learned his military trade as a young condottiere in Italy, John Hunyadi raised a fighting force to face the Ottomans, virtually leading a one-man crusade. In 1442, he defeated Turkish attacks on Sibiu, the Iron Gates and Ialomiţa River, and it was on 22 July, St. Mary Magdalene's Day, in 1456, that he counterattacked the Turks after they had failed to maintain their siege on Belgrade. He decisively routed them in savage hand-to-hand fighting, and such was the rejoicing at this victory, that all the church bells in Rome rang out together; even in far off England, a solemn mass was held in Oxford. The Pope bestowed upon John the title 'Athlete of Christ,' but he died of the plague soon after.

It was John's son, the 15 year old Matthias, who was elected king of Hungary in 1458 and went on to provide the last effective defence against the Turks until his death in 1490. Thirty six years later, weakened by the disaster at the battle of Mohács, where the Serbian peasant forces of Ivan the Black had inflicted terrible damage on the Hungarian army, the Turkish Army of Divine Light' struck and routed the remnants of the once mighty Hungarian army. Such was the history that swirled around the corridors and spiralling staircases of Hunedoara.

Sandwiched between a steel mill and petrochemical complex, its once commanding position on a rocky outcrop obscured by a towering forest of industrial smokestacks, tatty opaque polystyrene sheeting blanking out any view from its massive defensive slit windows, Hunedoara Castle still has immense menace and conjures up ghostly parades of history. Here are the Hussite knights, refugees from Bohemia, and experts in firearms; here, the heavy cavalry of German ritters, and the small horses of the Hungarian light cavalry, forerunners of the hussars, all rubbing shoulders together. Over there, in the Great Hall, John Hunyadi appears in the latest style of Milanese armour, including a great bacinet; he is *à la mode* with his Italian and German contemporaries. Later these same soldiers would form the core of Matthias's "Black Army," over 30,000 troops equipped in Blackened armour and skilled in winter warfare. One can hear the echoing clash of steel shod boots, the clank of shutting visors and metallic rattles of swords upon shields as knights returned from their bloody skirmishes. Now, a hurrah is heard as a sack of heads is held up to the prince. However, on the day of my visit, none of this was at the forefront of the minds of the hundreds of Romanians splashing about in the Cserna River below. Oblivious to the menacing towers above them, they were intent on being frisky and frivolous on a hot August day.

Although Hunyadi Castle was destroyed by fire in April 1854, Patrick Leigh Fermor[8] found in 1938 that:

> the fine state of the castle was an exception to the post-war neglect or abolition of Hungarian monuments which I had been hearing about, and for a very good reason. Janos Hunyadi, says the *Encyclopaedia Britannica,* and nearly all historians agree, 'was the son of Vojk or Vaic), a magyarised Vlach,' which means that the great crusader was of Rumanian origin... anyone reading the explanatory notices inside the castle might assume that Hunyadi was a purely Rumanian hero: the Hungarian activities with which his whole life was bound up were underplayed to such a degree that he might have had nothing to do with the kingdom.

What a shame such nationalistic fervour petered out when it came to granting planning permission for sprawling industrial complexes to be erected in the castle's grounds.

Forty miles to the north of Hunedoara lies the national town of Alba Iulia and it was near here that the first English traveller to Romania, Captain John Smith, best known for his dealings in Virginia and his relationship with the Indian princess, Pocahontas takes up his tale. Given 'leave and licence' as an 'English gentleman, captain of 250 soldiers' by Sigismond Bathory, Duke of Transylvania, at Braşov in 1602, Smith rose to fame when he killed three Turks — Turbashaw, Grualgo, and Bonny Mulgro — in a challenge of mortal combat, probably at or near to Alba Iulia. His success was short-lived for, after defeating a Turkish army at the Battle of Rotenthurn (The Red Tower) at the entrance to the Olt Pass, his army of 11,000 men was attacked by a Tartar force of 40,000 on 18 November 1602. It was a dreadful battle with over 30,000 killed on either side, "some headlesse, armelesse, and leglesse, all cut and mangled."[9] Smith was fortunate to be taken alive.

---

[8] *Between the Woods and the Water,* 1986.

[9] *The True Travels and Adventures of Captain John Smith,* 1630.

Sold as a slave in Constantinople to Bashaw Bogall, he was given as a gift to a pretty lady, Charatza Tragabigzanda, for whom he worked until, provoked by her brother, a particularly obnoxious pasha,

> he beat the Tymors brains with his threshing bat, for they have no flails.... clothed himself in his clothes, hid his body under the straw, filled his knapsacke with corne, shut the doores, mounted his horse, and runne into the desart at all adventure.

Smith made his way to Morocco via Transylvania where he described his experiences in Romania as

> in all this his life he seldom met with more respect, mirth, content and entertainment.... in Transylvania he found so many good friends, that but to see and rejoice himself in his native country, he would ever hardly have left them.

It was at Alba Iulia where, on 1 December 1918, Romanians gathered in their thousands to mark the union of Transylvania, Wallachia, and Moldavia. The significance of that day was stupendous for it was here, in 1600, that Prince Michael the Brave had so briefly reigned over a fledgling united Romania. The Church of National Unity, built in 1921, is testament to the efficacy of good, thoughtful design, making full use of the Brâncoveanu tradition with shady belvederes, elegant loggias, and well-laid out gardens. It was the scene of the coronation of King Ferdinand and Queen Marie in 1922.

The idea of a coronation had been mooted soon after the peace settlements but could find no consensus among the warring political parties, thus prompting Ferdinand and Marie to refuse to participate. The Coronation Church at Alba Iulia stood empty. When Brătianu, the architect of Greater Romania, was re-elected prime minister in 1922, the royal couple agreed to a ceremony. Yet the event was still beset with problems: the Transylvanians refused to take part and the Catholic Church forbade the king from being crowned by an Orthodox priest in a Romanian church. The latter difficulty was neatly sidestepped by Queen Marie who proposed an outdoor ceremony and for the king to crown himself.

Marie took on the project with her unique sense of theatricality and flair for design. On the day, after a private mass, the royal couple emerged from the church and were led by the bishops onto a dias in the centre of the public square. Under a canopy held aloft by six giant spears, the royal couple stood silently, Ferdinand in a cloak of deep purple velvet, edged with gold embroidery and trimmed with ermine, and Marie in a gold mantle studded with rubies in small roundels, bordered in purple with a trim of white ermine. Before a crowd of 300,000, Nando crowned himself with the iron crown of his uncle, Carol the First, made out of a Turkish canon which he had personally captured at the Battle of Plevna[10] in 1877. The king then turned to Marie, supplicant on her knees, and placed a huge gold crown, set with rubies, emeralds, turquoises and moonstones, on her head. Surrounded by the royal ladies dressed in gold and courtiers in mauve and silver, this was a glorious sight from medieval times, as had always been the intention of Marie. The guns roared, bells rang, and a huge cheer went up from the crowd.

Alongside the Coronation Church is the Gothic Roman Catholic Church, one of the most splendid churches in Romania, built at the same time as Notre Dame. Apart from its churches and its eighteenth century fortress, the town of Alba Iulia alas has few attractions, having been mercilessly 'improved' with banal modern apartment blocks flanking avenues which, inappropriately, all appear to lead to the old fort.

Equally significant in the story of the struggle for Romanian self-determination in Transylvania is the little town of Blaj, twenty miles to the west of Alba Iulia, on the junction of the rivers Târnava Mare and Târnava Mică. It was here, in 1848, that the Romanians of Transylvania published a manifesto, hand printed by students, affirming the need to recognise the Romania nation. On 30 April, 4,000 people gathered on the Field of Liberty to show their support; a month later their ranks had swollen to 40.000. In September that year 60,000 armed and distinctly militant peasants met there, rejecting the union of Transylvania with Hungary and demanding the abolition of serfdom and the election of a representative Diet. Civil war broke out the following year, only to end inconclusively. The status quo was maintained; Vienna kept control.

As I wandered its streets in the last rays of the setting harvest sun, Blaj had lost its once revolutionary fervour; it was a quiet, prosperous county town. There was one surprise awaiting me in the Greek Catholic Cathedral of the Holy Trinity built in 1750-1760. Its classic plain Baroque exterior belied an astonishing iconostasis inside. Its size — at least 35 feet high by 40 feet across — its proportions, the quality of its paintings suggested that this was one of the finest examples in Romania. Carved out of

---

[10] Carol had the distinction of being the last European sovereign to personally command his army in a battle on foreign soil. The English kings ceased this practice after George II fought at Dettingen in 1745.

wood, the iconostasis is topped by two silver dragons on their backs in submission to St. George, both interlaced and intertwined. The top tier of icons of the fifteen Saints are separated from the lives of the Saints below by an intricate border of scrolled-wood carvings. Each painting is framed by perfectly-proportioned wooden pillars. Over the knave, the rotunda has paintings of the Saints with their halos, waistbands, socks, and shoes picked out in silver which bestowed on them a glittering luminosity, attracting the eye upwards to this lively, heavenly host. It was a spectacular display of Byzantine art.

The artistic origins of these icons go back several centuries before the birth of Christ and continue until the beginning of the sixth century AD. Despite their initial antipathy to art in all its forms, which was widely associated with paganism, and their preoccupation with the Second Coming, the early Christians lived in a time of serious social and economic breakdown. With the old ideals of Roman republicanism in rapid decline, they despaired of life under a corrupt bureaucracy and the attendant widespread disorder and poverty, and they soon compromised, accepting the concept of pictorial theology so that the Christian message could reach the huge numbers of people who could not read.

The earliest art that is definitely Christian are the paintings in the baptistry at Dura-Europas in Mesopotamia. Only a handful of scenes remain: 'the Good Shepherd,' 'Adam and Eve in the Garden of Eden,' 'the Women of Samaria at the Well,' 'the Three Martyrs at the Tomb,' 'Christ Healing a Paralytic,' and 'Christ and St. Peter Walking on the Water.' These paintings were executed long before the establishment of Christian iconography, yet five hundred years later, strangely they would occupy the least important places in Christian religious art, if they were used at all. The 'Good Shepherd' of Hellenistic origin was dropped altogether.

No actual image of Christ was passed down in the early Christian Church, in contrast to the historically recorded likenesses of St. Peter and St. Paul in Rome. The earliest tradition of the images of Christ's life were passed down orally, hence the strong relationship between hymns and chants and the compositions of icons. This marked subordination to a text, the "literary imperative" characteristic of Byzantine religious art, accompanied by the shunning of individual creativity, led to the *Painters' Manuals* or *Pattern Books of Mount Athos* in 1468 and of *Stroganov* in Russia in 1552, which were used throughout the Byzantine world.

In their portraits of Christ, icon painters had the task of reproducing the ideal image — that is of combining the sublimity of the Divine Person with His true humanity. At the same time, the beauty of the humanity redeemed by Him was supposed to shine forward in the beauty of His image. Although pictures in icons are images of human beings — icon actually means: "image as the likeness of a prototype or model" — the paintings have deep mysterious meanings.

For instance, since time immemorial, the sun has been revered as the divine symbol of energy, without whose warmth-giving rays, all life on earth — plants, animals, and mankind — would perish. Thus, the halo behind the head of the human image on an icon represents the shape of the rising sun and the colour gold its light. This device was used by the Egyptians and Persians long before Christianity.

Many of the symbols of the early Christian Church are equally as old. The mother and child theme can be traced back to Osiris and Horus from Egypt. The cave, a landscape feature which appears in many icons, was also the scene of the birth of Buddha; Rhea's birth of Zeus in a cave in Crete; Venus's visit to Adonis in a cave; Mithras's birth in a mountain cave (indeed his followers worshipped him underground).

As St. Augustine of Hippo wrote in the fourth century:

> The very thing we now call the Christian religion was not wanting among the ancients from the beginning of the human race, until Christ came in the flesh, after which the true religion which already existed, began to be called Christian.

Icons are never seen as new in the sense of separate and recent. All icons of the Archangel Michael, for instance, are seen as the same icon. They are all of the same reality, of the one icon. No icon is ever copyrighted — one may freely copy an icon since it is not an individual work but the one work. When an icon is finished, the writer of the icon may add to the back his or her name — 'by the hand of' — but the image is never signed. No icon therefore belongs to the iconographer.

At one stage, the very existence of icons was challenged. In 725 the Byzantine Emperor Leo addressed the question: Is art the ally of religion or its worst enemy? Is the visual depiction of the godhead possible? And, if so, should it be permitted? Logically, he argued, if we accept the divine nature of Christ, we cannot then logically approve the two or three dimensional portrayal of Him as a human being. At the time of Leo, icons were openly worshipped in their own right and occasionally even used as godparents at baptisms. After some debate, Leo ordered that all icons were to be destroyed and so both the beards of intractable monks and their great libraries were set on fire. His motives were almost certainly more political than philosophical and were an attempt to break the power of the Church. Thus a vast treasure of icons was destroyed or dispersed to caches in the far corners of the Empire. It was sixty years before the conflict was resolved in favour of the iconodules and the great art reintroduced across the Orthodox Church.

Chapter Six

Gypsies, the Last Romantics

I left Transylvania along the valley of the Târnava Mică, heading northeast, past Târnăveni and Căpâlna de Sus until I reached Praid in the foothills of the Eastern Carpathians, the last bastion of the Hungarian language. Once over the first hills of the Munţii Gurghiu, I drove across the wide valley of the Upper Mureş until the border with Moldavia at Gheorgheni, where the farms changed in appearance, now with high fences and ornate wooden gates, a feature I would see again in Maramureş. Along the way, I met four young Gypsy women en route to the weekly child clinic and I persuaded them to pose for a photograph. They thought it a great laugh and, after striking a price with me, cavorted gaily in front of the camera in their bright flamboyant dresses. Further along, two little Gypsy girls in Gheorgheni insisted on being snapped for free.

Gypsies have long fascinated the traveller to Romania. Sitwell[1] enthused that:

> it is worth the journey across Europe to meet them ...their dark figures crouched or stood around a fire. A tent of sacking was in the background. These are the true Transylvanian Gypsies, swarthy as Moors, and with long hair reaching down to their shoulders... they are thieves and liars with the look of ascetics who have fallen from grace.

---

[1] *Roumanian Journey,* 1938.

He quotes extensively from Liszt's *The Gypsy in Music* written in the mid-nineteenth century, which had an enormous influence across Europe in portraying the Gypsies as the last of the true romantic characters.

> They are the outlaws of the human race, driven by their own will from place to place, and never staying in one spot after the ashes of their first fire had grown cold. The contemptuous trickery of their thefts, and the ironic sport of deceit they practised on all they met, bound them to this strange way of life they loved. Their wanderings took them away from the sunrise into the sunset, as if they were flying from a fate which threatened them.
>
> They stretched themselves to sleep upon low branches that made a hammock for their bodies, while every leaf seemed to have a nightingale's voice. Climbing down from the boughs, an eldertree blossom, or a branch of briar or hawthorn, caught their fancy. Their happiness lay apart from other men as they wandered. All their food they stole, raiding lonely farms, or robbing the woods. They shook the wild growing trees and brought the fruit down like savoury hailstones. When they came to the shrubs that strew the ground with trodden fragments, they gathered the sharp, red berries and ate them greedily straightaway, for this was their bread as rain was their water.

Konrad Bercovici in his book, *Love and the Gypsy,*[2] got quite carried away:

> the very thought of leaving the beautiful Gypsy girl chilled me to the bone. Those burning kisses, the round arms, the sparkling eyes, her throat, her bosom, her tall bare legs, and above all, her voice — all these were too dear to me to abandon without a supreme effort.

The *Glasgow Herald* commented in its review of this book: "We are led out to wolf-ridden forests, broad streams, and murmuring fields, to the company of Tartar and Gypsy chiefs, and their dark-haired, tanned-skin mistresses."

There is a Gypsy song about a nobleman who falls in love with a Gypsy girl and the words sum up the freedom so envied by those who came across these vagabond kings and queens:

Nobleman:

---

[2] 1923.

Maiden, wilt thou go with me?
I'll give thee pearls and diamonds,
I'll give thee a couch of purple,
I'll give thee a royal palace.

Refrain:

Free is the eagle in the air
Free is the salmon in the river
Free is the deer in the forest
Freer the Gypsy where'er he wanders,
Yuchza, Yuchza.

Maiden:

My pearls are my white teeth,
My diamonds are my black eyes that shine like lightening,
My couch is the green earth,
My palace the world.

Refrain:

Ditto

James Skene[3] was quite overcome:

> When we stopped to water the horses at a brook, we saw a Gypsy girl of rare beauty filling her jars; her olive skin was pure and fine as that of a duchess — her figure matchless, and her very movement full of grace... she was called Frumoasa Ioana or Pretty Jane.

In his *Singing Winds*[4] and *The Story of the Gypsy,*[5] Bercovici was more informative although hardly more objective. "There is more joy and more happiness, there is more poetry and deep emotion in a Gypsy camp of three ragged tents than in the largest city in our civilised world" and "I am speaking of people whose vocabulary lacks two words — possessions and duty." He traced their origins back through linguistic relation to the Jats of Hindustan in North India, living near the mouth of the Oxus River.

But the burning question is when did they — the Tziganes, Zigeuner, Gypsies, Czigany, Zingari, Bohemiens — arrive? Were they the Zotts who were deported by Prince Motasim to Ainzarba in Syria in 834? When the Byzantines, known as Roums, captured the city in 856, did the

---

[3] *The Frontier Lands of the Christian and the Turk,* 1853.

[4] 1927.

[5] 1929.

Zotts steal the nickname of their new masters, i.e. Romany? But Jats had been in Europe long before; Homer speaks of the Sygynes as skilled in metalwork. The Calo or Gypsy language spoken in Romania, Hungary, Russia and Spain still contains one third Sanskrit root words. Indeed, the exodus of the Gypsies might have happened at the time of Alexander's invasion for all Gypsies still count in Greek. Skene met some Greek professors who assured him that Tsingani was from Tsincali, "black men from the Tsend, Scinde or Jud, who had come from Hindostan in 1408-09 when Timur Beg was ravaging it." Beg's idea of a good ravage was to kill 100,000 people, so the timing of their exodus makes sense.

Most travellers are prone to attempt to classify the 500 to 600 wandering tribes of Gypsies into tribes and castes. Bercovici[6] identified the *ursari* or the bear tamers; and the Laeshi who

> have remained untainted, independent and have preferred death to slavery or domesticity. Darker than the other Gypsies, almost as black as full blooded Negroes, taller, broader, lighter on their feet, with long glossy wavy hair hanging over their shoulders, eves as black as coal and teeth as white as pearls, with arched noses coming straight down from their foreheads, full-lipped and long-necked, they are the handsomest species in Europe... They do not camp in open spaces. One finds them only in ravines, in the mountains and in the forests.... The fascination of their eyes is so strong they induce people to buy or sell things they have never wanted to buy or sell. They literally hold one in a spell by the fixity of their gaze. Their voices are so hypnotising, one is mesmerised into doing their will.

Emil Hoppe[7] listed four tribes: Loila, Kukuya, Ashani, and Tschale. He concluded it is safe to say their origins lay in Northern India. James Ozanne[8] noted three classes or tribes:

> Laiesi who follow a multitude of trades. The laoutari or musicians belong to them;
>
> Vatrari or servants employed in the great houses;
>
> Netotsi or atheists "half naked and living only by theft and plunder, they feed on the flesh of cats and dogs."

---

[6] *The Story of the Gypsy,* 1929.

[7] *In Gypsy Camp and Royal Palace,* 1924.

[8] *Three Years in Roumania,* 1878.

Referring to Serboianu's *Les Tsiganes,* Sitwell[9] divided the Lăieşi into fourteen corporations:

> *Oursani* or bear tamers, who travel round, though it is forbidden by law, with dancing and performing bears. They are nomads, but live in hovels in the winter;
>
> *Tehurarii,* makers of brooms and brushes;
>
> *Caldararii,* tinkers;
>
> *Ferarii,* ironsmiths;
>
> *Costararii,* coppersmiths from Turkey;
>
> *Kudari, Blidari* or *Lingurari,* makers of pitchforks and of wooden spoons The women wear their breasts exposed and are, often, naked to the waist;
>
> *Potcovarii,* blacksmiths;
>
> *Spoitoresele,* whitewashers of houses;
>
> *Mesteri-lacatachi,* ironsmiths selling keys and bars of iron;
>
> *Laoutari,* musicians;
>
> *Vanzatoare,* flower sellers;
>
> *Vrajitoarele,* sorcerers and fortune tellers;
>
> *Vaxuitorii de ghete,* cobblers;
>
> *Salahorii,* housebuilders.

Bercovici and Ozanne agreed about the Gypsy musical instruments: the *shah aldja* or violin; the *cobza,* resembling a mandolin; *naiul* or pan pipes; *moscalu* and the *cembalo (ţambal),* a sort of portable piano. Liszt described the latter as a *"zymbala,* a sort of square tablet furnished with strings ranged similarly to those of square pianos and struck by sticks." Hoppe found the Tzigane orchestra consisting almost always of two violins, a cello, a bass, a reed or flute, and a cymbal.

At the age of five, girls will know how to dance the Tanana, their racial dance consisting of leaps and lascivious poses. An endearing Gypsy proverb, 'a tent without a wife is like a fiddle without a string,' gives rise to much speculation about their sex lives. Bercovici stated that a Gypsy girl is usually a mother before she is eleven years old, the bride being bought and paid for. "Giving herself away for money" did not constitute

---

[9] *Roumanian Journey.* 1938.

adultery. William Wilkinson, who disapproved of virtually every facet of Romanian life in his *Account of the Principalities of Wallachia and Moldavia*[10] in 1820, sounded off:

> Both sexes are slovenly and dirty. The women are of the most depraved character. None of them follow the regular line of public prostitutes but at the same time none refuse their favours when the slightest offer of money is made.

Emily Gerard[11] made a less censorious judgement and stated simply that "the relations between the sexes are mostly free and unrestrained by any attempt at morality."

James Ozanne[12] wrote with authority about the religion of the Gypsies. According to the Tziganes, all religion is based on the harmony of astronomical phenomena; and Brahmanism, Judaism, and Christianity are but forms of the religion whose cosmogonic mysteries have been revealed to them by their ancestors. The sky is a vast sea of darkness from which light emanates and to which it returns. God is the ix or the invisible axis around which eternity revolves. The sidereal zone which we term the zodiac is the stole or starry robe which God puts on in the East when Pan sets in the West. It is from this stole, the apostole, that have proceeded all the grand voices which have made themselves heard throughout the ages. As in most religions, numbers are charged with meaning:

> The four points of the solstices and the equinoxes are the four principal heavenly messengers.
>
> The four seasons or times determined by the points are the four great voices or oracles of God, his four great prophets or evangelists.
>
> The twelve months which complete these four great times are the twelve little books of God.
>
> The twelve oxen or bulls of the night and the day sustain the ocean of the seasons and the brazen wall of Solomon's temple; the twelve tables of the laws of Moses and Romulus; the twelve sons of Jacob; the twelve apostles.

---

[10] This is one of the key eyewitness accounts of early nineteenth century Romania.

[11] *The Land beyond the Forest,* 1888.

[12] *Three Years in Roumania,* 1878.

Walter Starkie,[13] intrepid as ever, found himself in some difficulties with the Gypsies from time to time. He met up with one group and was dragged off to a party in a tent. His host

> muttered the words 'chai shukar' and I understood he wanted to bring a girl in for me. I shook my head but he laughed and ran out of the tent. In a few minutes he returned with a young girl who did not look more than thirteen years of age. She was a shy and wild little thing and the man had to drag her into the tent by force. She had nothing on but a dirty blue smock and was barefoot. Around her neck, however, she wore a chain of coloured beads. Her body was as lithe as a panther's, her skin hazel-coloured and her hair as jet-coloured as her eyes. The Gypsy stood there watching the effect the girl's beauty would have on me. She was his daughter...

Starkie then got indignant and started to moralise about this uncouth behaviour. His story ended when the Gypsy got drunk and attacked him. This man, he assured us, was a netotsi, "who are the most fierce of all when roused."

Gypsies today are much in evidence throughout Romania. Some still adhere to their traditional way of life, camping in woods and by roadsides; others of more entrepreneurial bent build large houses with exotic fairy tale tin roofs on the outskirts of towns. One camp I came across was a collection of huts, made of polymer sheeting propped up with sticks, erected on a village green. It was pouring with rain and a cold Easterly wind spread its chilly tentacles into every crevice of the rickety structures. It was hard to imagine a more miserable set-up as the water level rose, turning cart tracks into angry muddy rivers. Yet inside these tents of industrial debris, life was jolly, pots bubbled away on open wood fires, children scampered around, matriarchs gossiped, and dogs crept furtively about, determined to steal whatever was going.

An army of Gypsy ladies keeps the streets of Bucharest clean. Small, very dirty children beg for money at traffic lights. Collectively, the Gypsies, their women adorned in bright coloured clothes, still manage to defy the twentieth century dictat to conform and such defiance is hard to begrudge in a uniformed world of state supremacy, universal jeans, and tacky trainers.

---

[13] *Raggle Taggle,* 1929.

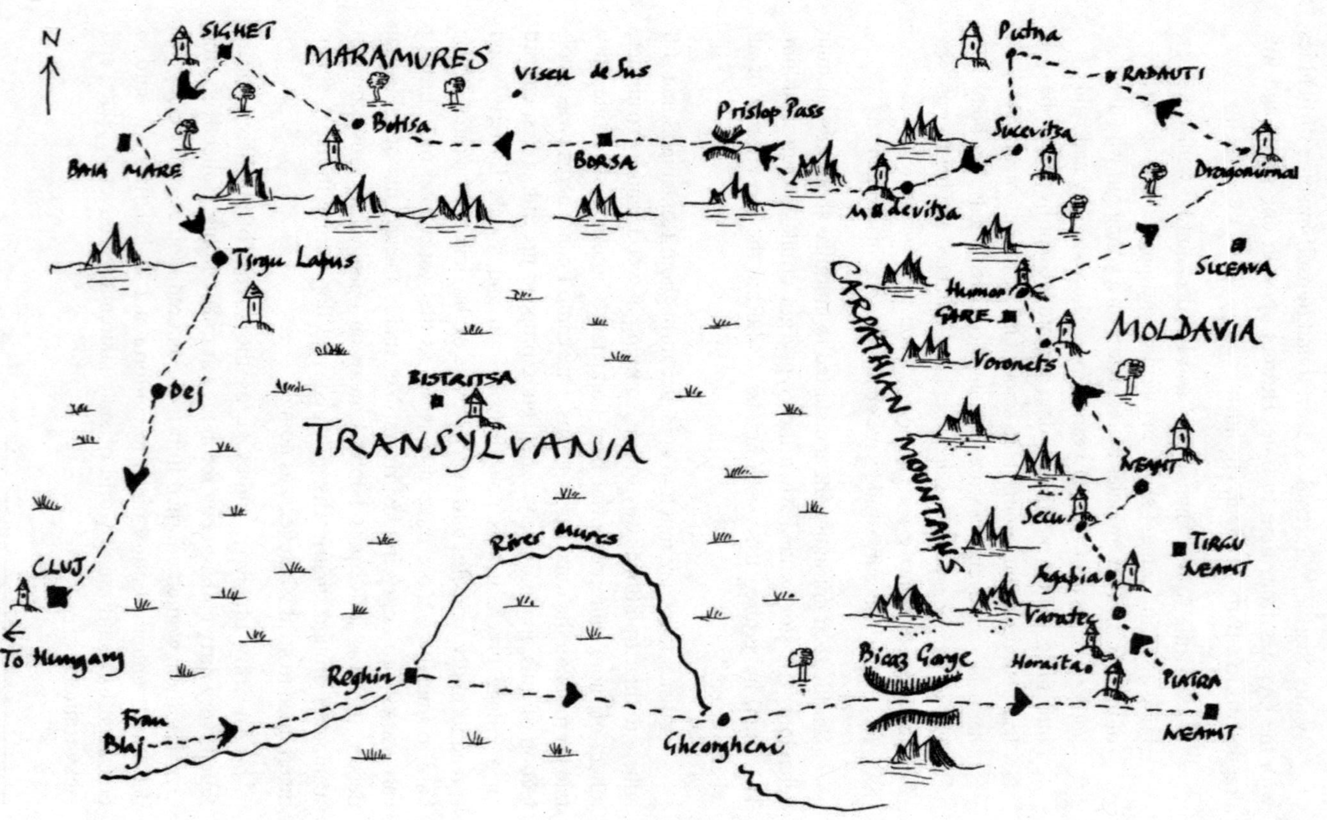
N
SIGHET
MARAMURES
Viseu de Sus
Botisa
Baia Mare
Borsa
Prislop Pass
Putna
RADAUTI
Sucevitsa
Dragomirnal
Moldevitsa
Tirgu Lapus
SUCEAVA
Humor
GARE
MOLDAVIA
Voronets
Dej
BISTRITSA
TRANSYLVANIA
CARPATHIAN MOUNTAINS
NEAMT
Secu
TIRGU NEAMT
Agapia
Varatec
River Mures
CLUJ
To Hungary
Reghin
From Blaj
Gheorgheni
Bicaz Gorge
Horaita
PIATRA NEAMT

Chapter Seven

Moldavia, a New Perception of the World

After a glorious stay in an almost tropical Transylvania, I headed to the northeast of Romania; driving through the night until, at dawn, I drew near to the Bicaz Pass, the entrance into Northern Moldavia. Adam Neale, a physician to the British Embassy in Constantinople, had set off on the Ayrshire Post Office packer on 19 July 1805 to Germany, Poland, Moldavia, and Turkey.[1] He wrote about the origin of the word 'Moldavia':

> The primeval Scythian inhabitants like the Hindus believed in the incarnation of the divinity in the person of a man called Xamolxis who, after being a slave in Greece and Egypt, returned to his native land and hid himself in a cavern for three years in the side of Mount Cogoeon. He attempted the civilisation of his countryman and as the most likely way to gain their confidence in his supernatural powers, he made them believe he possessed eternal life and was just raised from the dead. It was the custom of Scythian kings to retire to this holy mountain to consult the eternal priest or Mollah; and from this patriarch the country was called Mollah-div-ia or the territory of the immortal Mollah.

---

[1] His book, *Travels through Some Parts of Germany, Moldavia, and Turkey* (1820) is one of the best accounts of travelling in Romania at that time.

By any account, this was a preposterous if amusing explanation and conveniently overlooked the fact that the river running throughout the principality was called the Moldova. But why? James Samuelson's[2] answer was better if equally far-fetched: Bogdan, the voivode of Maramureş, went out hunting with his dog, Molda, and after crossing the Carpathians, found a beautiful country with a river flowing through its midst. What better than to call the river after his dog?

The Bicaz Gorge is where the Bicaz River cuts a dramatic, narrow swathe through the limestone mountains of Hăsmaş. Like an eighteenth century Alpine engraving, it beggars the imagination as its steep walls, or pietre, tower up three thousand feet, leaving a sliver of a passage of a mere thirty foot to squeeze through. The central part, known as Hell's Gorge, was peaceful on a warm summer's morning as I drove slowly through it, but in the torrents of spring the noise must be deafening. My arrival in Moldavia was a good deal less eventful than William Lithgow's[3] in the early 1600s.

> I entered Moldouia; where for my welcome in the midst of a border-wood, I was beset with six murderers, Hungarians and Moldavians; where hauing with many prayers saued my life, they robbed mee of threescore Hungar Duccats of gold, and all my Turkisk clothes, leauing me stark naked; save only they returned to me my Patents, Papers, and Scales.

Lithgow was left tied to an oak tree until rescued by friendly shepherds the next day.

Described by one biographer as "unamiable," Lithgow had the knack of getting himself into trouble. Born in Lanark in 1582, he left Scotland under a cloud, 'that delilah wrong,' after being found with a certain Miss Lockhart. Her brothers had taken umbrage and cut off young William's ears. From then on, he was on the road and by the end of his life claimed to have visited "forty-eight kingdomes, ancient and moderne; twenty-one Reipublickes, ten absolute principalities, with two hundred Ilands." The story of his travels is aptly called *The Rare Adventures and Painefull Peregrinations of William Lithgow.* The 'painefull' was a reference to the treatment dished out to him by the Spanish authorities with the enthusiastic help of the

---

[2] *Roumania, Past and Present,* 1882.

[3] *Rare Adventures and Painefull Peregrinations,* 1632.

Inquisition; he was so incensed by this that on return to England, he assaulted the Spanish ambassador and was jailed for eleven months!

Moldavia would have appealed to him for the two were about as ungovernable as each other. When his boyars refused to follow his orders in regard to the defence against a Russian invasion, the ruler, Nicholas Mavrocordaro,[4] was so incensed at their timidity that he summoned his grooms to bring thirty horses before him. He then, in the manner of Caligula, appointed the horses as his ministers. The list would have looked like this:[5]

Title	**Function**
Ban of Craiova	Viceroy of Little Wallachia
Vel-Vornic	Interior Minister; Governor of the Carpathians
The Great Vornic	Governor of the Lowlands
Logothet	Minister of Justice
The Great Spathar	Minister of War
The Great Vestiar	Treasurer and Master of the Robes
The Great Postelnik	Master of the Post
Paharnic	Chief Butler and Cupbearer
The Great Stolnik	Chief Cook
The Great Comis	Master of the Horse
The Aga	Chief of Police
The Great Pitar	Inspector of Commissariat

Imagine the difficulty of commentating on a horse race if this was the field.

On the far side of the Bicaz Pass lies Piatra Neamţ, a once small market town now defiled by dreadful tower blocks and a concrete town centre. It is the gateway to the magnificent monasteries[6] of Moldavia and the splendiferous painted churches of Bucovina. A remarkable English woman, Mary Walker, travelled here in 1888 and recorded her journey in

[4] 1711-1715.

[5] James Samuelson, *Roumania, Past and Present.*

[6] A monastery or *mănăstire* can either be occupied by monks or nuns but never both!

Untrodden Paths in Romania. She found Neamţ a "long, straggling, dirty, untidy place." My journey in these parts was to follow hers almost exactly.

Here was a world placed between the East and the West. At the time of the fall of Byzantium the greatest Christian capital of its time, the Wallachian and Moldavian princes, together with the Sreb 'krals' and Bulgarian 'tsars,' held the line of the Orthodox religion against the incursions of 'the heaven-chosen soldiers of Islam' and their legions 'forever in ecstasy before the grandeur of Allah.' Ascending the throne of Moldavia in 1457, Stephen the Great consolidated Bucovina or 'the country of the beech trees' as his political base and took stock of his options. His Western ally, Matthias Corvinus, was preoccupied with his European ambitions; to his north, Casimir of Poland was focused on the Baltic states and in the East, Ivan of Moscow was confronting the Tartars. Stephen's stark conclusion was that he would have to face the Turkish threat alone and therein lay his claim to greatness. A Romanian historian, Miron Costin, paints this pen portrait:

> Stephen was not tall of stature; he was irascible, cruel, prone to shed innocent blood, often at meals he would order people to be put to death, without legal sentence. But he was acute of judgement, sober, not proud, but a stubborn defender of his rights, in war always on the spot... generally favoured by victory, never depressed by misfortune.

It is strange to think that, despite these uncouth traits, Stephen became a saint.

Behind every great man, as they say, is a woman. In Stephen's case it was his mother. Before engaging the Turkish army at Războieni, Stephen sensibly installed his family in the fortress at Neamţ. The battle went badly and Stephen hurried back to organise the defence of the town. Somewhat to his surprise, he found the gates closed to him and his mother, standing on the wall, ordered him to go back and try harder "as she would never receive him again until victorious." He dutifully complied and the Turks, totally caught oil-guard by a man they thought they had just soundly defeated, were sent packing.

It was Stephen who ordained a series of churches including Voroneţ and Pătrăuţi as a cornerstone of the psychological defence against Islam. The sixteenth century was to bring a wave of brilliant decoration under his illegitimate son, Petru Rareş, who not only built monasteries but restored them as well, for monasteries had a short lifespan in those days. This was an age of transition from Medievalism to Modernism, when artistic, literary, and political individuality overturned and enlightened the dry style of medieval painting and manuscripts. The achievements of the painters who covered the exteriors and interiors of these churches are unique in the Christian world. Half a century later, the trend of exterior painting had disappeared and was replaced by sober white plaster covering the facades. Romanian academician Răzvan Theodorescu summarises this astonishing period as:

> Something more than a magnificent movement of Orthodox art. In this cultural space it expressed the search of an epoch of great faith, the changes of a certain mentality, the sharpening of a certain sensibility, the increase of knowledge, the assertion of a new perception of the world.

The great themes of the exterior paintings are common to most of the churches and monasteries. 'The Heavenly Hierarchy' or 'The Prayer of All Saints' is found on the apse of the chancel and on the exterior part that corresponds to the nave, depicting hundreds of winged characters, figures of seraphs, saints, prophets, apostles, fathers, martyrs and bishops who heralded, founded and perfected the early Christian Church.

A second theme, 'The Tree of Jesse,' is based on Isaiah's prophecy, proclaiming Mary's and Jesus's descent from Jesse, the father of King David. Reaching Moldavia from Saint-Denis and Chartres in France, it shows a dominant spread of a tree sprouting from Jesse's body, its branches supporting the figures of the Judaic kings and scenes announcing the birth of Christ. These vast compositions are 'guarded' by the figures of the pagan philosophers, Thucydides, Socrates, Pythagoras, and Plato, who through their wisdom heralded the triumph of reason and justice. The early Christians wisely counted them as the forerunners to Christ.

A third major theme is the "Akathistos Hymn," made up of 24 stanzas and attributing the rescue of Constantinople in 626 to the intercession of the Virgin Mary. In painting, it becomes a pictorial essay on the life of the Virgin from the Annunciation to all aspects of her adoration. In the centre of this mural, it is usual to find a large painting of the Siege of Constantinople, showing the citadel of Byzantium through which a procession, bearing the Mandylion[7] and an icon of the Hodegetria Virgin, slowly winds, whilst outside the city, the Persians of Chosroes the Sec-

[7] The image of the head of Christ.

ond[8] attack the walls. The significance of this event cannot be overstated in the sixteenth century Orthodox Church. John Julius Norwich in his marvellous *Short History of Byzantium* describes it as follows:

> On 29th June 626, the Persians and Avars were ready to mount their attack on Constantinople. The inhabitants of the suburbs sought refuge within the gates, which were closed and bolted behind them, and the long threatened siege began. The barbarian host of some 80,000 extended along the walls from the Marmara to the Golden Horn. The walls were defended by rather more than 12,000 Byzantine cavalry; and these were supported by the entire population, worked up by Patriach Sergius to a frenzy of religious enthusiasm. Day and night, catapults hurled rocks against the ramparts; but the walls held and the defenders stood firm. All through a sweltering July the siege continued, Sergius making a daily procession with his clergy along the whole length of the walls, carrying above his head a miraculous icon of the Virgin. On 7th August a fleet of Persian rafts, about to pick up troops and ferry them over the Bosphorus, suddenly found itself surrounded by Greek ships. The crews were either killed outright or thrown overboard to drown. Almost immediately afterwards, a collection of similar craft which the Slavs had gathered in the upper reaches of the Golden Horn attempted to force its way through to the open sea. It ran straight into a Byzantine ambush and was destroyed. After this second disaster the besiegers seem to have been overcome with panic. Their siege engines had proved useless, their subtlest stratagems thwarted. Now too the news reached them of Theodore's victory over Shahin (in Mesopotamia) and Heraclius's new alliance with the Khazars. There could be but one explanation: the Empire was under divine protection. The next morning they struck camp; the day after, they were gone.

It was, without doubt, a miracle and the Church was saved. But in sixteenth century Moldavia, there came news of a dire calamity. This time it was the Ottomans, not the Persians, at the gates of Constantinople. John Julius Norwich continues the story:

> On 29th May 1453, at half past one in the morning Mehmed gave the signal. Suddenly, the silence was shattered — the blast of trumpets and the hammering of drums combining with the blood-

[8] The besiegers are often depicted as the Turks of Mehmed II who attacked Constantinople in 1453, this time successfully.

curdling Turkish war-cries to produce a clamour fit to wake the dead. At once the church bells began to peal, a sign to the whole city that the final battle had begun...

Alter describing a fierce fight, Norwich continues:

It was early morning, with the waning moon high in the sky. The walls were strewn with the dead and dying; but of living defenders there was scarcely a trace. The surviving Greeks had hurried home to their families, hoping to save them from the rape and pillage which had already begun; the Venetians were making for the harbour, the Genoese for the comparative safety of Galata. They found the Horn surprisingly quiet; most of the Turkish sailors had already gone ashore, lest the army beat them to the women and the plunder... By noon the streets were running with blood. Houses were ransacked, women and children raped or impaled, churches razed, icons wrenched from their frames, books ripped from their bindings. The Imperial Palace at Blachernae was left an empty shell, the Empire's holiest icon, the Virgin Hodegetria, hacked into four pieces and destroyed. The most hideous scenes of all, however, were enacted in St. Sophia. Matins was already in progress when the beserk conquerors were heard approaching. Immediately the great bronze doors were closed; but the Turks soon smashed their way in. The poorer and less attractive of the congregation were massacred on the spot; the remainder were led off to Turkish camps to await their fate. The priests continued with the Mass until they were killed at the altar; but there are among the faithful those who still believe that one or two of them gathered up the patens and chalices and mysteriously disappeared into the southern wall of the sanctuary. There they will remain until Constantinople becomes once again a Christian city,[9] when they will continue the service at the point it was interrupted.

The dreadful news of the fall of Byzantium sent shock waves throughout Christendom, nowhere more so than in the countries in proximity to the Ottomans. The triumph of the Ottomans was to be the enduring political reality for Romania until the middle of the nineteenth century.

---

[9] The irony was that, after the fall of Constantinople, religious tolerance flourished (about 40% of the inhabitants were Christians) whilst in Europe Christian heretics were burnt at the stake in England and Germany, massacred in the streets of Paris, and tortured in Spanish dungeons.

The final great theme of the sixteenth century Moldavian churches is 'The Last Judgement,' placed almost without exception on the western wall where believers were guaranteed to see it on arrival. On the vertical plane of the wall, characters and imaginary scenes of 'the realm beyond death' are arranged one beneath the other; from the angels holding wrapped scrolls and zodiacal signs signifying the end of earthly life to the Deisis, with Christ as judge, with the Virgin and St. John the Baptist, with a suite of apostles and angels; from the throne of Etimasia, prepared for revelation, a river of fire flowing from under it which will consume the doomed, to the 'Psychostasia' or the weighing of souls by the Archangel Michael.

Eventually two big camps emerge: on one side, the righteous men stand in rows, sparkling with the glitter of halos, finding themselves at the gates of heaven where St. Peter and the patriarchs, Abraham, Isaac, and Jacob await them; on the other side, the sinful shuffle off, with allegories of the Sea and Earth giving back their dead, with groups of the doomed identifiable by their dress as enemies of Christendom: Tartars, 'lurks, Jews, and even Latins, such as Franciscan friars, and monophysite Armenians.

'The Last Judgement' is a vision displayed throughout the Orthodox world. When visiting the Batchovo Monastery in Bulgaria, 1 came across the paintings of Zahari Zograph. In 1840 he was commissioned to paint the new church at Batchovo and here for the first time, other than in the portraits of donors, he dressed his subjects in contemporary clothes. At the Last Judgement, the condemned women, standing, eyes agog, on the side of the River of Fire, are all dressed in the latest Plovdiv fashions of the time. Oblivious to her impending fate, one of the ladies is setting her hat straight so that she will look her best![10]

Much of his inspiration stemmed from the Revelation of St. John the Divine for how else could he have painted "a great red dragon, with seven heads and ten horns, and seven diadems upon his heads" in "a sea of glass mingled with fire;" or "locusts like horses arrayed for battle, on their heads were crowns of gold; their faces were like human faces, their hair like women's hair, and their teeth like lions' teeth;" and "the heads of the horses were like lions' heads and fire and smoke and sulphur issued from their mouths."

---

[10] In the same mural, Zahari has painted some female nudes of such perfect anatomical proportions. Since it is highly improbable that any woman would have posed as an artist's model in those days, it is a mystery why they are so accurate.

Arriving by horse, saddle bags crammed with paints and brushes, the advent of an icon artist at a monastery must have caused quite a stir. By the rime he had finished, the local populace would inherit a collection of painted macabre monsters, together with gory scenes of the inferno, designed to deter them from sin forever. And they were left in no doubt as to who was for the high jump — adulterers, thieves, lechers, sorceresses, millers, grocers, drunks, and tavern-keepers were just the start of the list.

A secondary theme which follows many of the visual elements of the 'Last Judgement' is the 'Ladder of St. John of Sinai,'[11] not to be confused with 'Jacob's Ladder.' Based on the text of a seventh century hermit, the oblique line of the ladder has thirty rungs symbolising the virtues required to enter heaven. The sinful monks topple off into a fiery river leading to a black-violet hell where devils, some with masks and the others with very unpleasant faces, are wriggling with excitement at the prospect of their arrival.

About fourteen miles to the north of Piatra, along a gentle valley which climbed up into a forest of spruce and beech, lay Mary Walker's 'little monastery' of Horaiţă. I found a new building there with a glittering steel-sheered roof: no one appeared to be there, the garden untended and the church locked. Disappointed, I moved on across country, until I came to a long, precarious wooden bridge over a deep river. After watching the farmers with their horses and carts confidently move through the water which was too deep for the Landrover, it was with an air of impending disaster that I steered onto the dilapidated wooden structure. Gingerly feeling my way and praying hard to St. Christopher, it was a huge relief when the wheels touched the far bank.

This was but a mere hiccup, though, compared to the adventures of Mary Walker and her companions. When they visited the nearby Durău Monastery, they returned by rafting down the Bistriţa River. Caught by a sudden torrent of a rainstorm high in the mountains, their raft capsized and "we reached Piatra in a fearfully limp and helpless condition." As an afterthought, she added: "I have, unexpectedly, collapsed."[12]

Văratec, where our nineteenth century lady travellers had found "men and women of all sorts lounging about; Jewish pedlars spread their wares and... engaged in vociferous bargaining," is a charming convent with

---

[11] Also known as St. John Klimakos, which is Greek for 'ladder' and is the derivation of the modern word climax.

[12] *Untrodden Paths in Roumania,* 1888.

a beautifully tended garden. Possibly because of its remote location, the design is not defensive and the outer facing walls have balconied rooms for guests. There was a service taking place, the soft singing of the nuns at their devotions gently reverberating around its hallowed walls. Around the courtyard are dotted small bungalows, which could have come from a nineteenth century Raj summer town in Northern India, their verandahs covered in hanging flower baskets and pots of bright geraniums. Văratec, being a relatively late foundation started in 1781, has no exterior paintings.

Mrs. Loughborough in her *Roumanian Pilgrimage*[13] found:

> all round it were grouped almost fairy-tale little houses, one storey high, with a balcony in front of each, covered with flowering-plants, and a garden bright with flowers on either side of the crazy pavement, and each one fenced and gated with low, vivid green paling.
>
> As we came in, a group of the figures in their bunchy, brown and black habits and funny round black caps and veils, came and stood at the top of the steps on our right. Those quaint little hats they wear, right forward on their foreheads, their bright eyes, and little excited chattering, made them look exactly like a flock of birds, as they hopped down the steps and path and surrounded us, with cries of surprise and pleasure.

Queen Marie loved these churches in their pastoral surroundings and in her diary used the same ornithological simile.

> We visited the convents and monasteries, which were occasions for crowded and picturesque receptions when nuns or monks flocked around us like great dark birds.[14]

In the next valley along from Văratec stood the Agapia Monastery, another convent, where Mary Walker discovered "order, peace, and quiet" in contrast to my visit, when the monastery was under noisy restoration and its church temporarily decommissioned. Back in 1888, she described it thus:[15]

> Agapia was a nunnery devoted to noble families. There are over 400 in the community. The Maica Fundaricu, who attends to trav-

[13] 1939.

[14] *The Story of My Life,* 1934.

[15] *Untrodden Paths in Roumania,* 1888.

ellers, is exceedingly handsome, tall, slender and distinguished looking with a noble cast of countenance; the shrouding drapery of the black veil is wonderfully becoming to the pale complexion, slightly acquiline features and soft dark eyes of the wearer.

Originally, in 1437, Agapia was situated "in the middle of a glade on the peak of a mountain" and then moved, because of its in accessibility, further down the valley in the seventeenth century. The present church dates from 1935 and the whole place seems rather new. What was of interest to me were the nineteenth century panels of Grigorescu on the Rococo iconastasis, particularly the Virgin and Christ who has a small child kneeling by his feet, pointing out the Pantocratic passage in the Bible on his lap. Grigorescu had won a competitive tender to redecorate the church and this of course was his original trade before he went to study in Paris. His paintings are superbly executed in a high Victorian fashion of neo-classicism. In the museum, there is a good collection of nineteenth century Moldavian rugs with their traditional patterns and a charming small oil painting by Grigorescu of the wooden walls of the monastery at the turn of the century. Much to my chagrin, there was no sign of the rose leaf jam that Derek Patmore had found the nuns selling to visitors in the summer of 1939.[16]

From Agapia, it was a short drive to the Monastery of Neamţ through the town of Târgu Neamţ, similar to Piatra with its ugly modern apartment blocks. Approaching from the south over a tree-lined causeway, I passed by the white fronted Vovidenia hermitage, then the imposing buildings of the theological seminary and infirmary, until, after the holy water font with its enormous cupola, I came to the monastery and God's Ascension Church. Founded by Peter the First, who built and endowed the church in 1380, and restored by Alexander the Good in the following century, the monastery received its assets from Stephen the Great who sought to establish it as a centre of learning. From the beginning, education was key to the way of life at Neamţ; one can still see some superb calligraphy of the fifteenth century. At the beginning of the last century it became a printing house with the quality of its books renown throughout the Eastern Church.

The good Mrs. Edward of the Iaşi Mission to convert the Jews to Christianity, was not exactly welcomed with open arms at Niamto (Neamţ) in 1847, the Archimandrite surreptitiously referring to her group as possi-

[16] *An Invitation to Roumania,* 1939.

bly 'the Apostles of the Anti-Christ.' This provoked her to exclaim:[17] "Such a multitude of monks!... I was glad to get away from them. Fancy 2,000 idle men; out of this number only sixteen choose to learn."

Through the gateway, a large walled courtyard with an elegant balconied cloister leads to a church of classic fifteenth century design, offset to one side. The interior of the church is entirely painted with traditional mural designs: the effect was inspiring. The icons on the iconastasis are richly covered in gold and silver with inlaid jewels. In the museum there is a superb example of a hand-picked wooden cross with three dimensional miniature figurines. The most famous of these crosses is to be found in the museum at Rila Monastery in Bulgaria, carved by the monk Rafael. Taking a small piece of wooden board, he spent twelve years picking out an 18 inches high cross with 140 biblical scenes and over 1,500 tiny three-dimensional human figures. He finished it in 1802, totally blind at the end of the twelve years it had taken him to make.

Between the wars, the author, Gregor von Rezzori, came here with his father. The Von Rezzoris were typical of the fallout of the Hapsburg Empire, finding themselves abandoned in Bucovina as it changed hands after the First World War. His father described them as "cultural compost, envoys of the civilising administration of an empire" that no longer existed. In his memoirs, *The Snows of Yesterday,*[18] von Rezzori writes:

> We are guests of the abbot; with paternal kindliness the prior shows me 15th century illuminated manuscripts in bindings of chased silver; sunlight falls through the high windows, in broad stripes alive with dancing motes of dust... outside, jays are heard quarrelling in the pines.

Mary Walker found Neamţ with 376 monks but "countless empty guestrooms and the stables for 300 horses in ruins." She pressed ahead with her two companions in an ox cart and arrived at Secu Monastery on a small tributary across the valley from Neamţ. Typically English, she remembered the names of the oxen — Douman, Pluvan, Yello, and Tchokolan! The ladies were the first English visitors to Secu and there was a mutual fascination. In those days, the monks made their income through selling fish traps.

---

[17] *Missionary Life amongst the Jews of Moldavia,* 1867.

[18] 1991.

Further upstream from Secu, I stopped at Sihăstria Monastery, a place of utter stillness and repose as its name suggests — 'a holy, isolated place.' The monastery itself was far from quiet with over 120 monks going about their duties. This large population has led to the building of a second church and it was my good fortune to meet the Archimandrite who was personally painting the new iconastasis and ceramic wall hangings. In his studio on the hill above the monastery, he showed me the panels of the Deisis and St. Theodora which he had painted in a contemporary minimalist style. Across the top of the iconostasis he planned to position the traditional twelve saints; he had just finished St. Peter. We discussed the possibility that of all the early figures of the Christian Church, there may well have been an actual likeness recorded of Peter. For him, the jury was still 'out' on this issue. The gates in the centre of the iconostasis were to be of St. Michael and St. Gabriel.

Whilst we were talking, the 'toacă' started up; this is a drumming on a suspended wooden plank, an extraordinary, mesmerising noise, requiring great skill on the part of the 'drummer.' It came about according to James Noyes:[19]

> As the Turks were never partial to the sound of bells, the Christians were formally called to the house of worship by a wooden hammer rattled upon a board.

The range of tones, tempos, and even notes comes as a surprise. The primitive sound, almost African, echoed round the valley in the late evening, the setting sun burnishing the copper towers of the monastery. I stopped to give a lift to a young woman who was touring the monasteries on her own, contemplating a future as a nun. According to Aida, there were stiff entry requirements which involve passing exams to a high standard.

That night, with the guest rooms of Secu all full, we camped in a grassy valley by a mountain stream, closed in by beech woods. Around a fire of beech logs and pine cones, wrapped in the dark mantle of the woods, I came to understand the lure of the monastic life spent in the beauty and isolation of these ethereal places. It was of no surprise to me to learn that never has the monastic vocation in Romania been more popular than today.

---

[19] *Roumania, the Borderland of the Christian and the Turk,* 1858.

Chapter Eight

Revelations of the Byzantine World

At dawn, I headed to Fălticeni across the Moldova River valley, along straight roads lined with whispering poplars until I reached Gura Humorului, a hurley-burley market town in the pass between the Munţii Stănişoara and Obcina Mare. A few miles out are the first of the Bucovina painted churches, Voroneţ and Humor.

Voroneţ is considered by many to be the Sistine Chapel of the East. Founded in 1488 by Stephen the Great, the original form of the church can be seen in the votive picture of Stephen, his wife, Lady Maria, and his heir, Bogdan, who are depicted giving the monastery to Our Lord through the mediation of St. George. Placed on a stone pedestal with the tower rising from a central square base, the monastery rises into the sky, slender and graceful. The exonarthex was added in 1547 when the exterior paintings were begun under the direction of Grigorie Roşca.

The magnificent fresco on the west wall, 'The Last Judgement,' is unique in the art of the Christian East. The artist's originality can be seen in his use of Moldavian musical instruments — the bucium or alpenhorn and the cobza, the ten-stringed guitar — and in the local attire and landscape of the composition, all against a background of a startling, vivid blue which has been designated 'Voroneţ Blue,' ranking along Titian Red and Veronese Green as one of painting's great colours. This colour is made from ground down lapis lazuli, a most precious and expensive commodity of its time, reflecting the wealth of the princes who financed this foundation.

It is worth contemplating how the artists' colours were produced, for this was not the modern era of ready-made enamels, oils, and acryllics. Of the most important colours and pigments, ochre was obtained from soils and deposits and used as the basis for all flesh colours. White, used to highlight faces and hands, was obtained through the oxidisation of lead using vinegar, a process which took about four weeks before it was ground into powder. Black was produced by burning wood or bones, hence 'bone' black. Red came from quicksilver, known for over three thousand years in Georgia. Carmine red was discovered in 1517 through processing the cochineal louse and was mass-produced in the seventeenth century when it came into popular use in icon painting. Indigo came from a dye plant, widespread in the forests of Europe, and was extensively used because of its affordability. Green was obtained from glauconite and volconsconite soils found in Bohemia and Verona as well as in Novgorod. The colour purple was obtained from the purple snail and yellow from the fruit of the buckthorn tree, cooked with other plant juices and combined with chalk or alum. Gold colour, auripigment, is an arsenic sulfite and ranges from pale to reddish yellow. And of course, gold itself came from the precious metals and was not, in itself, regarded as a colour but as 'a shining,' a radiance to which all other colours were subordinated. Modern analysis shows that the colours were mixed with lime, egg, gall, vinegar, honey, some turpentine, and water.

When Bucovina was annexed by the Hapsburgs in 1785, Voroneţ fell into disuse until 1991, when a community, led by Mother Prioress Irina Pantescu, took it on and the nuns are now fully immersed in farming and painting as well as their religious life. When rung skillfully, its two bells call out the name of its founder: 'Ştefan-Vodă, Ştefan-Vodă.'

Sitwell[1] came here and found

> a tiny church, lost in its bucolic distance, but the purity of its style is in harmony with its unspoilt woods and meadows. Its romantic history associates it forever with Stephen the Great, whom it is not difficult to imagine, here, with his train of Boyars, clad in their fur robes and wearing their enormous headgear of fur. We may think of them coming to Voroneţ in a snowstorm, in a little medieval

---

[1] *Roumanian Journey,* 1938.

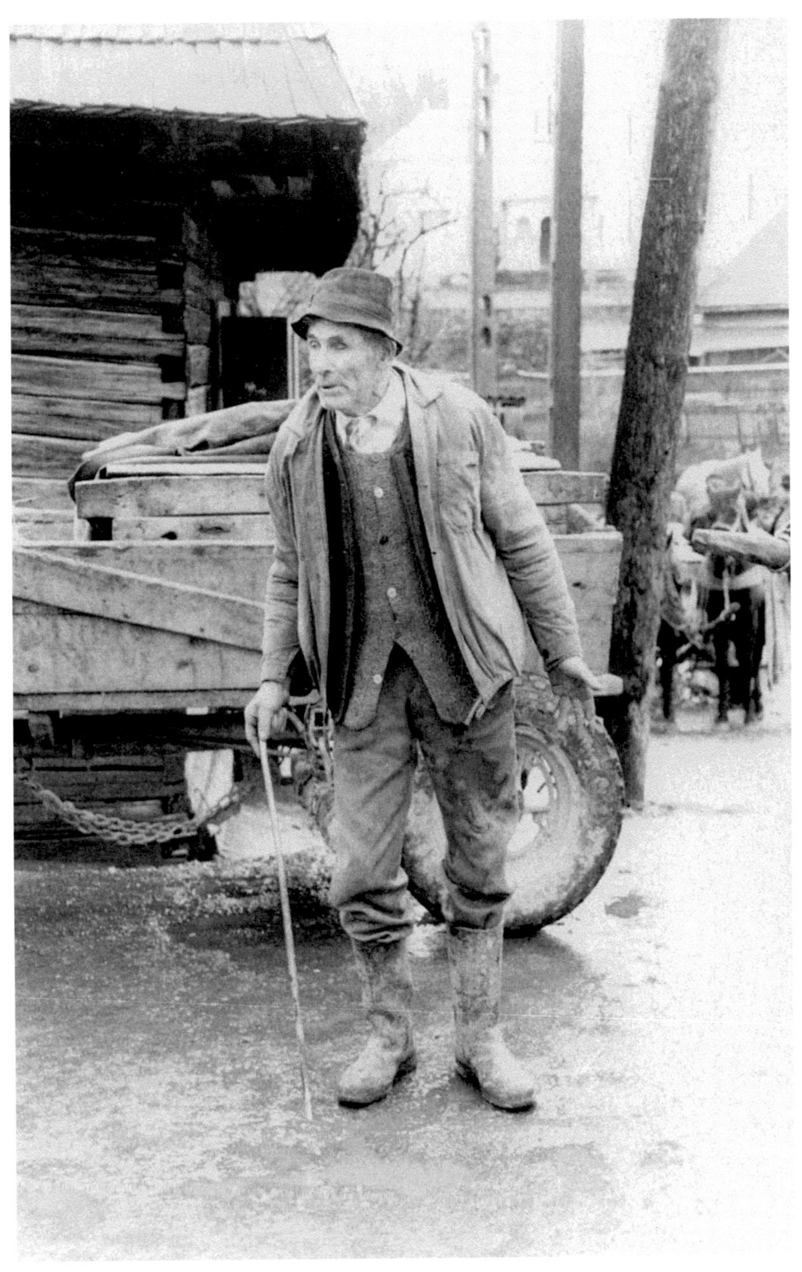

XVII. Maramureş: Village Elder

XVIII. Maramureş: Villagers Homeward Bound

XIX. Maramureş: Village Children

XX. Maramureş: Ioan's Mother

XXI. Maramureş,: Village Street

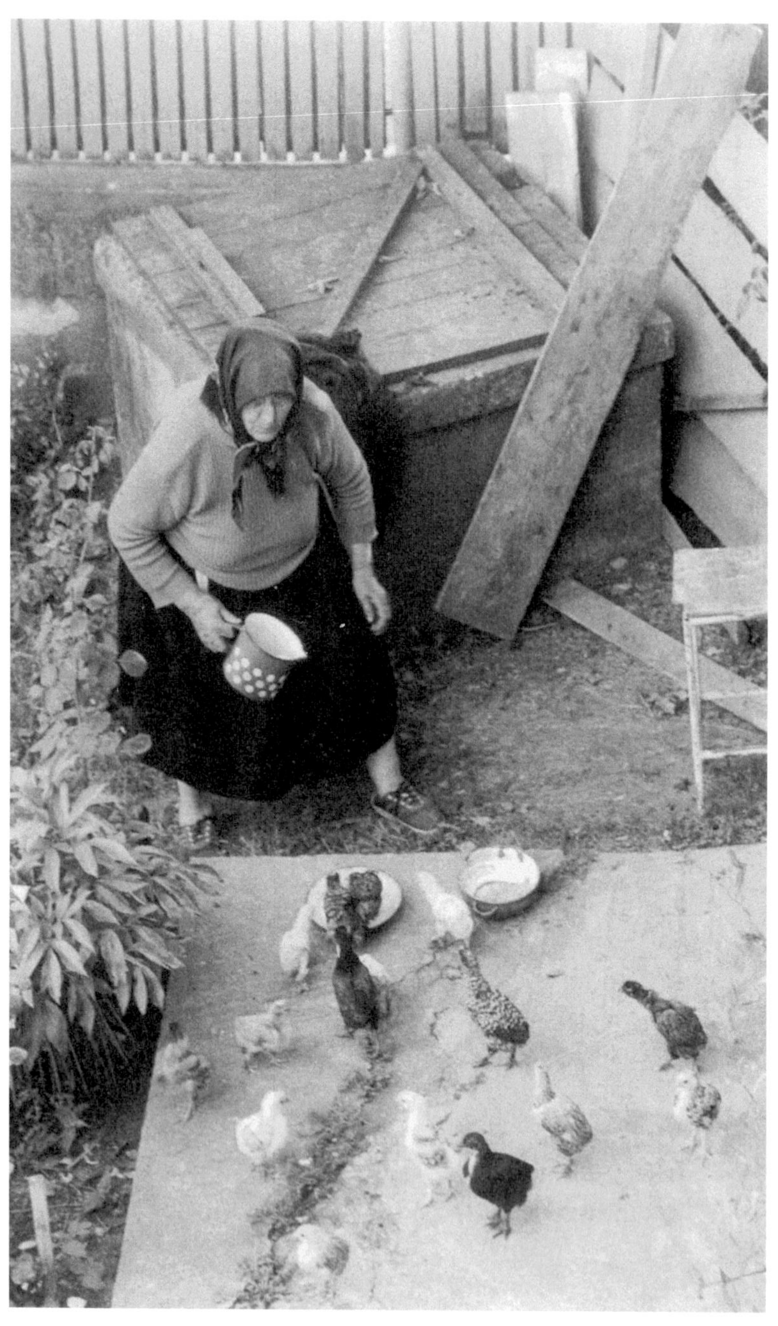

XXII. Maramureş: Granny and Chicks

XXIII. Maramureş: Gypsies Leaving the Market

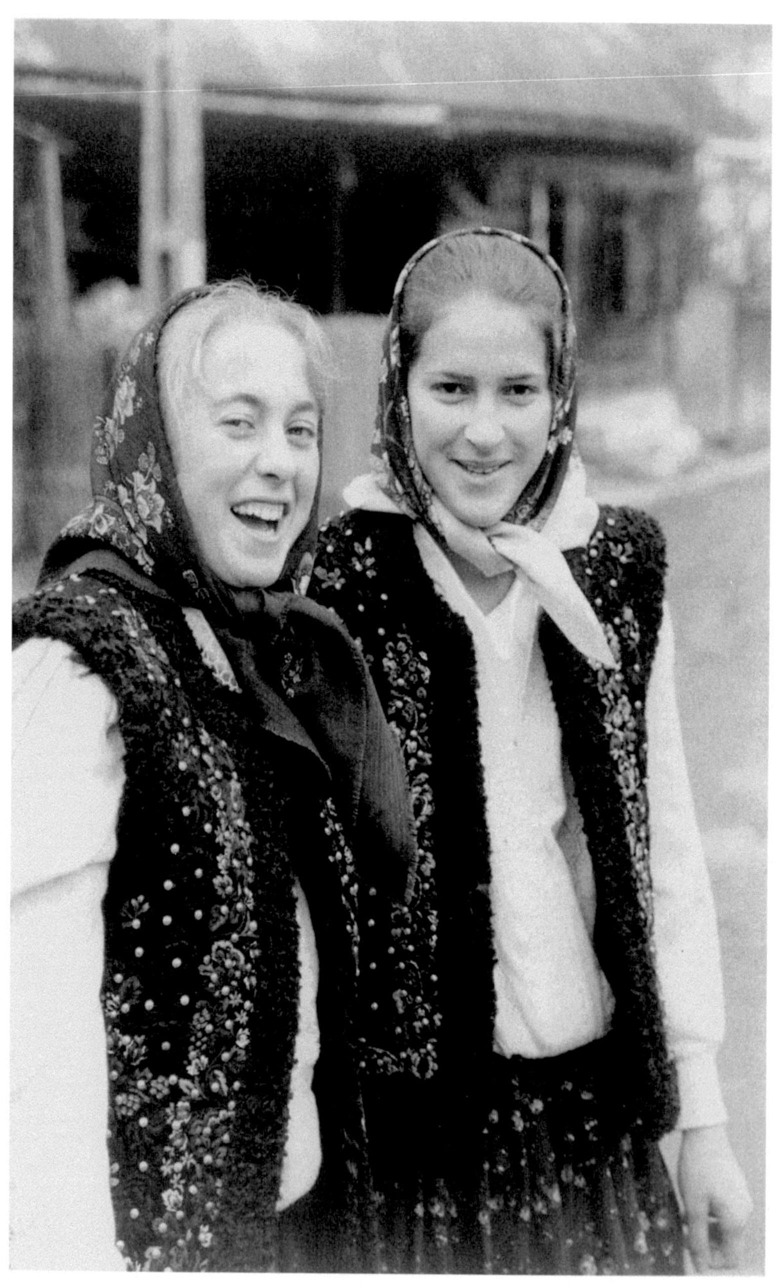

XXIV. Maramureş: Unmarried Girls after Church

XXV. Maramureş: Wooden Church at Botiza

XXVI. Maramureş: Saturday Market in Botiza

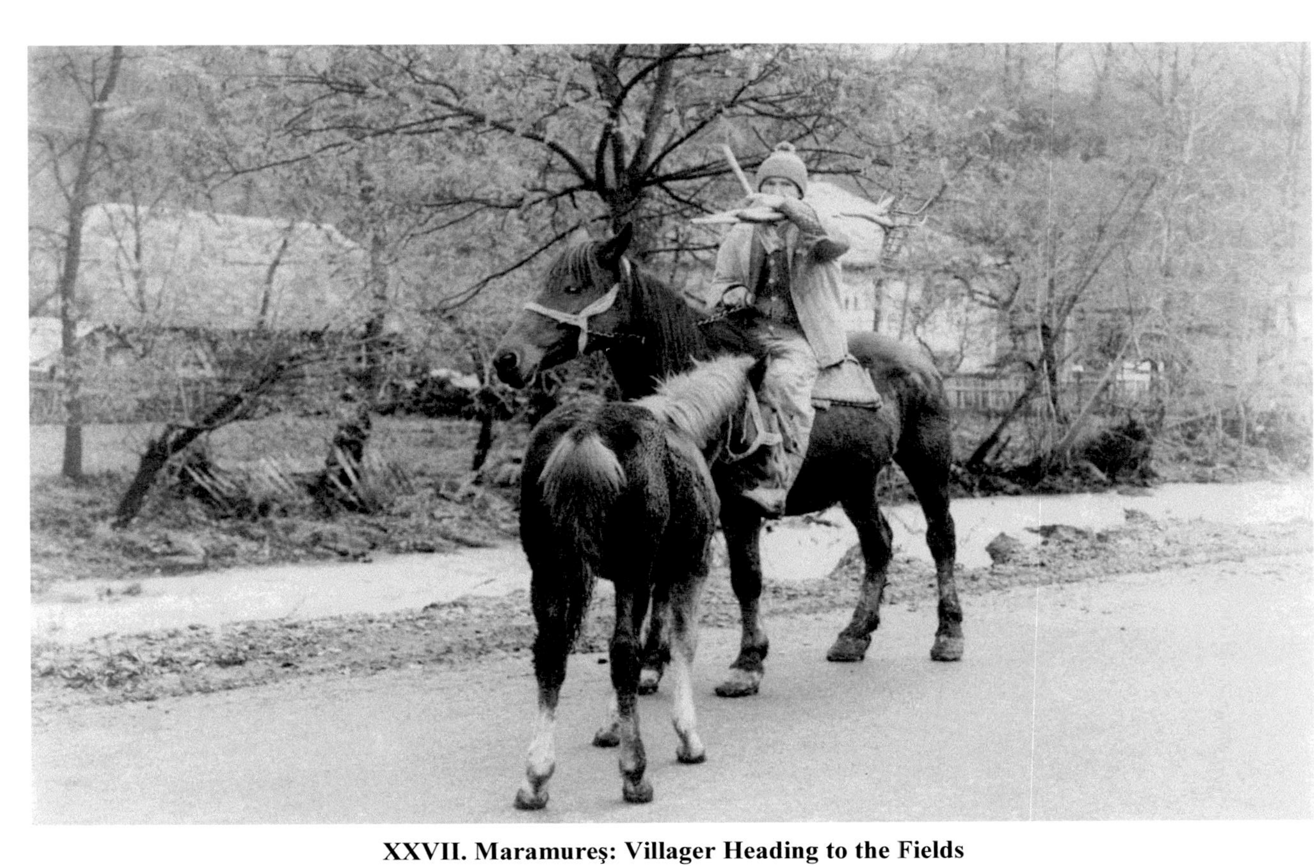

XXVII. Maramureş: Villager Heading to the Fields

XXVIII. Transylvanian Landscape

XXIX. Gypsy Lady

XXX. Gypsy Girls

XXXI. A Transylvanian 'Truck'

XXXII. Transylvania: Bran Castle

> world which was enclosed, for that day, was fenced or palisaded, by the snowflakes.

He gave it the accolade of "the most beautiful and touching of the painted churches of Bucovina."

A few miles away, Humor Monastery is just to the north of Gura Humorului and was founded in 1530 by a Moldavian Boyar, Toader Bubuiog, in the reign of Perm Rareş, Stephen's bastard son. The architecture of Humor is different to Voroneţ. Built on a trifoliate plan, there is no tower to the nave and the porch is open and arcaded, a style only repeated at Moldoviţa. This may well have been influenced by the Wallachian loggia where it was introduced into the religious architecture of this time. In contrast to Voroneţ Blue, the artist at Humor used a red that gives a glowing warmth to the other colours. The paintings were started in 1535 by Toma Zugravul and follow the classic Bucovina patterns: the 'Akathistos,' 'Jesse's Tree,' the 'Last Judgement,' and the 'Saints' Procession.' There is a most unusual painting of an elephant who had found himself, together with a lobster, on the wrong side of the River of Fire. The 'Sea Allegory' always produced more flights of the imagination than any other scene; I recalled the little ninth century monastery of Boboshevo in Southern Bulgaria where the unknown artist depicted the sea populated with grotesque fishes and reptiles with the goddess Aphrodite on a walrus-like animal with a scaly body and tail of a fish. She is holding a large sea-shell in her hand and seemed oblivious to the fate of the sinners, one of whom is being gobbled up by her monstrous mount.

The surrounding walls of Humor and its defence tower were erected in 1641 under the Moldavian Prince Vasile Lupu. He was an enthusiastic legislator[1] and was famed for his Code of Forty Articles, which included:

> 28. The slave, the salaried man, and the servant who may ravish a woman shall be condemned to be burnt
>
> 30. He who carries off an adulteress with her consent shall not be punished in any way
>
> 37. A judge may extenuate a penalty where love is concerned. Love is the same as intoxication or madness. It is indeed even worse than madness. That is why this law has been made
>
> 39. He who, yielding to love, meets a girl in the road and embraces her, shall not be punished at all.

---

[1] And procreator — he had twenty-seven children.

Like Voroneţ, the monastery of Humor fell into abeyance in 1774, when the Hapsburgs took over, and it was only in August 1991 that a little community of nuns re-established themselves there. They were much in evidence during my visit, sweeping, deadheading roses, and beating carpets, all done with cheerful and happy smiles.

Heading eastwards through Suceava, along roads choked with overloaded harvest carts pulled by sweating horses wearing red bell tassels on their bridles to ward off evil spirits, I arrived at Dragomirna, a dramatic fortress monastery with a unique three storied church. Unlike the others I had seen, Dragomirna stood on the shores of a lake, alone in gentle rolling parkland, no village as yet encroaching on its privacy. Built of raw, unpolished stone in the first three decades of the seventeenth century by Anastasie Crimea, the church is almost 150 feet high, yet only thirty across, giving it a slender, modernistic shape. The thick defensive walls with their battlements, buttresses, and four corner towers were added in 1627 to stave off Turkish and Tartar attacks, for Dragomirna, lying in the valley floor, was exposed from afar, unlike its peers hidden in impenetrable woods up narrow re-entrants.

Inside the church the pronave is stark and undecorated, giving the feel of a Norman church, and contrasted to the fully decorated nave, tall and narrow 'like a beautiful box of holy relics.' Here one can look up into the well of the Gothic windows of the stone steeple and watch the light play in intricate geometric patterns. A Romanian writer, Comarnescu, described this experience:

> On looking to the cupola and arcade with the unbelievable splendour resulting from the matching of the architecture with the painting and the natural light, one feels like writer Procopie felt on contemplating the huge cupola of Justinian's foundation, St. Sofia... that it rests less on the walls, rather hanging on the end of a golden chain directly from the sky.

Dragomirna must be viewed from afar and, as I walked up onto the hillside, a monk, Bible in hand, came into view, leading his flock of sheep across the pasture by the pond. It was indeed Arcadia, a world long since vanished in Western Europe.

In the far north of Romania, on the border with the Ukraine, lies the Monastery of Putna, reached either by road or by a tiny single-track railway. On my way to it, I passed two funerals; the first was led by a shuffling procession of mourners carrying wreaths of fir branches. The hearse, a cart drawn by an old white horse, bore the body of an old lady laid out on the harvest hay, hands clasped, eyes shut, her face to the sun. She looked serenely happy as if snoozing on the haywain coming back from the fields after a long, tiring day. A cortege of 200 people followed silently on foot. When I reached Rădăuţi, I passed a similar scene but this time the body was in a coffin with the lid on, for the ritual changes after the church service en route to the cemetery.

Putna is a fortified monastery with no exterior decoration on the church. Founded by Stephen the Great between 1466 and 1469, it is now his final resting place, his tomb covered with a masterful white marble canopy. Entering the sturdy stone church of a trilobate plan, I was struck by the murals either side of the door from the pronave into the nave. On the right was a crowned Pantocratic Christ, dressed in fifteenth century robes. He sat on a wooden throne decorated with grapes and red flowers and surely the artist copied this from real life, for it is too realistic to be from the imagination. On the other side, was the Mother of God sitting in an identical chair. Their icons were repeated on the iconastasis but here the Christ wore an elaborate silver halo.

Attacked many times by Polish intruders and local brigands over the centuries, not to mention subjected to three tires and an earthquake, Putna had just been given a facelift when I was there and had a thriving community of over seventy. The church is supported by six buttresses on either side to re-inforce it against earthquakes, which give it a slightly clumsy look compared to the slim four buttress arrangement of Voroneţ and Dragomirna.

From Putna, I drove down an appalling road to Suceviţa. Sometimes I managed 100 metres without having to stop to avoid a cavernous pothole; other times, only two or three. I caught sight of a girl in a field, white blouse, bright blue skirt, intent on winding the wool on her distaff; she could have been the subject of a Grigorescu painting. As the long evening shadows lengthened their hold on the valleys, the fabulous monastery of Suceviţa came into view, set amidst hay meadows and beech woods.

As his car rounded the bend and the monastery came in sight, Sitwell was overwhelmed:[2]

---

[2] *Roumanian Journey,* 1938.

> This first view of Suceviţa is amongst the most impressive revelations of the whole Byzantine world. That is to say, that where the Classical world has its Partenon, its temples of Girgenti, its Colosseum; the Gothic world, its facades of Chatres, of Wells; the Renaissance its colonnades of St. Peter's, or the foundations and parterres of Versailles; this painted church of Suceviţa is of parallel importance in the world of art to which it belongs.

Suceviţa was the last of the painted monasteries, marking both the end of this great post-Byzantine artistic cycle and the beginning of decorativism of the seventeenth century. How apt that the family which founded it, the Movilăs, epitomised this transition in their scholarship and patronage of the arts. Started in 1586, the large church follows the trilobate plan with a "closed" porch fed from either side by two little open porches, a 'Wallachian' architectural styling. The steeple projects upwards from the nave with a distinct Wallachian hexagonal tower, inset with overlapping arches. The precinct is marginally quadrilateral, well over 100 metres each side. The twenty-foot high walls with their four corner towers, capped in black pointed roofs, must have presented awesome defences to passing marauders.

The paintings of Suceviţa are worth special study, for they represented the last stages in a tradition that had started 150 years earlier. The votive or donors painting brings together numerous characters related to the Movilă family, a departure from the simplicity of Voroneţ and Humor. Externally, the predominant colours were green and blue, used to separate the fresco panels. The Russian theme of 'Pokrov' appears with the 'Akathistos Hymn' on the south wall and the 'Ladder of St. John of Sinai,' on the north wall, is quite magnificent. Placed against a grey background, the ochre steps of the ladder are the centre of a very large composition where the horizontal arrangements of the angels' green and red wings balance the vertical line of the sinners, falling into a black, purple hell. At the porch, the traditional place of the 'Last Judgement,' there are some wonderfully strange fishes in the 'Sea Allegory;' the two little side porches also have curious friezes of primitive animal motifs. The seven registers of the 'Prayer of All Saints' on the exterior wall of the apse are of a unique brilliance, the interwoven crosses of every conceivable combination — black on white, the piebald and the skewbald, blue on white and white on blue. The west wall remained unpainted, legend having it that the painter fell off his ladder and died before he could start it.

It is impossible not to agree with Sitwell's conclusion:

> Sucevitsa is the paradise of the Orthodox Church, approached by suffering and contrition, and with an added beauty because of its isolation in this distant place among the meadows. Its sacred and hieratic character is implicit in every one of the painted figures upon its fabric.

Climbing the hill to the south of the monastery, I presided like a VIP over a sunset tattoo, whose brilliant illuminations bathed the dark green Carpathian hills in gold. The landscape was soft and gentle, yet never without a hint of menace, for what threats this buccolic scene once held for the guardians of this outpost of Christianity.

Aida had found us lodgings with Madame Abraham who ran a small guesthouse by a little stream half way up a neighbouring alpine valley. Despite its half-finished appearance, the rooms were spacious and comfortable with polished wooden floors and a profusion of windows. The communal bathroom, waiting for its door to arrive, proved an hilarious meeting place for the inhabitants of the house.

Madame herded her geese and chickens into the garage as the sun slid behind the hills and treated us much the same way, ushering us into a warm basement kitchen. Here was a scene of intense activity for her daughter was to be married on the following Saturday and a constant stream of villagers arrived unannounced, bringing glasses and plates to support the imminent reception for 200 people. I bought a jug of *vin alb* which Madame tapped from a large dusty barrel — it was strong and clear, tasting of pine, with an oily, sharp aftertaste.

Robert Bargrave,[3] who was in Romania in the mid-seventeenth century, was not so fortunate as me in his choice of lodgings. He was shocked at one wayside halt.

> We went through delightfull woods but toilsome to the Carres; and took our noon bait at a poor village in a house steevd with women that were almost naked, having in lieu of clothes only a stove to keep them warm.

Thomas Thornton had a similar shock:[4]

> The inhabitants of a dark cottage were dislodged to make room for us, and I had ordered the chamber which we were to occupy to be cleared and swept; but on approaching the fire I observed a person

[3] *Narration of a Journey from Constantinople to Dunkirke,* 1652.

[4] *The Present State of the Turk,* 1809.

> sitting among the embers of the hearth... a naked mummy, for so it appeared to me: the body wasted to supply the enormous excrescence on the neck, the spindle shanks shrunk up, the long arms hanging down the sides, and showing no sign of life except a vacant and frightful stare. I confess I felt horror.

In the bright light of dawn, through fir and beech forests, I crossed over the 3,000 foot Obcina Mare Pass and descended down into the village of Moldoviţa, where on the site of an old wooden church, Petru Rareş had ordered the building of a painted monastery. The church was the second and last to have an open porch; other than that, it followed the trilobated structure of its time, save the bema rested on eight arches instead of four. Although the precinct is fortified with a vigil way and towers, the stylistic similarities with Humor are obvious. Yet Moldoviţa has richer colours and is altogether brighter. The exterior paintings, characterised by a dark yellow gold unique to the monastery, are lavish, with a splendid 'Final Judgement' in the porch which includes Mohammet among the heretics. On the south wall is probably the best depiction of the 'Siege of Constantinople;' the artist has introduced a landscape of armies moving between the hills and seashore as well as inserting a minute Slavonic graffito on the city walls, questioning whether this was a Christian victory of 627 or a Byzantine defeat of 1453.

A luxuriant 'Tree of Jesse,' the first appearance of this motif in Moldavia, completes the decoration on the south wall.

A visiting American lady was convinced that the names of nineteenth century tourists irreverently stencilled on the walls of the porch were the signatures of the artists. I persuaded her that this was not the case but a legacy of those long years under the Hapsburgs when all the monasteries fell into disuse and disrepair, open to the mild vandalism of Romantic students and adventurers.

In the tympanum of the portal, there is a most moving fresco of the 'Mother of God,' more humanised and tragic than any other I saw. Likewise the votive painting in the nave is of the highest standard, the yellow ochre cloaks of the donors having such an enduring vibrancy that they could have been painted yesterday. The 'Crucifixion' is often compared to Italian contemporary art or the Novgorod school in Russia, and the humanistic 'Last Supper' has Christ turning to John in the intimate manner of close friends. The iconostasis has an interesting device in that the uppermost icons are angled at 90 degrees, allowing the viewer to see their small round panels quite clearly. On the lower panels of the iconostasis, the

'Pantocratic Christ,' wearing a bejewelled crown, is seated on an ornate throne with its top corners decorated with a carved eagle and cherub's head and the arms with the head of a lion and a bull, a mixture of pagan and Christian symbols.

The monastery museum contains the throne of Petru Rareş, a plain and simple chair of heavy wood-carving. Its other treasures include a magnificent silver covered Bible, a gift from Catherine the Great, and a collection of beautifully illustrated books such as the Four Gospels of 1613 and a Psalter of 1614. All stem from the work of the monks of the monastery when Bishop Efrem erected a clisianitsa for use by copyists and illuminators in 1612.

As I left, I nearly collided with the Mother Superior as she overtook me in her car, the interior decked out with gaudy leopard skin seats. She heads a vibrant community of 34 nuns who are re-invigorating the monastery with their energy and devotion.

How does one sum up the experience of visiting these exquisite shrines of the Orthodox world and how does one account for their astonishing revival today as thriving communities and popular places of worship? John Julius Norwich gives a clue in his masterly summary of Byzantine civilisation:[5]

> The Byzantines were a deeply religious society in which illiteracy — at least among the middle and upper classes — was virtually unknown, and in which one Emperor after another was renowned for his scholarship; a society which alone preserved much of the heritage of Greek and Latin antiquity, during those dark centuries in the West when the lights of learning were almost extinguished; a society, finally, which produced the astonishing phenomenon of Byzantine art. Restricted this art may have been, largely confined to the great mystery of the Christian faith; within this limitation, however, it achieved a degree of intensity and exaltation unparalleled before or since, qualities which entitle the masterpieces... to be reckoned among the most sublime creations of the human spirit. The instructions given to the painters and mosaicists of Byzantium were simple enough: 'to represent the spirit of God.' It was a formidable challenge, and one which western artists seldom attempted; again and again, however, in the Churches and monasteries of the Christian East, we see the task triumphantly accomplished.

---

[5] *A Short History of Byzantium.*

This surely is the context in which we must see today's Moldavian monasteries and the painted churches of Bucovina. After the fall of Constantinople, the torch of the Christian faith was passed to the fledgling churches of Eastern Europe and it was their challenge to uphold the traditions of Byzantium. It is still blazing.

Chapter Nine

Maramureş, where Time Stands Still

From Moldoviţa, the scenery became more dramatic each mile as I followed the Bistriţa River up towards the Prislop Pass. The forests and alpine meadows grew cooler as the road climbed up into the hills. At Ciocăneşti, the village architecture changed to double-storied houses with latticed windows on the right angle of the upper corners, forming conservatories full of flowers. The top of the pass lay deserted, a lonely and windswept place except on the second Sunday of August when it is the scene of a great Gypsy fair. I made my way down the pass into the mountain spa of Borşa towards my destination, the Maramureş Depression.

The name 'Maramureş' first appeared in documents towards the end of the thirteenth century when Hungary was expanding into Transylvania. In the fifteenth century Orthodox Ruthenians emigrated to the area, settling near the Tisa River. After 1688, Maramureş became part of the Hapsburg Empire, along with Transylvania. In 1920, the region was divided between Czechoslovakia and Romania, and the northern part integrated into Sub-Carpathian Ruthenia.[1]

The Land of Maramureş is one of the largest depressions in the Carpathians, its border with the Ukraine marked by the Tisa River, and, to the south, defined by its four tributaries, the Iza, the Vişeu, the Cisla, and the

[1] This territory was occupied by Hungary in 1939 and by the Soviet Union in 1944; since 1991 it has been part of the Ukraine.

Mara. All life revolves around these rivers, with their narrow and steep-sided valleys in the upper reaches, opening up as they descend into small plots of land, for centuries cultivated with hayfields and potato plots.

The villages in Maramureş are generally large, laid out along a road, with orchards, pastures and woods around and above them. The larger villages are divided into *Susani* or Upper, and *Josani,* Lower, abbreviated into *Sus* and *Jos.* Each part of these villages has a church, the oldest being in the Sus. There are only a few homesteads[2] away from the heart of the village; the occupants of such houses are sniffily said to 'live in the fields.'

The people here are a mixture of ethnic populations; the Slavs or Houtsoules are found in the Vişeu and Ruscovà valleys; on the Tisa River, there is a mix of Romanians, Poles, Slovaks, Ukrainians, Magyarised Germans, Hungarians, and even Italians who came to work the salt mines in the early nineteenth century; the villages of the Iza, Mara, and Cisla are purely Romanian.

The first village I came to was Ieud, a magnet for ethnological and architectural students. I was offered lodgings in a house newly constructed out of breeze blocks, the legacy of some well-meaning Belgian aid workers. This was surely the equivalent of staying in a bungalow in Manhattan since the glory of Maramureş is its wooden architecture. For the fir, spruce, and pine of the Vişeu and Iza valleys, the beech and oak of the Mara and Cosau are the very fabric of all life in these parts. Oak is always used for the massive wall beams and for the walls, beech for the roof frame, the ceilings and window frames. The houses are pegged with yew, oak, elm, and ash whilst the doors are mostly of oak or lime. An old saying in these parts is: "One day wood is in the forest, the next it is in pieces, and the third day it is up on the church roof."

The village I finally chose as my base, Botiza, was the epitome of Maramureş life. Situated on the junction of two gushing mountain streams, along which followed two diverging roads, the village houses had their principal façades facing towards the yards which are the centres of daily activity. A second facade looked out over the lane where the entrance was a large gate, usually with a little covered bench beside it, a customary resting place for young and old alike and a meeting place on feast days. The fence and gate are essential elements in Maramureş architecture, delimiting the family space and providing social and cultural indicators through their

[2] 'Homestead' is the best description of the small farms which make up 90% of the villages.

dimension, form, and decoration. For instance, small gates, simply constructed with a single leaf, mark the entrances to humbler homesteads; the addition of a second opening and of tall posts generally mark those of well-to-do families. The inscriptions carved on the gate record the date of its erection and the name of the craftsman or owner.

The motifs carved on the gates can be cosmic or animal symbols of pagan or Christian origin and place the homestead under Divine protection. The twisted line, found on bronze age sickles and well-known in the Celtic world, is frequently used on the door frames and the same twisted rope motif carved in a single piece of wood guards the cntrance like a belt. The sun is represented by a rosette or by a square inscribed inside a circle. Often it is in close association with the cross symbol, typical of the Eastern tradition, that marks the centre of the inhabited universe and is placed above all other designs. The symbol of the cross[3] precedes Christianity for in the ancient East and in Pre-Columbian America it was used as a defence against opponent's magic or against any kind of harm, either as a picture or as an amulet. Another popular symbol, the 'Tree of Life,' is usually a fir tree but the rope motif can be adapted to include horizontal branches

The barn, which shelters the animals as well as storing fodder, is set at right angles to the house or facing it. Separated from the rest of the house by a small wooden fence, the garden of the Maramureş home is given over to vegetables, such as lettuces and onions, a few fruit trees — apples, pears, and plums — potatoes, and beans for the animals. Around the homestead are a number of other wooden buildings, the larder for basic foodstuffs, the well, often shared by several families, the hay store, and often a workshop.

En route to the village, I stopped to pick up an old lady with *opinci*[4] on her feet who was patiently waiting by the roadside for a lift. Her load of three sacks of vegetables was formidably heavy as I heaved them onto the Landrover. Her name was Maria and she was 71. Married at 22, she had been a widow for the last twelve years and lived in a one room wooden house up a steep, rutted track on the fringe of the village. In winter, she said, it was often impassable. Her single living room contained traditional Maramureş spaces with specific purposes. The corner by the door was for cooking because it was warm and light. Her bed was

[3] The followers of Mithras demonstrated their allegiance to him by having a cross tattooed on their bodies.

[4] Homemade medieval rawhide galoshes.

placed in the darkest corner of the room. There were long benches that doubled up as chests of drawers. In past times, the bench positioned by the door was called the 'bench of cooking pots' and that by the window and table, 'the bench of good fortune.' If suitors coming to visit the daughter of the house were given seats on the bench of the cooking pots, it was a sign that they were rejected. A small cupboard and table completed the furniture. Woollen rugs were hung on the walls and an icon shared pride of place above her bed with a photograph of ex-President Iliescu. One half of the house belonged to her animals, two cows, two sheep, and a piglet.

She told me how her husband had died in hospital with 'no lights,' deeply upsetting circumstances for Maramureş people for without a candle at death, there may well be problems on the Day of Judgement. Maria still worked on the hillside all day in the summer and, although her face was deeply lined from hard labour and the scorching sun, her blue eyes shone with youthful beauty. She was, by nature, a poet and recited to me a long poem she had composed in her head on the loss of her husband. It was about her feelings of how hard it was to cope without the presence of someone she had loved and cared for, and as she spoke the rhythms — the *trohaic* — in a fluent, melodious, lilting voice, her eyes filled with tears and her words became choked with emotion. To rejuvenate her, I took her photograph and she embraced her "new friend from London."

I found lodgings with a family in the centre of the village in a two-storied wooden house set in an orchard of apple trees, the preserve of a dozen scrawny chicks and three small pigs. All around, I could hear the competing noises of cockerels, pigs, and small children. Everything here was made out of wood, the fence, gate, the house, barn, workshop, even the tools for the fields like pitchforks. The entrance to the house was through the *prispa* or verandah, a sheltered space extending across the front of the house, affording shade in the sun and protection from snow falls in the winter. Inside the house, the main living room was the focus of life, with benches along the walls and a central tiled heating stove.

My hosts, Ioan and Maria were *nemes,* a sort of caste placing them at the upper end of village society through their hard work and ambition. He was a driver for the local lead mines and Maria worked at home, making patterned Maramureş rugs. Their son was a forester and daughter a librarian at the National Library in Bucharest. Ioan's elderly mother, aged 84, was in charge of the chickens which were trained to obey every whistle and shoo she vented at them. It reminded me of Ivor Porter's story[5] about how Romanian countrywomen would make a purring sound as they passed a farmyard and all the turkeys, cocks, hens, and chickens would march out of the farmyard and follow them.

Granny asked Aida where she came from.

"Bucharest," Aida replied.

"Is that in Romania?" she enquired .

"Yes. It's the capital."

"Goodness, one learns something new every day."

Maria picked *roşii, ceapă, castraveţi,* and *mirodenii* — tomatoes, onions, cucumbers, and herbs — from the garden and cooked a delicious dinner of pork and potatoes over a fire of maize husks in the garden. Half way through, we were joined by three hedgehogs, *arici. Ioan* picked one up and stroked it gently, murmuring 'cush-coo-u, cush-coo-u, cush-coo-u' until it unfurled and gazed attentively around. Then he placed it gently on the grass and with an amazing burst of speed, like a small racing car on the starting grid, it scuttled away into the night to the next door garden.

Tereza Stratiloesco[6] told the Romanian folk tale of hedgehogs in her book, *Pictures of Roumanian Country Life:*

> When God resolved to make the earth, he took a ball of warp and another of woof, and after calculating the heaven's size set to work, giving the ball of warp to the hedgehog to hold. But the cunning little beast let the ball go loose, so that the Creator, unawares, made an earth much too large to be fitted under the sky. What was to be done? The Almighty stood there, puzzled and annoyed, when the industrious bee came to the rescue. She quietly flew round the hiding-placc of the hedgehog, and heard him say: "H'm, if I were God, I would simply take the earth with both hands, crush it together, and thus produce on its surface mountains and valleys, and tit it under the sky." The bee informed God of what she had heard, and He, following the hedgehog's hint, crushed the earth and gave it its present shape, with mountains, hills and valleys, instead of the even surface He had at first decided upon.

There was no street lighting in the village at night, so I duly collided with two horses being driven home from drinking in the river, appearing to mc like mounts without their knighted riders. Then a horse and can, with no lights of course, came cantering through and I had to fling myselt into

---

[5] *Operation Autonomous,* 1988.

[6] 1906.

the ditch. I was learning about village life the hard way! Passing shadowy bodies in the lanes, the evening was full of friendly *'bună seara'* or just *'seara,'* spoken like a password. The village, cloaked in the night, felt a safe place, surrounded by ragged walls of dark hills. The 'collective' here was a natural state, not the imposition of some political or ideological dogma. The clear heavens gave whatever light I needed, once my eyes were accustomed to the gloom. I sat in a small *grădină,* under a vine plump with ripening grapes, talking to the villagers about the harvest. The men slouched in contented poses with their tummies exposed, cooling off in the chill night air. The *vin roşu* was sweet and cooling.

There followed days of delay whist Ioan and I struggled to mend a mechanical fault in the Landrover. Finally, we prevailed and I drove up to Sighetu Marmaţiei on the border with the Ukraine. A factory belched thick acrid black smoke over the town, a horrendous reminder of the pollution once prevalent over much of Eastern Europe. Sighetu has little character and is infamous for its prison where the entire "cabinet of 1945" was incarcerated, executed and despatched to paupers' graves.

To the south, through the villages of Călineşti and Budeşti, renowned for their elaborate gates, I took the road to Bârsana on the Iza River. It was the most bucolic landscape imaginable; if a giant had reached out and stroked it like a cat, it would have purred. Girls were balanced on top of haystacks, catching the loads thrown up by their men; Gypsy women dazzled the village streets with their coloured skirts; small children marched solemnly in their twos and threes homewards from the fields after a hard day's work.

The following day, I followed the Vişeu Valley road from Sighetu. crossing the Northern Maramureş Valley. Rising through steep banked woods of beech, the road cascaded down into a broad valley into the busy town of Vişeu de Sus, which was full of the tremble of excited country people out to enjoy themselves. It was 15 August, the Feast of the Dormition, when the villagers all headed for Moisei to pay tribute to the Virgin. Nearly every village would send its young girls and boys, often in long crocodile formations, church banners held high, on the long march to Moisei. Earlier I had taken three villagers, Johanna, Maria, and Vasili, about ten miles to the main road, where they planned to walk the remaining fifteen miles.

The site of the celebration in Moisei was a busy monastery set high on a wooded hill, overlooking the village. On one side of the hill, Gypsies had set up their stalls, hammering rough pieces of wood together to form frames that were then thatched with broad poplar leaves. Their wares were rather mundane — cheap plastic toys, soft drinks, and the odd stall of designer jeans — but their sheer activity made it a glorious summer sight. Some of the men had tired quickly of building and sat in the newly-erected shade playing cards with great gusto. The bearded priests and tight-capped nuns were equally as animated as the pilgrims, chatting vivaciously with each other. The faithful knelt on the grass outside the church, poised motionless in intense prayer like stone statues draped with colourful rugs. Outside the monastery gates, the limbless and chairbound with their alms bowls had begun to gather. It had been a gruelling climb for them up a steep, dusty mountain track of maybe a mile or more. All around, faith prevailed, tinged with the necessities of material survival.

On my return to Botiza, I had promised my hosts that I would pick up some water from the village spring. When I arrived there, I found a woman heartily cursing a small boy who had been washing his feet in the drinking bowl. She stared at the bubbling spring water, as if waiting for the bacteria to safely disperse. Given the strong sulphorous taste of the water, it was hard to divine what the difference would be.

That evening I was a guest of another village family, Vasili and Maria and their four children. Vasili was a master builder of wooden houses, 'the finest in Maramureş.' They had been fasting for two weeks prior to the Feast of the Dormition and had prepared two plump Muscovy ducks for supper. In the sitting room drapped with rugs, the television was showing a black and white version of Elizabeth the First with Glenda Jackson in the role of Queen Bess: no one understood a word. Over supper, I asked him about the construction of the wooden churches which are the distinctive architectural hallmark of the Maramureş. He explained that, like the construction of a house when a family is helped by its friends and neighbours, the erection of a church involved the whole community. There was little difference in the materials and techniques of construction, except the vaults and the domes. The church porch and little gallery in the tower were joined in the same way as a *prispă.* The division of space was similar to the larger houses; the pronaos being the 'women's church' whilst the naos was 'the men's church' where there was often a platform installed to increase the space and introduce a choir. The apse was usually polygonal and fairly small. The care of the cemetery and the preparation of the graves of the dead on commemoration days remained the responsibility of the women who also looked after the 'house'[7] and donated towels and rugs woven at home to decorate the walls and iconostasis.

The structure of the tower is based on an oak framework, assembled using traditional techniques without metal nails. Its weight is distributed onto the walls through a vertical structure of beams and posts. There are three types of roof — a single roof covering the whole building; that with secondary eaves all around the church at a lower level and the third with only the main body of the church having the lower caves. The individuality of the tower design is one of the distinguishing features of Maramureş churches, ranging from tapering tetragonal steeples to circular and, on occasions, bulbous towers, with two or four smaller subsidiary bell towers.

The Maramureş villagers are profoundly religious and continue to commemorate those who have died as part of the living family. The Day of the Dead celebrated throughout the Eastern Orthodox Church is known here as *Luminaţie.* A few days before women and children tidy the graves and decorate them with flowers. Ritual loaves are prepared as are candles to be lit on the graves. All the names of a family's dead are written on a *pomelnic* or paper which is placed, with the bread, on a table in front of the church. When night comes, the priest chants the scores of names whilst families stay beside the graves. As soon as the *pomelnic* is ended, cakes are shared around and the cemetery and surrounding hills transfigured by the light of the candles.

Early the next morning, I bade my farewells to Ioan and Maria. A white blanket of mist lay over the valley floor, slowly peeling back as the sun rose over the hills. I sat in the garden breakfasting on eggs, *slănină* — small squares of pork fat — and cold sausages with slabs of cake left over from Maria's name day on the Dormition. The sounds of awakening life — roosters, dogs, and the impatient neighs of horses — echoed all around.

I had made an inventory of the village's resources and calculated how their sum amounted to virtual self-sufficiency: dogs for herding and guarding; cats for pest control; goats for milk, cheese and fine hair; chickens, ducks, and geese for eggs and meat; sheep for milk, cheese, and wool; pigs for meat; cows for milk and meat; horses for traction and transport; oxen for traction; hay and maize for fodder; plums for *ţuică;*[8] wood for houses, furniture, farm implements and fuel; grapes for wine; berries for jams; blackberries for more wine; corn for bread; water for salt and drinking; apples, root vegetables for roughage. There was little for want among these hardy and resourceful people.

---

[7] As in 'The House of God.'

[8] The Romanian equivalent of schnapps, made from plums.

The way of life in the villages of the Maramureş has remained unchanged for centuries. Its English equivalent is described in Henry Bennett's classic study[9] of fifteenth century England, based on the Paston letters of Norfolk.

> The good wife was her own baker, brewer, weaver and dyer. Her husband and his friends were... continuously engaged in their various farming occupations, and, as a result, could supply most of the simple needs of their households... he grew his corn and other crops on his arable land; his cattle fed on the commons or in his untilled fields; his dairy supplied him with milk, butter and cheese, while his oxen and sheep ensured him a certain supply of meat. When he wanted wood to mend his barns, or to burn on the hearth, he found it near at hand on the edge of the woods and forests which he was usually allowed to make use of... During the long winter months when there was little farm work to be done, they mended the broken harness, repaired hoes and rakes, cut shingles or new ox-yokes, made new hurdles for the fields, and chopped up spare pieces of wood to burn in the house.

Maria had explained to me how much of her summer was spent collecting the dyes for her winter-woven carpets. The light green came from the wild cornflower, with some copper sulphate blue-stone from the mine added. The middle greens were a combination of lilac leaves and calican whilst the dark green were brewed from the bark of the Romanian maple tree and tea tree, with onion skins and branches from the nut tree. This mixture produced a yellow which when added to the blue-stone gave a darkness to green. Brown started with the maple tree branches, then *cruşin* or All Saints' Wort and ash was added to bring out the red coloration. Grey and black were from selected strands of wool whilst hazel was made from onion skins mixed with leaves from the walnut tree. The colours were fastened using cucumber vinegar and then the wool was washed in detergent before being woven into carpets, bags and clothes. The patterns on the rugs were sometimes representational like the *hora* dance but usually symbolic, using simple motifs of the fir tree, stags, and houses.

I left Maramureş by the high pass to Baia Mare, through woods of towering beech trees which soared upwards like perpendicular columns in a Gothic cathedral into a canopy of vaulted foliage, speckled with intricate patterns. Passing by Târgu Lăpuş in the centre of the Lăpuş Depression

---

[9] *The Pastons and their England,* 1922.

and then by Dej, I completed the full circle of my journey at Cluj. A final act was unexpectedly played out as the Land Rover came to a sudden halt to the west of Cluj, having suffered a complete power failure.

It was pitch dark and the surrounding countryside a black wall save for the light of a small farm a quarter of a mile away. I knocked on the door and explained my predicament in a mixture of French, German, and Romanian. The Romanian phrase for 'my car has broken down' — *Maşina mea are o pană de motor* — sounds like the line of a tenor's libretto in a tragic Italian opera, yet it meant nothing to the occupants, an old man and his wife, since they only spoke Hungarian. Their son appeared and I managed to make myself understood in broken Russian. Although, by now it was 10:30 at night, he towed me to his workshop where he rolled up his sleeves and started dismantling the alternator. At midnight, he looked up from the engine and announced:

"Me, English lord."

He produced a photograph of a 1634 family crest and told how his family had been stripped of their title by the communists in Hungary. On this maudlin note, we closed the evening with several toasts of *palincă*,, double strength ţuica, and I was woken a few hours later by the sounds of the 'count,' busy at work again under the bonnet. With an infectious smile that radiated optimism, he worked on a trial and error basis until the engine, with all manner of jury-rigged electronics, looked like a Heath Robinson invention. His mother came over to inspect his progress; I suspect it was she who had taught him his skills, *A Mother's Guide to Tractor Maintenance.*

By now the sun had heated up the farmyard and its inhabitants like eggs in a frying pan, yet still my guardian angel mechanic toiled on. We had been joined by two dogs, a horse and several chickens who had come to watch. With a grunt of satisfaction, the 'count' invited me to switch the engine on and it fired first time. All attempts of remuneration were contemptuously dismissed. Instead I received hugs from each member of the family and was despatched on my way over the border to the frenetic Great Plain of Hungary where tractors charged like hussars across the vast fields as they gathered in the last of the summer's harvest.

Winter

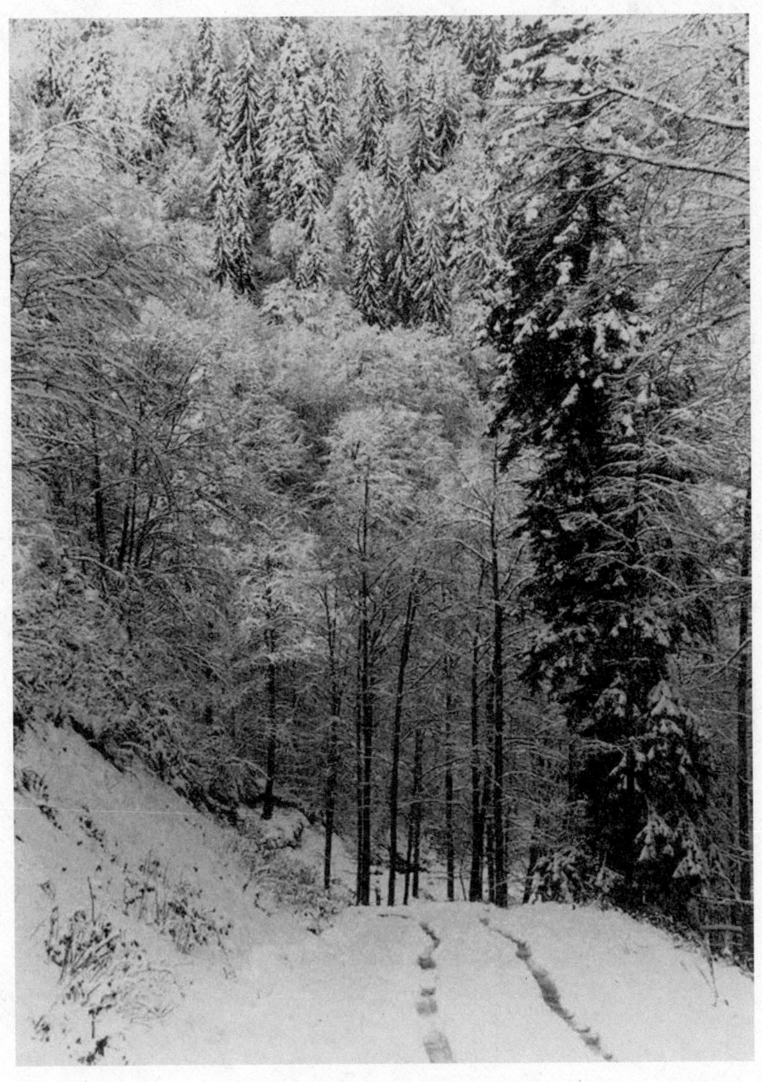

A high pass in Maramureş

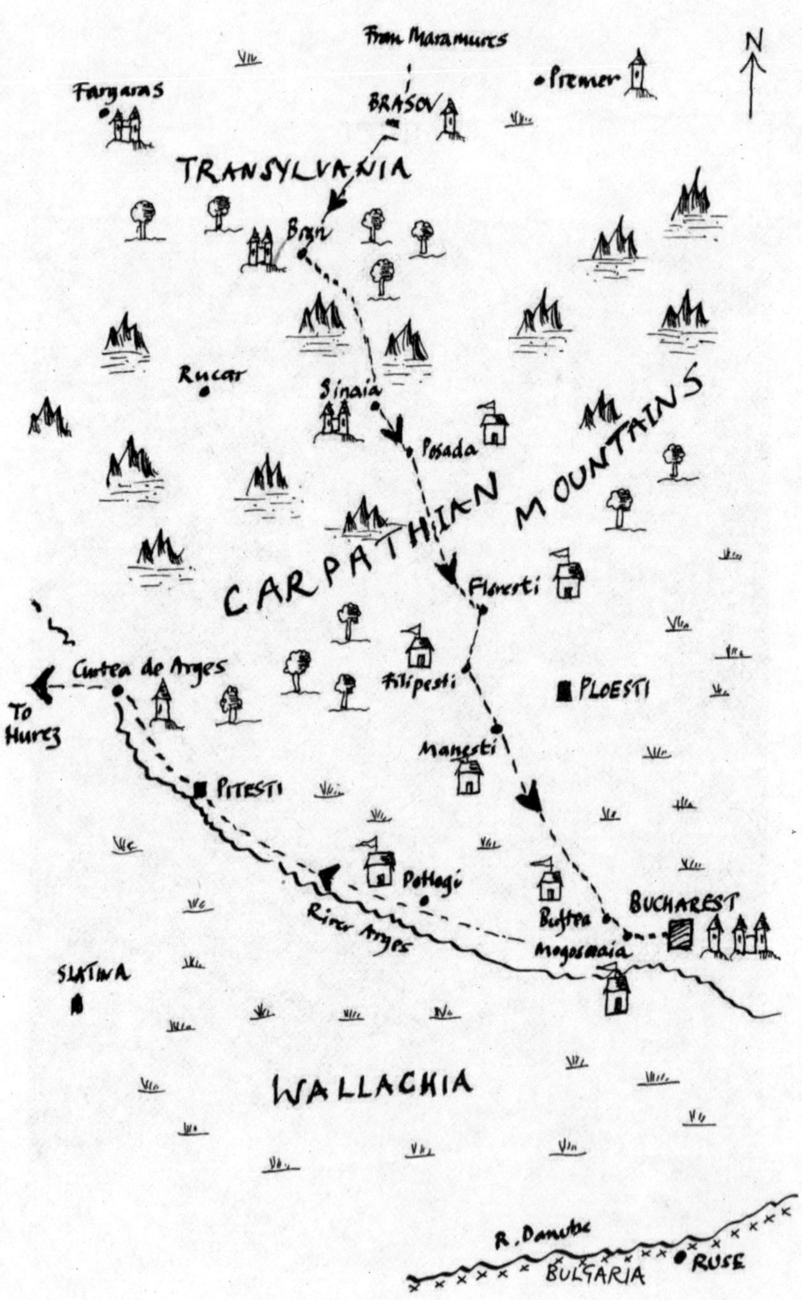

From Maramures
N
Premer
Fargaras
BRAŞOV
TRANSYLVANIA
Bran
Rucar
Sinaia
Posada
CARPATHIAN MOUNTAINS
Floresti
Filipesti
PLOESTI
Curtea de Arges
To Hurez
PITESTI
Manesti
Potlogi
River Arges
Buftea
Mogosoaia
BUCHAREST
SLATINA
WALLACHIA
R. Danube
BULGARIA
RUSE

Chapter Ten

Return to Maramureş

It was early November when I returned to Maramureş, along the same route across Europe as the summer. The piles of luscious fruit along the roadsides had been transformed into mounds of ruddy autumn apples. The countryside was shorn, clipped of its midsummer coat of swaying maize and bobbing sunflowers. Where the ploughs had been at work lay deep, black scars.

Everywhere, people were preparing for winter. The loads on the carts had changed from hay and fat watermelons to logs and dried stalks of withered maize, fodder for cattle in the snowbound months ahead. I passed a tractor and trailer ladened with sedge grasses for basket weaving in the long nights of darkness. Some of the horses now grazed idly on the verges after their long summer exertions, a blanket draped on their flanks for the cold had arrived. Gone were the bright Gypsy dresses, replaced with sheepskin waistcoats and dark woollen jackets, a weave of red or green giving them token colour. The men wore black or grey lamb's wool hats of traditional inverted flower-pot shape.

The hills and woods were a patchwork of rusts, russets, yellows, and oranges, sprinkled with coniferous greens as the autumn leaves clung grimly to their rigging of spindly branches. In the villages there was a sense of urgency as cows, goats, oxen, and buffaloes were chased into farmyards before dusk snuffed out the weak sun. No attention was paid to passing cars during this purposeful round-up, steam gave way to sail as the iciness of night descended.

I met up at Cluj with Aida who had come up on the train from Bucharest. There had been considerable progress in the bar of the Hotel Continental — the management had taken my disappointment of the summer to heart and invented a 'cocktail Hotel Continental.' With great ceremony, I was ushered into the bar and served a sticky green mixture in a tall, thin glass. Shaken in a container like a castanet, the recipe was:

1 pt Rum Bacardi
1 pt Marie Brizard
Suc de lămâie
Sirop bar

The effect? After two, a pleasant haze enveloped me and the world became a gentle blur of warm colours. This was a good excuse to change horses and I was proffered a 'Septembrie 3,' which consisted of:

Gin Gordon
Suc de roşii
Worcester Sauce
Suc de lămâie
Tabasco
Ţelină
Piper
Sare

The effect of this brew was like a thunderclap and necessitated a brisk walk around the town. Since the summer, Cluj had come alive with students, scurrying, dawdling, kissing, darting in and out of dark alleyways. The music schools pulsated with the sounds of piano and violin, wafting over the town on the cold, night air towards the edges of the universe.

The next day, I took the rainswept road north to Botiza, through the villages of Chiuza, Salva, and Coşbuc, across mountains already coated in a thin, chilly layer of snow. The rivers had awoken from their summer slumbers and rushed noisily down the valleys in their new guise of angry mountain torrents. Rain is a recurring topic in the travellers' storybook. Andrew Crosse[1] got lost and was miserable.

---

[1] *Round about the Carpathians* (1878).

> Darkness set in, and with it a cold drizzling rain — not an animated storm that braces your nerves, but a quite soaking rain, the sort of thing that takes the starch out of one's moral nature.

James Noyes,[2] the man who "used an urchin for a pillow," meets his match with a peasant on the subject of rain.

> I noticed a peasant crouched in the corner of his cabin, to keep dry.
> 'Why don't you repair the roof of your hut?' I inquired.
> 'It rains too fast, master,' was the answer.
> 'But why not repair it when the weather is good?'
> 'Oh, it's of no use then.'

Noyes was inclined to overdramatise the weather: "The revolving squadrons of heaven's artillery whose reverberations became more terrific every moment" — was his description of a Transylvanian thunderstorm.

At the top of the Şetref Pass, just over 2,700 feet, I ran into a blizzard, passing ghost-like carts loaded with hay from the high pastures. Neither man nor horse could see further that a few feet, such was the intensity of the driving snow. The windscreen wipers on the Landrover chose this moment to pack up, so I tucked myself in behind a haywain and inched my way slowly into Botiza. A market was in full swing when I arrived, with stalls of red and yellow peppers and mounds of red sweet paprika powder. Now that oceans of mud had settled in for the duration of winter, everyone was wearing the ubiquitous black rubber gunboot. A noisy altercation between a Gypsy cart and a car as to whose right of way it was nearly ended in blows. Threats, curses, and spells were exchanged with an old one-eyed Gypsy man emerging the clear winner.

The Maramureş was ready for winter, rotted wooden shingles replaced with new ones, logs piled high around the yards, fences repaired, ditches dug. It began to rain heavily, so I retired to Ioan's house and, over a hospitable bottle of *pălincă,* asked him about the days ahead. He was expecting snow for the next five months and was planning to use the time to extend his house. Most days were devoted to 'transport,' by which he meant the removal of dung from the barns to the fields. Was there any hunting? Yes, there were deer and bears but it was very restricted unlike the days of his childhood when the villagers were able to roam in the forests and take their pick of the old and decrepit beasts.

---

[2] *Roumania, the Border Land of the Christian and the Turk,* 1888.

Christmas in the Maramureş is much looked forward to, except by the family pig who is served up at table. It starts on the morning of Christmas Eve and finishes on the morning of Boxing Day: in between, no one sleeps! Early on Christmas Eve, the children go out and about and sing at neighbouring houses. The first visitor must be a boy. If it's a girl, Ioan hinted, his luck would be out for the next year. Little presents of cookies, apples, nuts and money are given to the children and, much to their excitement, a glass of *pălincă* is allowed, the theory being that they must learn to drink it at some stage, so why not at Christmas.

Church starts at 10 p.m. on Christmas Eve and by midnight, Scottish style, it is time to visit other families. This is the moment for practical jokes like taking your neighbour's gate off its hinges and hiding it By ten on the morning of Christmas Day, it is time to go back to Church, where, after the service, the village stages *Viflei* or a nativity play acted by both grown-ups and children. There is no script as the tradition is purely oral, based on a mix of characters such as Christian good and bad angels, Pagan Death and a wandering Jewish miser.

The rain clouds had lifted, giving way to startling shafts of sunlight from the setting winter sun. I had heard about the church at Polienei about six miles from the village and set off to see it whilst the weather behaved. Set on a hill to the cast of Polienei village, this miniature wooden church, surrounded by a wooden stockade, was built in 1604. It has an open porch, a small pronave, and a barrel roofed nave with a tiny gallery. The iconastasis is a simple painted wooden panel. What was exceptional about the interior were the frescoes in faded reds and greys, dating from 1783. The first thing that catches ones attention is their facial artistry, be it the eyebrows, upper lids or oval shape of the eyes. They have an incredible softness, almost invoking a docility, yet other features like jaws and mouths are firm and full of fortitude.

No longer in use, Polienei had been a segregated church, only men being allowed into the nave with its hundred hat pegs set like rake pegs around the walls, and the women restricted to the gallery or pro-nave. This was why there are two iron grills in the separating wooden wall for the women to look through and why, on the walls of the pro-nave, there was a group of frescoes depicting what happened exclusively to 'female' sinners.

Painted on the wooden walls of what is known as 'The Devil's Gallery,' these pictures are quite specific in their message, according to my guide the verger. If you break the fast, a wooden stake is driven up your bottom; for ironing on a Sunday, you yourself are ironed by a devil; if you are late for church, you can expect a rather hirsuit and good looking devil, with horns and a goatee beard, to sit on the end of your bed and play the violin: this will make you ill.[3] If you steal from another's field, you will be literally ploughed up. I wasn't sure about what sins deserved bellows blowing up one's backside or being force fed a baby; I was later told that farting in church and abortion fitted the bill.

'The Final Judgement' is disappointing. A circle with four faces in the quarterly points blowing into the centre, the inside is of indeterminate illustration although the outer has the usual fishes of the 'Sea Allegory.' The lower frieze of the pro-nave has a diametrical pattern with four-cornered stars on the intersections and red dots in the centre of the quadrangles. The picture of the votives is unusual in that it is a landscape with figures; on the right, wearing a low-cut dress, red necklace, and splendid medieval bonnet is the votive's wife, drawing a pitcher from a pond.

That evening I called on Maria whom I had befriended that summer. Wearing archaic felt boots bound with thongs, she had spent the day burying her potatoes underneath her house, so that they would freeze and keep for the duration of the winter. I had had her poem translated into English and she asked me to read it to her by the light of a solitary candle.

"But you won't understand a word," I exclaimed. "I only had it done, so that I myself could understand it."

"Never mind, I want to hear it in English." And that was that and I began to read.

A poor little cuckoo and I
We both want so badly to die
So we'll both go away
And leave my darling behind
For I'll never find another like him.
Even if I go with the nightingale,
And leave my darling behind,
I can never go back, never go back.

My poor little heart whispers at midnight
So I stay awake as it asks me why I can't sleep.
Then I know what I am missing,
And so I must die, and so I must die.

---

[3] Another source states this is a punishment for adultery.

I want to be a sister of the earth
If I don't have my darling by me.
I want to be a brother of the earth,
If I don't have my darling by me.
For a long time ago, I had a beloved
But my enemies have taken him from me.
They didn't let me stay with him,
Choosing to leave me all by myself,
Like a little bird perched on a fence
So that all can attack me, all can attack me.

So may God help them the way that they help me.
They should live like I do, alone on the planet,
That way they would see how bad it can be.
For it's hard to be on your own,
Picking up the debts of the world,
So nobody likes one anymore.
I wish that all the world's fortunes
Would burn ablaze in hell
For people are like leeches with riches
Bringing only bad, bad things.

"Hey, Floran, you broke my heart,
My heart and yours,
And nobody can undo that."

Death, oh burning hell, you bring only evil.
You burn us humans to our hearts
But nobody can undo you.
I can never be alright
Because you have taken my husband
And put him in a coffin.
And I feel so sorry for him
Because he was mine alone.

"Hey, Floran, what have you done?
Where have you been?
You have been sick in bed
And I searched everywhere for you.
But I couldn't find you,
Because you went away
And left mc alone.
You left me alone.
How can I live anymore?"

"Hey, Floran, poor thing, come back from death
So I can tell you how hard it was on me
After you died, after you died.
Because you died without a candle,
Without somebody you knew,
Nearby you, nearby you.
It must have been very hard for you
And your heart,
Sitting there on a hospital table
Where nobody saw you,
Where nobody saw you.

Worse than a dog. I feel so sorry for you
Because you died without a candle."

"Hey, Floran, what have you done?
What was in your mind
When you thought about dying?
With whom did you talk to?
And who let you die?
When the time came,
Who was by your bed?
I couldn't be there.
There was no one to wake you
And there was no one to ask what hurt you
And there was no one to tell you to eat
And there was no one to offer you a drink
When your mouth had run dry."

"Hey, Floran, what have you done
Since I found out that you were dead?
My eyes have never dried
Since I found out that you were planning
To rust away.
My eyes have never dried
Neither in the day nor in the night
Without you.
And all that is your fault
Because I didn't know where you were.
I found you in a dark grave,
A very dark grave.
And I'm afraid I'll never see you again:
Maybe just at the day of Judgement.

When you were first at the hora,
I just looked at you,
And since then,
I've missed you each minute
Of the day and of the night.

Since the first time I saw you on the road
I couldn't look at another man
And I keep looking on the road
To see at least your footprints, if not you.
That way I can quench my love."

So I keep looking on the road
To see at least your footprints
That way I won't feel so sad.

The only one that was close to me
Now sleeps with a cross on his head.
The only one I cared about
Now sleeps with his hands clasped.
He sleeps and he doesn't know
How dear he was to me;
He sleeps and he doesn't worry
How sad I am for him.

"Hey, Floran, wake up from your grave
So I can ask you just one little word —
Why did you spurn me and
Go away from my house?
Was it because you thought I wasn't worthy of you?"

Franz Liszt recorded how he overheard Gypsies constantly using the diminutive: "Oh, you poor little darling;" "You poor little soul;" "You poor little dove." There is an obvious connection with Maria's diction although she was not a Gypsy herself.

Charles Boner[4] at a party near Bistriţa, a few miles to the south of Botiza, heard a village 'Sappho' sing a ditty with similar lyrics:

My love has eyes like blackberries,
And eyebrows like the wing of a raven,
And teeth like jewels. His face
Is like a rose that has been dipped

---

[4] *Transylvania: its People and its Products,* 1865.

In milk, and his figure is as if
It had been turned by a turner and
Drawn through a ring. His moustache is
Like cars of barley

The structure of Maria's poem is similar to the ballad of Mioriţa.[5] Here is an excerpt when the Moldavian shepherd is talking to his little sheep, Mioriţa:

Mioara, little pet,
Plump little darling.
For three days back
Thy mouth is no longer silent.
Does the grass no longer please thee?
Or art thou sick,
Mioara, little Mioara.

I left Maria with a large supply of shortbread biscuits and found out from Ioan the next day that she had eaten all of them that night.

The next day was a Sunday and after church, the main street in Botiza became a promenade for families and clutches of unmarried sisters. There were 'uniforms' of a sort according to sex and age: the older women wore woollen aprons of red and black horizontal stripes, the young girls floral skirts, just above the knee, and sheepskin waistcoats trimmed with fur. The men all dressed in a nondescript fashion, a sad retreat from their former sartorial glory.[6]

That afternoon I drove with Ioan up into the beech forests now layered with snow. The forest tracks were hallmarked with the cloven hoofs of deer. From the top of Vârfu Secului, we looked out over the wild mountain ranges of the Ukrainian Carpathians, which stand like a great white wall on the northern border of Romania. It was here that during the German occupation of Poland, the Countess Gizycka, nee Krystyna Skarbek, established a ski escape route through the Carpathians. She told Ivor Porter about her adventures when she met him in Cairo:

> how once, when the German troops were after her, she had met a wood-cutter who, with great presence of mind, had taken her in as his daughter, and how she laid 'sick' in bed until they went away. An authentic fairy tale. She was a slim, fair girl, very fit, beautiful

---

[5] From Stanley's *Rouman Anthology,* 1856.

[6] Wonderfully captured on camera by Kurt Hielscher in 1931.

and optimistic about the course of the war. She was later awarded the George Cross for her outstanding bravery and initiative in France.[7]

The Countess was murdered[8] in 1952 by a crazed lover who was a steward on a ship which she had been working on. It was a tragic ending to a life which had discovered courage and valour in these desolate mountains.

---

[7] *Operation Autonomous,* 1988.

[8] Liane Jones, *A Quiet Courage,* 1990.

Chapter Eleven

Houses and Gardens in the High Carpathians

It was mid-night when I reached Braşov where Emily Gerard[1] had found

> in the streets, beside the usual contingent of fiery Magyars, stolid Saxons, melancholy Roumanians, ragged Tziganes and solemn Armenians, other figures, red-fezzed, be-turbaned, or long-robed... only a few steps from such things as camels, minarets and harems.

Paget's[2] description of Braşov was similar though more flowery:

> The sober plodding Saxon is jostled by the light and cunning Greek; the smooth-faced Armenian, the quaker of the East, in his fur coat and high kalpak, meets his match at a bargain in the humble-looking Jew; and the dirty Boyar from Jassy, proud of his wealth and nobility, meets his equal in pride in the peasant noble of Szeckler-land. Hungarian magnates and Turkish merchants, Wallach shepherds and Gypsy vagabond make up the motley groups which give life and animation to the streets.

Emily also told a story of how in the fourteenth century church, where there was a collection of the most exquisite Turkish carpets, an

---

[1] *The Land beyond the Forests,* 1888.

[2] *Hungary and Transylvania,* 1834.

Englishmen stayed an entire month trying to buy "that pale-blue one up yonder."

Sitwell[3] described it as

> a pleasant town with most of the character removed from it owing to the Austrian rule, which has left large public buildings in the manner of those to be found all over the Hapsburg Empire. This might be Graz or Klagenfurt or Linz... the chief sight of Braşov is the Black Church, built in German Gothic by the Saxons and called by that name because of its walls that are stained with smoke. Its Protestant interior is rather bleak and uninteresting, though there are some good oriental or Turkish rugs, of a pattern which is said to have been made especially for export to the Saxons of Transylvania. Apart from the shops and the Black church, there is but little of interest at Braşov.

I found this description as accurate today as it was in its time and sadly did not experience Emily's sense of the Levant. Andrew Crosse[4] rather priggishly observed in Braşov:

> The Wallach maiden is adorned by her dowry of coins hanging over her head and shoulders, and with braids of plaited black hair — mingled, I am afraid, with tow, if the truth must be spoken.

Charles Boner at Braşov, to his astonishment, found "English bricklayers were at work, and everyone told me of the astonishment which their quickness occasioned... one gentleman said he had counted that they laid six bricks whilst the native workman laid one."[5]

South of Braşov, in the mountains, is the Castle of Bran, granted by Ludovic I D'Anjou to the good burghers of Bran to defend the southwest approaches to the city. Before the pass at Predeal was completed in the late nineteenth century, Bran was the front door to Transylvania from Bucharest. Lord Paget's embassy passed through Rucăr and onto Bran in 1702 and Edmund Chishull recorded:

> we arrive at the castle of Bran, a small fortress which defends this pass; where His Excellency was saluted, as he passed, with three different salvos of about twenty one guns. Within canon shot of this fort we find a fair set of huts...[6]

---

[3] *Roumanian Journey,* 1939.

[4] *Round about the Carpathians,* 1874.

[5] *Transylvania: its Products and its People,* 1865.

[6] *Travels in Turkey and back,* 1747.

Given as a present to Queen Marie in 1920 by the citizens of Braşov, this once uninhabited jumble of towers and battlements became famous as her country house, where everybody who was anybody seemed to get invited to tea. Starting with Sitwell,[7]

> Queen Marie led the way to a delightful summerhouse where we had tea. This is built in the style of a peasant house and during the course of conversation there was much laughter.

The summerhouse is now the castle shop.

Dudley Heathcote took tea with her in 1924.[8] He recalled her wearing

> a pale green grey swathed turban of lightish material that hung down slightly at the back; a white blouse that was embroidered in red; a red pleated skirt and round the waist a lovely hand-wrought buckled belt. Over the blouse a three quarter length embroidered coat, most exquisitely made with a band of fur at the neck; white shoes and stockings completed her costume.

Derek Patmore, a journalist, who like Sitwell was a guest of Princess Callimacki, had a couturier's eve and found that[9]

> Marie's clothes were designed to set off her beauty — that fine head with golden hair, fair complexion, and expressive blue eyes, and the fine athletic body — and she wore them with a majestic sweep which captured the imagination of all who saw her.

And during Emil Hoppe's visit[10] to Bran where the Queen was in residence, he noticed, in every room, flowers in profusion, Madonna lilies, roses and dahlias from her famous collection. As the evening drew on,

> a golden glamour spread over the land, and soon the glories of sunset were like a tremendous palette steeped in a splendid blaze of light. A vivid shaft of light touched the Queen's face and its dying flicker trembled in her hair.

In Hoppe's opinion, she put everyone, from artist to peasant, at case, and 'made them her intimates without losing her noble dignity.'

---

[7] *Roumanian Journey,* 1938.

[8] *My Wanderings in the Balkans,* 1924.

[9] *Invitation to Roumania,* 1939.

[10] *In Gypsy Camp and Royal Palace,* 1924.

Bran was very much a private house. As far as Marie was concerned, "there is no court, not even a lady-in-waiting. And I ask here only the people I like." This privacy allowed her to act up to her surroundings. Mabel Daggett was sitting with the Queen in the library one night, a furious storm raging outside:

> And now it is time for good night," said the Queen. She held high against the shadows a lighted silver candle stick her maid had brought. She stepped to the wall beyond the bookcases. A panelled door flew open at her touch. In the threshold she waved her hand to us. And she disappeared down the secret staircase in the thick stone wall.[11]

When she died, Marie left Bran to her youngest daughter, Ileana, Grand Duchess of Austria. After the war, in 1948, the castle and gardens were seized by the state and left neglected until 1958 when it reopened as a museum. Only in 1993, after extensive repairs, did the ancient citadel recover its reputation, though currently there is a spurious 'tourism' plot to market Bran as Dracula's castle, a ploy of appalling pretence.

Marie's garden has disappeared but, as in all her homes, her spirit still lingers on. Pause in the enchanting library and music room with its painted floral doors and whitewashed inglenook and you will find Marie sitting there by the fire, book in hand, poised to make a funny or flirtatious remark.

Marie was a most unusual and talented person. The grand daughter of Queen Victoria and Tsar Alexander II of Russia, Marie had a thoroughly English upbringing at Eastwell Park in Kent before, at the age of fourteen, she moved with her parents to Coburg where, at one time, she was promoted as the bride of the future George V.[12] James Pope-Henessey in his biography of Queen Mary was delighted this never happened.

> She developed into a very theatrical person, authoress of an extremely clever book of memoirs, but as neurotic and self-satisfied as her cousin Kaiser Wilhelm II, whose character indeed hers slightly resembled.

---

[11] *Marie of Roumania,* 1927.

[12] Prince George was having a good time as a bachelor in Southsea and London when his elder brother unexpectedly died and thus he was heir to the throne. So influential were the supporters of Mary of Teck, his dead brother's fiancee, that George ended up marrying her.

Anyway, her Russian mother had different ideas and on the evening of her first formal appearance in society, Marie found herself sitting next to Ferdinand "Nando" Hohenzollern-Sigmaringen, the nephew of King Carol of Romania, who had recently been adopted by his childless uncle as heir apparent. Nando was in trouble at the time; he had fallen for a plump and witty authoress, Helen Văcărescu, with the encouragement of his aunt, Queen Elizabeth. His uncle had forbidden any idea of marriage, so young Nando was on the lookout for the right royal princess. The two were duly married and Marie, pregnant within two weeks of the wedding, delivered a boy, Carol, on 15 October 1893, and the Romanian succession was assured.

As I crossed the Carpathians south of Braşov, I picked up the thread of Marie's life on reaching Sinaia. It was here at Peleş that the Romanian royal family had their summer residence in the mountains, a veritable Balmoral of the Balkans. Indeed it could be the mansion of a nineteenth century English industrialist, high up in some Scottish glen. The building had been started in 1873 by King Carol I when he instructed Wilhelm Doderer, a German architect, to draw up plans. Doderer proved somewhat dogmatic in adhering to his original plan, so he was replaced by Johannes Schultz in 1876, a man more amenable to change or "interference." Although completed in 1883, many more alterations were carried out between 1893 and 1914 by the Czech architect Karel Liman and today's castle is a riotous hybrid of all their designs.

On the outside, Peleş is attributable to the German neo-Renaissance style: vertical, slim profiles, asymetrical, irregular shapes, and an abundance of timber frames and decorative elements. The steep gabled roofs are reminiscent of medieval Nurnberg. The terraces of the castle, overlooking the fir covered mountains, were conceived in the Italian Renaissance style, crowded with statues, urns, vases, and columns, a blend that is marginally successful in working with the house.

I entered the castle to find an eclectic mixture of styles: German neo-Renaissance, Italian, English Renaissance, Baroque, Rococo, Moorish and indeed Turkish. In the hall of Honour, inspired by the "Fredenhagen" at the Palace of Commerce in Lubeck, the wood decoration by Bernard Ludwig and his Viennese workshop typified the excellence of the "fin-de-siècle" craftmanship used throughout the castle. The names of the rooms signified their style — the Turkish salon, the Mooresque Hall, the Florentine Hall.

For many years Peleş was the home of Marie's mother-in-law, Queen Elizabeth, alias the authoress Carmen Sylva, a most sensitive and artistic soul. The daughter of two highly educated and cultured parents — Prince Hermann of Wied,[13] a philosopher and Princess Marie of Nassau, a poet and healer — Elizabeth never dreamt in her Rhineland childhood she would marry Karl de Hohenzollern-Sigmaringen, the second son of the southern German branch of the Hohenzollern family, and be Queen of Romania aged twenty. Karl was some way down on the list of Ion Brătianu, the Romanian politician sent in 1866 to trawl Europe for a foreign prince to occupy the newly created Romanian throne.

Leslie Gardiner in his book, *Curtain Calls,*[14] wondered:

> How the solemn king came to fall for a pantomime dame was one of the romantic mysteries of 19th century court life. Rumour said she fell for him — literally, tripping over a stair-rod and landing in his arms.[15]

Up at four every morning, the hour her young daughter, Princess Marie, had died, an event from which she never recovered, Elizabeth combined her role of Queen with that of an artiste extraordinaire, for she was a poetess, speaking and writing fluently in seven languages. She completed over fifty volumes of literary oeuvres of one type or another. Great hearted and greatly gifted, her spendthrift ways caused awful trouble with the Exchequer and she was often in her husband's bad books as a consequence. Although surrounded by armies of 'artistes,' she considered her existence "distinctly unpleasant" and told Marie she felt like a caged tiger. Her biographer, Elizabeth Burgoyne, pithily summed up her life:[16]

> Carmen Sylva would, one must suppose, have been a more perfect Queen if she had not been an artist; she would certainly have been a greater artist if she had not been a Queen.

The story of her "pen name" is legend. One morning she said to her doctor: "I should like a nice pen name! As I now belong to a Latin people, I must have a Latin name. It must, however, recall my origin. How do you say forest in Latin or rather, of the forest?"

---

[13] Author of *The Unconscious Life of the Soul and the Manifestation of God.* Writing and spiritualism ran in the family.

[14] 1976.

[15] This was in Berlin when she was eighteen — she married him when she was 26!

[16] *Carmen Sylva,* 1941.

"Forest," Dr. Kremnitz replied, " is *sylva* and of the forest is *sylvae.*"

Elizabeth was delighted. "That is beautiful. How do you say bird?"

"Bird, your highness, is row."

"I don't care for that," she said, "it doesn't sound very pretty. How do you say song or singing in Latin?"

"Song or singing is *carmen.*"

She clapped her hands. "My name is found! In German I am called Waldgesang and in Latin, Carmen Sylvae; but Sylvae doesn't sound like a real name, so a little mistake must help out and I wish to be called Carmen Sylva!"

All over the castle of Peleş are poignant reminders of Carmen Sylva: 'The Old Music Hall' where she held her literary evenings, with its canvases of diaphanous ladies by Dora Hitz, illustrating German fairy tales and its stained glass windows with scenes from Romanian folklore. In her 1896 book, *Legends from River and Mountain,* Carmen drew widely on both, starting with Romanian stories of Furnica, The Maiden, The Cave of Jalomitza, and finishing with German tales from her Rhenish homeland.

Above the fire place in the Concert Hall, which was added in 1906, is a portrait of Elizabeth by Jean du Nouy, depicting her, pen in hand, as a poetess at work. Music was yet another artistic arrow in Carmen's cultural quiver. Wiliiam Curtis glowingly reported:[17]

> She is a brilliant pianist and was a favourite pupil of Rubinstein and Clara Schumann. She is equally accomplished as an organist... she has composed symphonies and other pieces. She plays the harp gracefully

One of the few rooms with any enduring charm in the entire palace is the Theatre Hall, an enchanting hall seating sixty people with a wonderful frieze by Gustav Klimt and Franz Macht. It was here that Carmen gathered around her a coterie of neophytes, the Tragic Muse attended by her adoring handmaidens. She dressed these young women in Oriental robes, referred to them as her children, and led them fearlessly in the pursuit of beauty.

Princess Anne Marie Callimacki, Sitwell's hostess, remembered meeting Carmen Sylva:

---

[17] *Around the Black Sea,* 1911.

> As a mere baby, I remember attending Queen Carmen Sylva's musical seances, where, dressed in long flowing robes, her white hair bearing a sort of halo covered with long lace draperies hanging down her back and shoulders.[18]

The irony of Carmen's luxurious and indulgent life at Peleş was, according to Queen Marie,[19] that she hated it.

> The Queen had been allowed little part in the plans of the castle; her conception of life being ardently fantastic, she was seldom consulted about things that had to be built of brick and stone. Indeed, I had always the impression that Carmen Sylva never really loved the castle; its sumptuous magnificence seemed to oppress her.

In the *Golden Thoughts of Carmen Sylva, Queen of Romania,* a plaintive pensee of Carmen's reads: "Hope is fatigue ending in deception." I suspect that Carmen was more often on a 'low' than a 'high,' whatever glossy external shell she presented to the world. Such ups and downs were consistent with Marie's observation that "she never saw anything small, everything had to have dangerously huge proportions." Of her many poems, 'The Kiss' epitomises this welter of emotions she lived in:

> Ah! The kiss that I once gave thee,
> Such a hot and loving one,
> That the moon, our only witness,
> Stood enchanted at the fun.
>
> When at length our lips consented
> From each other to withdraw,
> Birds were singing in the branches,
> And the rising sun we saw.
>
> But I cannot now remember
> If the kiss which I did give,
> With its warm and heavenly feeling,
> Did indeed the night outlive.
>
> Or if, when I kissed thee, dearest,
> With such ardent, burning love,
> 'Twas the sun that was our witness
> Or the moon on fire above.

---

[18] *Yesterday was Mine,* 1952.

[19] *The Story of My Life,* 1934.

The "plump ghost of the Romanian Sappho"[20] seems to hover over the castle, even to this day.

Marie found life at Peleş with her parents-in-law both overpowering and dull, so her solution was to build a small home for her family, at Pelişor, next to the Great Palace. Using the Czech architect, Karel Liman, to design it, Marie imposed her own ideas on Pelişor with great success. It was an intimate as opposed to grand house; it was personal as opposed to official; and above all it was stamped throughout by her endearing personality. Marie hated the sterility of the neo-classical movements and together with Bernhard Ludwig devised an Art Nouveau style tinted with Byzantine and Celtic motifs. The result can be seen in the Golden Room where the walls are embossed with thistle leaves, a symbol dear to her both as the emblem of the town of Nancy in France, the home of Art Nouveau, and of her native Scotland. The ceiling has a skylight in the shape of a Celtic Cross, another device most precious to Marie who was always conscious of her English roots. Much of the décor and ornament was made specifically to Marie's instructions and includes work from the best designers of the day — E. Galle, the Daum brothers, J. Hoffmann, and L.C. Tiffany.

But life in Bucharest and Sinaia for this high spirited, blue-eyed princess was extraordinarily dull and it was not long before Marie found a let-out in riding. Her father-in-law, impressed by this equestrian streak, appointed her colonel-in-chief of a cavalry regiment, the Fourth Rosiori or Hussars. Her uniform was splendid: a dark red tight-waisted jacket with black brocade, an ankle length white riding skirt and a little blue-grey pepper box hat. She would have looked quite irresistible and it was only a matter of time before she was rumoured to be having an affair with Lieutenant Zizi Cantacuzino,[21] a scion of the Cantacuzino clan. Her reputation in ruins with the King, she was sent with her husband to the South of France. The flirtation continued until she was hauled up before the King who famously remarked: "We all know that Nando may not be so very entertaining. But that does not mean you may find your entertainment elsewhere." Lieutenant Zizi was promptly posted as far away from Bucharest as possible.

---

[20] Leslie Gardiner, *Curtain Calls.*

[21] There are various spellings of this name: Cantacuzenus (Byzantine); Cantacuzino (Romanian); Cantacuzene (French); Cantauzen (Russian). I have used the Romanian spelling throughout.

Not one to be cooped up for long, Marie struck up a friendship with the young multi-millionaires Waldorf and Pauline Astor. Hannah Pakula, her biographer, wrote that "as they spent more time in Romania, they came to understand and share Marie's irritation with her husband and his family — their pomposity, humourlessness, and insensitivity to others."[22] When Waldorf married Nancy Shaw, an American divorcee, Marie had to slowly withdraw from the intensity of her relationship but remained lifelong friends.

It was in the spring of 1907 that Marie went up to Pelişor with her children and accepted an invitation to stay with Princess Marthe Bibesco in her nearby country house, Posada.

Marthe Bibesco's biographer, Christine Sutherland, described what happened:[23]

> The Crown Princess's stay was memorable for it was in Posada that her lifelong affair with Prince Ştirbey began... Two years older than Marie, Ştirbey was tall and slim and carried himself with great authority. Reserved and rather elusive, he had great charm and a "hypnotic quality" in his dark brown eyes which made him very attractive to women. Educated in Paris like most aristocratic Romanians, he had studied law at the Sorbonne, was a brilliant businessman and ran his farms at great profit, becoming one of the richest and most powerful men in the country... for both, it became the commitment of a lifetime, and their partnership, which had the tacit approval of the monarch, brought immense benefit to Romania.

At the end of the First World War Marie forged another close friendship, this time with a Canadian adventurer, Joe Boyle. A man out of the pages of fiction, a mixture of Richard Hannay and James Bond, in 1917 Boyle had delivered to Iaşi, the Romanian wartime capital, a small part of the Romanian archives and currency that had been sent to Moscow for safekeeping after the fall of Bucharest to the Germans. Marie found him "a curiously fascinating man who is afraid of nothing, and who by his extraordinary force of will and fearlessness manages to get through everywhere." This was no exaggeration according to the account[24] of Captain George Hill DSO, a British Secret Service agent.

---

[22] *Queen of Romania,* 1984.

[23] *Enchantress,* 1996.

[24] *Go Spy the Land,* 1932.

In 1917, after calling in a favour with a Red commissar, he and Boyle had loaded 100 million lei, together with some of the crown and royal jewels, into whicker baskets and set off from St. Petersburg in a train. Their journey took them across Russia and the Ukraine, everywhere in the grip of revolution. After beating off drunken Cossacks, mainly with Boyle's fists, Hill ordered the train driver to crash through a blockade in the middle of the night and finally the pair reached safety.

After hearing that he had suffered a stroke in the summer of 1918, Marie sent for Boyle and installed him in Bicaz when she was determined to supervise his recuperation. Pakula said it was here

> that Joe Boyle fell in love with Marie and that love changed his life... For the first time in his fifty one years, Joe Boyle had found someone to live for and from then on he devoted himself to the Queen and her family.[25]

Five years later he was to die of heart disease in England, just months after rescuing an old friend from a Communist jail in Tiflis.

In summarising Queen Marie and her impact on the Romanian people. Princess Anne-Marie Callimacki, her close friend, described her as[26]

> simply breathtaking. To radiant beauty she added intelligence, wit, passion and a deep understanding and love for her adopted country... her love affairs were never considered a grievance by the people. On the contrary... the Romanians with their natural lack of morality, felt relieved at not having a saint for their queen.

The town of Sinaia which lies at the foot of the royal castle had that faded grandeur of Biarritz, the hotels aged like Dowager Duchesses. When Derek Patmore passed through it in 1939,[27] he stayed at the Palace Hotel where "at night, the large rooms are crowded with fashionably dressed women and their escorts, who sometimes are their husbands and at other times their lovers or admirers." The hotel is still there but has most definitely shed its notoriety.

On the road to Bucharest from Sinaia, I passed Princess Callimacki's house at Măneşti, her ancient family seat near Ploieşti and Câmpina. From 1920 to 1940 Anne-Marie farmed a 14,000-acrc estate at Cocargea, left to her by her grandfather Kazotti When Patmore met her in Bucharest in

---

[25] *Queen of Romania,* 1984.
[26] *Yesterday was Mine,* 1952.
[27] *Invitation to Roumania,* 1939.

1939, he wrote: "She is small, dark, with a fine classic head and great dark eyes; her vivacity is dynamic."

She painted some wonderful vignettes of Romanian life in her memoirs, *Yesterday was Mine,* centering on stories of unbridled passion. Princess Stourdza jumped on a horse into a ravine to her death because of falling in love with a neighbour, Count Candriano de Roma. Adele Cantacuzino-Paşcanu sat up waiting for her first love, Georges Ştirbey, to return to her although she had since married and had children. As an old lady, each night in her isolated country house, she changed into full evening dress, grand decollete with some of the famous Paşcanu jewels — cabochon emeralds, rubies, Cantacuzino opals. The house ablaze with candle-filled chandeliers, curtains drawn back, windows wide open, the old lady waited hopefully for her lost love, who never returned. One night on such a vigil, she was murdered and all her jewels stolen, it was rumoured, by her son's redheaded Russian girlfriend.

Her father a Văcărescu,[28] her mother's grandmother a Mănescu, Anne-Marie recalls the grand quail shoots in her childhood at this great estate. She remembers the "silver pine, hornbeam alley, two huge lime trees, poplars, old elms, walnuts, apples, and pears and masses of acacias." Sirwell[29] recorded on his visit there

> moorish verandas and a tower of lattice work as a prelude to the interior which is furnished in large part by the fournisseur or ebeniste to Napoleon the Second and has the stamp of Imperial patronage upon the underneath of many of the chairs and sofas.

It's hard to imagine Sacherverell of all people on his hands and knees looking for such stamps but he goes on:

> It has a lake and weeping willows and more than one classical temple. This is the park of so many of the novels of Turgenev, in a country house or chateau where the ladies read Byron and had just discovered Chopin.

A year later, Derek Patmore found

> peasant boys in long white tunics and coloured embroidered belts... watering the grass, and the air heavy with the scent of the roses which grew in terraced beds in front of the house.

---

[28] An old boyar family.

[29] *Roumanian Journey,* 1938.

It was a life that the forces of the twentieth century were closing in on and even then, before the storms of war erupted, one can detect a poignancy in the hearts of the visitors. When I visited Măneşti, it was a dilapidated ruin, teetering on the verge of collapse. Its once welcoming rooms were crammed full of fallen timbers; the garden and park lay overgrown. The only inhabitants were stray dogs, nesting in piles of leaves beneath the beech trees. The great house was nothing more than an aristocratic skeleton, the flesh of legendary hospitality eaten by Stalin's worms.

Nearby to Măneşti, on the western bank of the Prahova river, was the magnificent ruin of a Cantacuzino house at Floreşti. Started in 1913 by a Cantacuzino nicknamed the 'Nabob' on account of his huge wealth, this neo-classical house, fit for an eighteenth century English duke, would have been the greatest house in southeastern Europe in its day. Never completed, it lies in ruins, its stone facade defiantly protecting its interior of rubble and fallen beams. A few miles south, at Filipeşti de Târg, there was a classic Brâncoveanu period house, Filipescu, in the process of restoration. The house now stands alone without the surrounding building of its curtea but its revival lifted my spirits after the horror of the scene at Măneşti.

Anne-Marie Callimacki was less than flattering about Marthe Bibescu, whose famous houses at Posada and Mogoşoaia were my next stop:

> At this early stage Marthe was not yet an author of repute, not even the lovely ornament of cosmopolitan salons: just a beautiful young woman under twenty, lovely and gay... a mere girl, strikingly handsome, with a scheming nature, faulty ankles, great intelligence, steady willpower and an incomplete education[30]

Another acquaintance wrote of Marthe: "She had to be right there with the right people on the right spot at the right moment... she was ready to compromise any kind of situation just because she wanted to be on the right side and what the right side was." This steely determination led her into an affair with the Kaiser's eldest son, which backfired on the outbreak of the First World War, a liaison with King 'Nando,' a steamy tryst with Henri de Jouvenel, editor-in-chief of *Le Matin,* a long love affair with Colonel 'Kit' Thompson, later Lord Thomson, the British air minister, and a platonic relationship with Ramsay Macdonald when he was prime minister. Queen Marie saw her as "a born adventuress."

---

[30] *Yesterday was Mine,* 1952.

Thomson's infatuation with Marthe was told in his thinly disguised story of 'Smaranda.' Meaning emerald, Smaranda was the alias for Marthe and Smarandaland code for Romania. For a stiff-lipped British officer of the old school, Thomson was touchingly romantic in his writing, unable to suppress his emotions in spite of his Britishness:

> The heat in the Capital has been appalling, and I have escaped to these cool forests for a few day's in Smaranda's mountain home (Posada)... No one else is staying here at present... we went for a ride in the forest. As Smaranda rode beside me I thought of those lines by Tennyson, in Lancelot and Guinevere, which begin — 'She looked so lovely as she swayed the rein with dainty finger-tip...' and misquoted them rather badly. The surroundings and the woman I was with were enough to make any man sentimental.
>
> With Smaranda one enjoys a rare companionship wherein romance and mental stimulus are combined. She listens, laughs at British jokes, suggests their parallels in French, makes stupid men, with dull, fagged brains, feel brilliant, draws out the best one has to give, and talks our language by translation; to hear her speaking English is the best way of learning French and certainly the nicest... As the sun set a hush fell on the forest, and we too were silent. A bird flashed across the glade before us, and, in the fading light, I thought I saw the gleam of azure on its breasts and wings. Was it a mere fancy, or, indeed, that swiftly passing and elusive bird we all pursue?
>
> Four questions come into my mind:
>
> How may she catch the sunlight and wear it in her hair?
>
> Where is the golden apple whose core is not despair?
>
> How may one cull the honey and yet not pluck the flower?
>
> And how can man, being happy, still keep his happy hour?
>
> Smaranda has told me to write something about a forest, and I will. It would be sloshy if I wrote about bluebirds, so I will write about an owl.
>
> We heard an owl's cry as we were dismounting, a harsh, strident note that struck a chill. But we soon forget it in the warmth and light of the great house.[31]

Prophetic? Thomson died in the R100 airship crash in 1929.

About five miles south of Sinaia, 'Smaranda's mountain home' had burnt down in 1915. What happened was that Colonel Kit Thomson had stored the bulk of the British Embassy's secret documents at the house on 15 September that year; ten days later German intelligence agents set tire to it and the house was devastated. And still the war had not finished with Posada — in December 1916 soldiers of a Hungarian regiment stationed there found family portraits stored in an attic. They used them for target practice and thus destroyed a family Renoir.

The setting is still magnificent but long gone are the ascending paved terraces of roses and lilacs, sheltered by giant chestnut and acacias trees. The house has survived in the form of the converted stable block which still makes for an ample country house. Alas, the main road from Bucharest to Braşov passes almost on its doorstep and, ironically, next to the house is a hideous oblong concrete and glass structure, which contains Ceauşescu's hunting trophies from the surrounding mountains. Its stark and ugly presence serves to prevent the most vivid of imaginations from conjuring up the Posada of old.

Mogoşoaia was and is one of the great houses of Romania or more specifically Wallachia. It was Constantine Brâncoveanu's attempt to create a unique style for his court, both in scale and design. As Anca Brătuleanu put it in her treatise on *Romanian Princely and Nobiliary Courts:*

> no more camping with tents in a place determined by the length of travel decided all of a sudden, or chance stopovers at noblemen's courts, but a framework to cope with specific necessities.

Mogoşoaia was part of a series of houses — Doiceşti was visited at vintage time, Sâmbata de Sus a refuge in case of Turkish invasion — designed to give the prince a place to walk and rest. He started the house in 1702, based on the 1698 design of his house at Potlogi, and it incorporated all his favourite Palladian features of flowing staircases, loggias, and belvederes.

Brâncoveanu owed many of his ideas to Petru Cercel who ruled Wallachia from 1583 to 1585. This remarkable man had lived in Constantinople where the works of Italian artists were well-known; indeed, Mehmed the Second had had his portrait painted by the Venetian Gentile Bellini,[32] contrary to the ruling of the Koran. At the beginning of the six-

[31] *Smaranda,* 1926.

teenth century, Leonardo da Vinci, then Michelangelo, had both been invited to build a bridge over the Bosphoros. Petru then lived for a while in Poland where the Renaissance form was gaining popularity before he moved to the French court of Henry the Third and its splendid feasts at Blois and Chenonceaux. For good measure, he dropped in on Venice where Palladio had published his critical treatise on good taste, *Four Books of Architecture,* in 1570. Petru brought back ideas for loggias, that device designed by Palladio for the reunion of Italian families, the concept of a garden, and even cages for wild animals. It was the beginning of an era of borrowing from Western design, of experimenting initially within the old defensive court and then successfully without it.

Marthe Bibesco came into Mogoşoaia when she married Prince George Bibesco and in 1912 she began to supervise its rebuilding. Unhappy in her marriage and worn out by her tempestuous affair with Prince Charles-Loius de Beauvau-Craon in Paris, she put all her formidable intellect and energy into the project and soon, under the direction of the Venetian architect Domenico Rupolo[33] and the famous decorator Fortuny, the house was nearing completion when war rudely intervened.

In December 1916, a few months after the fire at Posada, Marthe was told that Mogoşoaia had been ransacked by German soldiers. Christine Sutherland recounts the scene that Marthe found:[34]

> The long poplar drive, along which a battle must have taken place, was strewn with the decomposing bodies of farm horses. Inside, the house was in a shambles: pieces of antique furniture, some stacked in the fireplace to be used as firewood, curtains torn from the windows, a sea of valuable china littering the floor, carpets stained with soldiers' excreta. The Byzantine chapel of the Brancovan princes... had been turned into a stable. "I am deeply ashamed of my men," said the local commander, Von Diergard, "and I apologise — poor Princess." Whereupon a young German soldier, looking at Martha's lovely face, exclaimed with a sudden surge of re-

[32] In 1479, the Doge had sent Bellini over in response to the Sultan's request for 'a good painter.' Bellini also painted the 'cose di Iussuria' — erotic murals — on the walls of the Sultan's inner chambers.

[33] The project manager was Georges Cantacuzino (see Constanţa), who was later criticised for removing the original stucco, thus leaving the brickwork exposed. In his defence, Cantacuzino argued that the stucco had only been applied in the first place as a surface for murals which had long since flaked off or faede. Was he supposed to repaint them?

[34] *Enchantress,* 1996.

> gret, "We had no idea that the owner was a young and beautiful woman — we would not have done it had we known." "Should I have put a notice on my house advising that I was not an old woman?" Martha remarked bitterly to herself.

It was from Mogoşoaia in 1945 that she was finally forced to flee her beloved country. At a lunch party for her birthday on 28 January, Marthe tartly informed the Soviet ambassador who was haranguing her on the advantages Romania would derive from a close relationship with the USSR:

> Don't forget, Ambassador, that you are in the house of a prince who, together with his four sons, was beheaded by the Turks for pursuing policies friendly to Russia. That's where it got him.

The prince Marthe was referring to was none other than Constantine Brâncoveanu.

Sitwell[35] felt at home at Mogoşoaia.

> the beauty of Mogoşoaia is a tribute to the skill and good taste of its owner (before that time it had been empty and derelict for many years.) An outside staircase and a pillared loggia... make of this house the unique essay in its style. The material is a close whitish brick, not unlike the brick architecture of Lombardy. At the other side of the house there is another loggia, and a series of flowered terraces go down to the lake which is full of lotuses. The interior of the house, which we were allowed to see by kind permission of the owner, is simple and beautiful and must be the ideal retreat for a torrid summer.

And a young Stephen Runciman[36] was a guest at a dinner with a bizarre menu:

> A young peacock had somehow fallen out of a great cedar tree in front of the house and had broken his leg and had to be put out of his misery; he was served up for this dinner. And he was served up in the proper manner, on a golden platter with his head sewn on to his body and the long tail feathers stuck into trail behind the dish. It was, I thought, macabre; and he tasted like a tough, coarse old turkey.

---

[35] *Roumanian Journey,* 1938.

[36] *A Traveller's Alphabet,* 1991.

When I reached Mogoşoaia, the gates were closed and a small crowd of excited Gypsy women and children were craning their necks over the low wall. It was the visit of Prince Charles that had drawn their attention. Once his motorcade had swept out of the grounds, the waiting little girls rewarded with a beaming royal smile and friendly wave, I presented myself to the gate keeper, a red-faced lady of obvious and enormous self-importance.

"May I go in now, please," I asked.

"No. We're now closed. Go home and come back tomorrow," was her peremptory response.

I nodded sympathetically for the work that goes into any royal or presidential visit must be massive. However, there was, I thought, a misunderstanding in the offing.

"I quite understand but the difficulty is that my home is 2,000 miles away in London. Actually, it's the same place Prince Charles lives."

This threw the guardian of the gate into much confusion and, after a telephone call, a pretty girl came down the drive, walking very slowly and stiffly in her new "royal" high heels.

"Is it you who lives with Prince Charles?" she asked archly.

Sometimes, misunderstandings can be positively advantageous.

The house looked like an advancing army was only hours away; vans and cars were being loaded up at a frenetic pace. The grounds were empty, so I was able to enjoy the setting of the Curtea as it would have been as a private house. The land on the far side of the lake now sprouted a large modern villa, some sort of industrial yard and several ramshackle houses, so the prospect was well and truly ruined. But the miracle was that the Mogoşoaia estate had survived in one form or another for over 290 years and that the house itself had been so successfully preserved.

There was one most annoying 'gremlin' which had crept into the upkeep of Mogoşoaia. The whole beauty of the position of the house by the side of the lake rests on their interdependence. From inside the house one should be able to look out, unimpeded, across the lake; from the other side, one should be able to see the house and its reflection in the water. This was how it was when Karl Hielscher photographed it in 1931. For some reason, a high screen of evergreen trees has been allowed to grow between these two principle components of the landscape and this entirely defeats the original purpose of their juxtaposition.

XXXIII. Transylvania: Shepherds

XXXIV. Sinaia: Peleş.

XXXV. Sinaia: Peleş

XXXVI. Sinaia: Pelişor

XXXVII. Prahova Valley: Floreşti

XXXVIII. Prahova Valley: Filipescu House

XXXIX. Prahova Valley: Măneşti

XL. Sinaia: Posada

XLI. Bucharest: Mogoşoaia

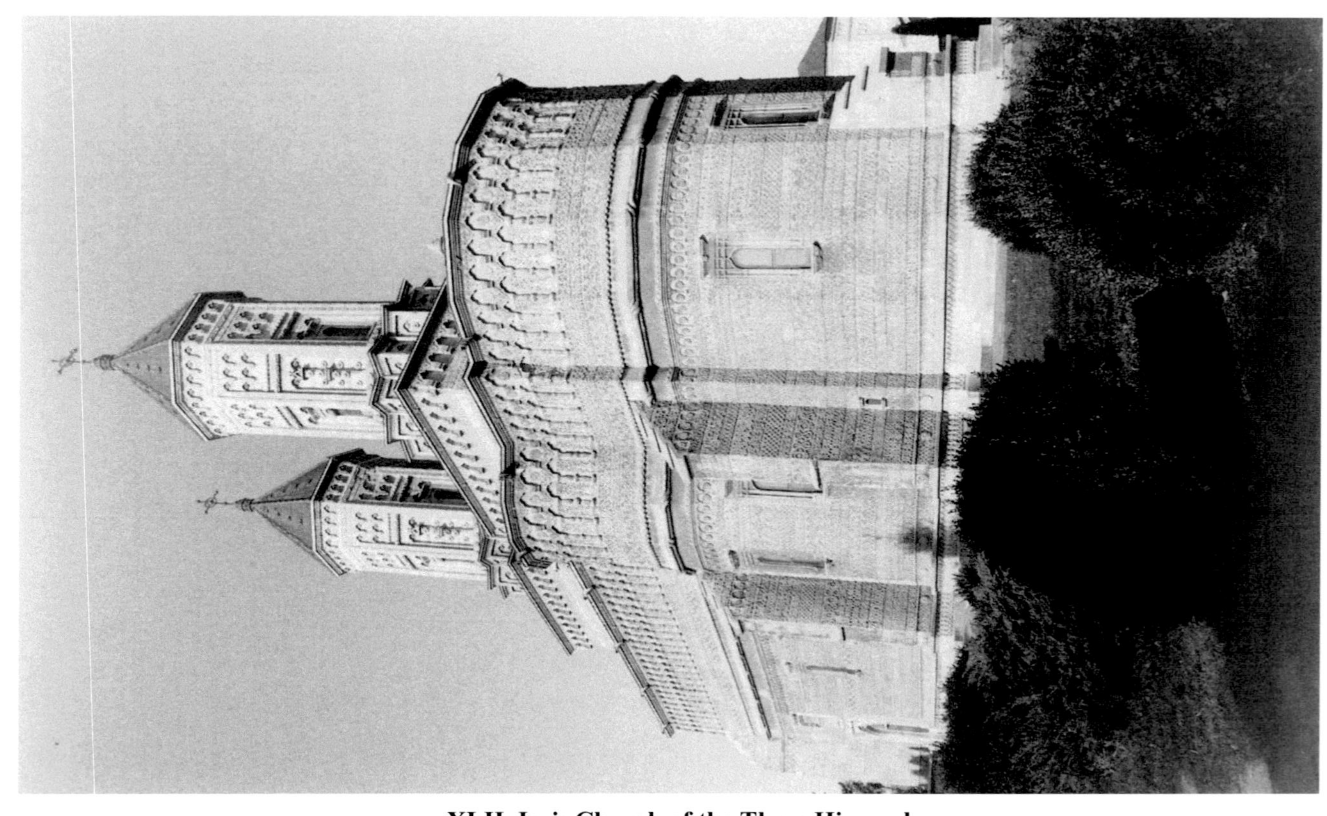

XLII. Iaşi: Church of the Three Hierarchs

XLIII. Constanţa: Saligny's Casino

XLIV. Constanţa: Hotel Rex (Mamaia)

XLV. Bucharest: The Old Stănescu Hotel

XLVI. Bucharest: King Carol II's Palace

XLVII. Bucharest: ARO Block

XLVIII. Bucharest: Caru cu Bere Restaurant

About three miles to the north of Mogoşoaia, I discovered the palace of Prince Barbu Ştirbey at Buftea. Built between 1855 and 1864, the palace was a mixture of Scottish baronial and German neo-Gothic, the sort of house a prosperous Victorian businessman might have built for himself in the Lake District Standing in thick woods, it is now a hotel, well reviewed in the guidebooks. The great avenue of chestnuts down which Ştirbey would ride with Queen Marie was still just discernible but much truncated.

On the road to Bucharest, I drove by a small military cemetery for Allied soldiers of the Second World War. Most of them were fliers who had been shot down in the great air battles over the Ploieşti oilfields but there was a headstone to a Captain David Russell of the Scots Guards which looked singularly out of place. It was in reading Ivor Porter's account of his work for SOE[1] that I came across Russell's story. Porter recalled

> I shared a flat with David Russell who, wearing German uniform, had just rescued two officers and eight other ranks from Tobruk. David had a Sudanese servant who would sometimes wrestle with him after dinner.

Commissioned into the Scots Guards in 1940, Russell was posted to SOE in April 1942 and awarded the MC in January 1943. On the night of 15 June, he was dropped into Homolje in Yugoslavia with Nicolae Ţurcanu to "open up W/T communications, effect contact with Maniu's[2] organisation and organise a reception area in the Romanian Carpathians." He crossed the Danube on 2 August with a Serb chetnik guide and towards the end of the month made contact at Varciorova with Maniu's representative. On 4 September Russell was killed, generally thought to have been murdered by his guide for the gold sovereigns he carried on him. Such is war.

---

[1] *Operation Autonomous,* 1990.

[2] The leader of the Peasant Party and the main Allied contact.

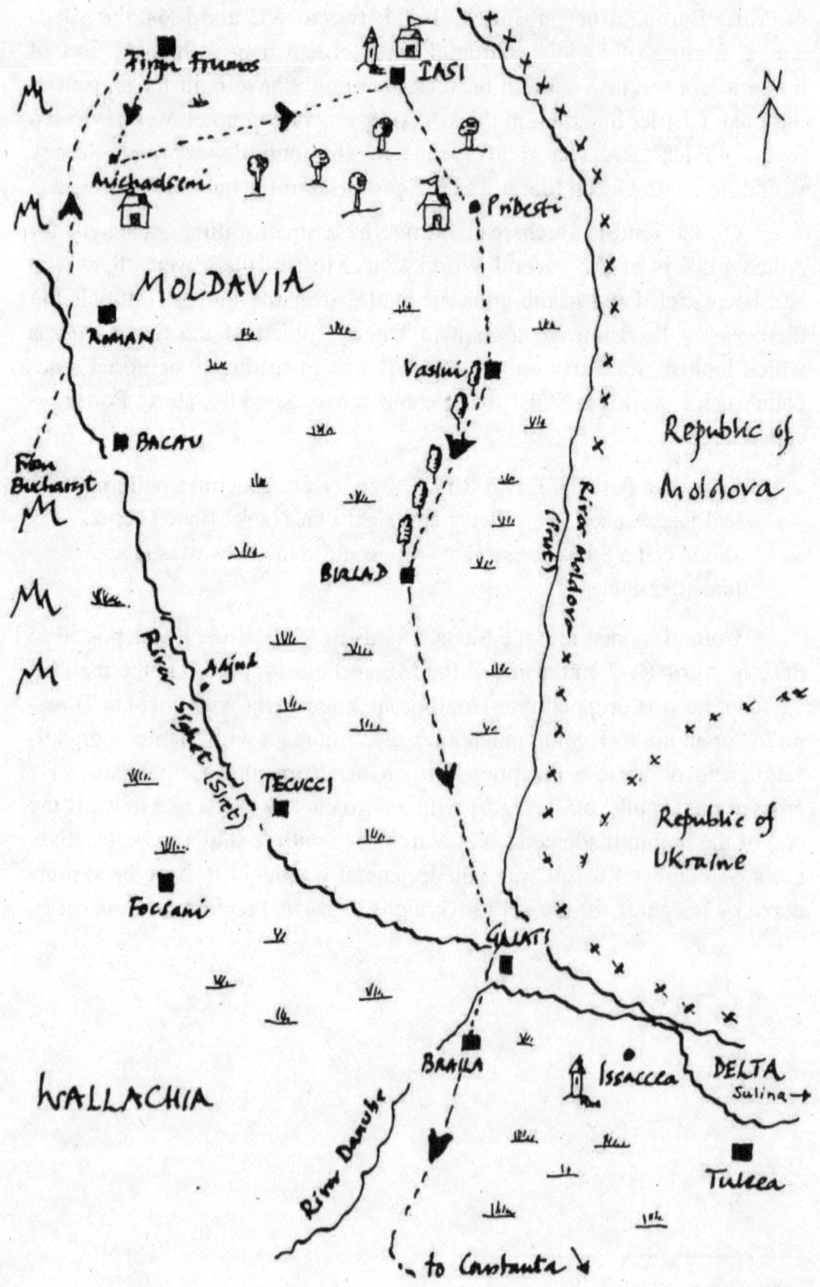
Tirgu Frumos
IASI
N
Michadseni
Pribesti
MOLDAVIA
ROMAN
Vaslui
BACAU
From Bucharest
Republic of Moldova
River Moldova (Prut)
BIRLAD
River Sighet (Siret)
Adjud
TECUCCI
Republic of Ukraine
Focsani
GALATI
BRAILA
Issaccea
DELTA
Sulina
WALLACHIA
River Danube
Tulcea
to Constanta

Chapter Twelve

Bucharest: One Street, One Church, and One Idea

Bucharest has always evoked colourful responses from its visitors, some favourable, some highly critical. On her arrival in Bucharest, Elisa Craven wrote to her Margrave that she was met by a "kind of Chamberlain, with a gold robe on and a long white stick in his hand" who took her to see the prince of Wallachia. She found him dressed à la Turque[1] — "over his head were ranged the horses tails,[2] the great helmet and feathers,[3] the magnificent sabre and other arms that I had seen parade in the streets of Constantinople." Half way through the audience, Eliza's ears "were assailed by the most diabolical noise she had ever heard." A secretary leant over to her and whispered : "C'est pour vous, Madame — c'est la musique du prince." She looked into the court and saw:

> trumpets of all kinds, brass plates striking together, and drums of all sizes were ranged on the ground, and the strikers of them squatted on the ground to beat them. Each musicians was endeavouring to drown the noise of his neighbour, by making a louder one if possible and I do not know that my nerves ever were so tried before; for my

[1] In the eighteenth century, the princes of Wallachia and Moldavia were Greeks, known as Phanariots, who both dressed and ate like Ottomans.

[2] The bey of Wallachia was allowed two: more important beys had three.

[3] *Cuka* or jewelled crest with ostrich feathers.

> companion, who saw the difficulty I had to refrain from laughing, was saying, for God's sake do not laugh.[4]

After this impromptu concert, to show Elisa "an extraordinary mark of respect," the prince invited her travelling companion, Henry Vernon, to come into his harem where they sat down together to inspect the concubines, presumably under the watchful eyes of the black eunuchs. Elisa did not relate what happened in the harem but neither the prince nor Mr. Vernon probably possessed the stamina of Sultan Ibrahim, "The Depraved," whose "strength so faithfully kept pace with his immoderate desire that twenty four slaves could visit his couch successively in the space of twenty four hours."

The anonymous traveller in Richard Phillips's *Book of Journeys* must have arrived at Bucharest with some sort of high-ranking embassy, for they were afforded the red-carpet by 'Alessandro Moroozi,'[5] the ruler of Wallachia.

> The state coach which he sent for us was drawn by six horses, and eight tehoadaars or pages walked at our side. They were habited in close white dresses of cotton, with green silk sashes, tyed in large bows, and high fur caps on their heads.

He was looking forward to a square meal since, until Bucharest, he had politely bemoaned the standard of food.

> The common diet of the country is black bread, very moist and sour, with which the post-horses are likewise fed. We were favoured with white manchets, which would have been very good but for the sand which is mixed with the flour in grinding the wheat.

William Wilkinson, the British consul in 1820, hated it:[6]

> Bucharest is an extensive dirty town, containing 80,000 inhabitants, three hundred and sixty six churches, twenty monasteries and thirty large hanns or caravanserays.

The pavements in those days were wooden or bridges, underneath which were "large kennels which collected the sewage." Wilkinson got on famously badly with the inhabitants:

---

[4] A *Journey through the Crimea to Constantinople,* 1789.

[5] Alexander Moruzi, 1799-1801.

[6] *An Account of the Principalities of Wallachia and Moldavia,* 1820.

> Man, the chief work of nature, is here of a dull and heavy disposition: with weak passions, no strength of mind and betraying a natural aversion to a life of industry or mental exertion.

He did however find something nice to say about the ladies who

> dress entirely in the European style; but they combine the fashions with oriental richness and profusion of ornament. Their persons, in general, have not much beauty; but this deficiency is made up by a great share of natural grace and pleasant humour, and by a particular neatness of shape.

On the subject of girls, Captain Socivizca[7] had his ear to the ground:

> Their ornaments consist of Ear-Rings of white or yellow Brass, of coloured Glass, Beads, Pearls, Feathers, and Pieces of Money, fastened to a string, and tied round the Head and Neck. These Ornaments making a ringing Noise, so that a fine dressed Raize or Wallachian Girl, may very often be heard sooner than seen.

Wilkinson was scathing in his assessment of the boyars, the aristocracy so-called from the title of the Roman colonists who went into battle in chariots armed with scythes and drawn by oxen, every master of such chariot being a boier *(bovis herus).* "They consider it derogatory to their dignity to make use of their legs and leave to the mob the vulgar practice of walking" and "Those who hold no place in government, spend their leisure in absolute idleness, or in visiting each other to kill time." He disapproved of their lax morals:

> In the habitual state of inaction, brought on by a natural aversion to every serious occupation which does not immediately relate to personal interest, both sexes, enjoying the most extensive freedom of intercourse with each other, are easily led to clandestine connexion: the matrimonial faith has become merely nominal.

William Macmichael in his *Journey from Moscow to Constantinople* in 1818 was more measured in his account:

> As a proof of the state of morals in the capital, the son of the Hospodar entered the club, where sat his mother and sisters, having on his arm his mistress, a beautiful Wallachian lady, who had lately deserted her husband and six children; there appeared to be nothing extraordinary, or that was considered indelicate, in his conduct.

[7] *The Life and Extraordinary Adventures of Captain Socivizca,* 1778.

Wilkinson obviously dreaded dining with the inhabitant:

> The kitchens of the Boyars are, from the filthy habits of the cooks and the inattention of the masters, not less disgusting than the common receptacles of swine.

Over a hundred years before, Edmund Chishull had arrived in Bucharest from Constantinople. He was met on 24 April 1702 by Constantine Brâncoveanu, a prince "of an affable, mild and courteous temper." The prince received Paget "at the head of the stairs" of his palace which, "with the appartments and gardens adjoining," Chishull found "truly noble and magnificent."

Chishull, unlike Wilkinson, was an observer, devoid of opinions. He records in his diary:

> Bucharest is a large straggling town of a very peculiar make, the outward parts very mean, consisting of houses, the greater part of which is underground like our cellars, and covered over at the top with straw or bark of trees. The better sorts of houses are about the Palace of the Prince, which are covered with handsome wooden tiles, the walls built of substantial stone, and the yards and gardens always very wide, enclosed with intine trunks of oaks set as near as possible to each other.[8]

The French point of view was altogether more 'laissez-faire,' particularly if a good party was in the offing. Anatole de Demidov[9] arriving in Bucharest in 1837 was initially unimpressed: "The houses, for the most part, are little better than barns of rotten timber, among which are seen edifices of the most pretentious style of architecture." But he mellowed when asked to a party:

> I know of no city in Europe in which it is possible to find more agreeable society, or in which there is a better tone, united with the most charming gaiety. This delightful ball was kept up until far into the night and it was a pleasant sight to see the master of the house, the Aga Philipesco, in his ample Boyard dress, his fine head fringed with a long, silky-white beard, surrounded by a swarm of young and pretty women, whose gauze and ribbons, long tresses, and charming faces, were so well matched with the gentle physiognomy of the stately old man.

---

[8] *Travels in Turkey and Back,* 1747.

[9] *Travels in Southern Russia and the Crimea,* 1853.

James Noyes[10] found Bucharest in 1858 "resounding with an incessant concert of fetes, of sports, of the neighing of horses, the howling of dogs and the weeping of slaves." In 1864 W. Beatty-Kingston[11] bemoaned that "social immorality had attained its apogee, not only amongst the higher classes but throughout all strata of the formation." By 1878, these deprecatory views were beginning to change and James Ozanne[12] found

> the Chaussee lined, two or three rows deep with vehicles of very description... such a display of velvets and satins and lace as is to be met with nowhere else... we pass a pair of thoroughbred Hungarian bays... a superb Arab, ridden by some Moldavian belle.

Maude Parkinson, who had set off to Romania as a governess in 1889, described Bucharest[13] as "a town of one street, one church, and one idea." She justified this statement because in those days, the main street, Calea Victoriei was practically Bucharest, the Greek Church knew no dissenters and the prevailing idea was the spending of money. Ruing the fact that "Roumania is a breakfastless country," Maude determined that

> We must always remember, in considering the Roumanian people, that their civilisation is more suggestive of the East than of the West... for instance no one ever dreams of starting on a journey or commencing any particular work on a Tuesday (the day that Constantinople fell).

My favourite story, which she recounted about her life as a governess, was when she once gave a pupil a portion of the fourteenth chapter of St. Mark to turn from French into English. The pupil's translation read: "The ghost is agreeable, but the meat is feeble."

Breakfast was obviously an issue for the English. Gertrude Mendl[14] pursued this in her mysterious statement:

> English habits must be modified whilst visiting the provinces. It is, for instance, best for breakfast to be served in the bedroom, unless there happens to be a decent coffee house in the neighbourhood.

Was it that frightful?

---

[10] *Roumania, the Border Lands of the Christian and the Turk,* 1858.
[11] *A Wanderer's Notes,* 1888.
[12] *Three Years in Roumania,* 1878.
[13] *20 Years in Romania,* 1921.
[14] *Roumania Calling,* 1933.

Dorothy Kennard,[15] the wife of the British ambassador in Bucharest in the First World War, had a more enlightened view of its people. She recalled meeting a peasant when out riding and asked him whether he has seen an aeroplane; after all he lived by an airfield.

> Yes, I have seen a machine. It stopped on the road where Mitru lives and left a pool of liquid in the road which was not water. Mitru's pig drank it there and it died.

Living in "an absolutely distracted whirlwind of uncertainty" waiting for the advance of the German army, she prepared for evacuation to Iaşi. She recalled one evening that "the cook has appeared quite ready to start with six dead chickens hanging on a string from her arm. She says they will be useful."

Lady Hoare, the wife of the British ambassador in 1939, was somewhat more eccentric. Ivor Porter[16] told how she carried an alarm clock in her handbag, which rang when it was time to say goodbye to her hostesses. She also flew a small aeroplane. Porter was a British Council lecturer at Bucharest University and was a witness to the Bucharest of Olivia Manning's *Balkan Trilogy.* He knew her and her husband Reggie Smith who was No 2 at the British Institute.

> Cut off from her own country with war approaching, without friends or even the language to help her, she watched her young marriage breaking up, seemed incapable or unwilling to do anything about it, and hated the place where it was happening.

Two of her novels, *The Great Fortune* and *The Spoilt City,* are thinly disguised autobiographical accounts of life in pre-war Bucharest, yet they remain fiction.

Pre-war visitors were enthusiastic about the city; Dudley Heathcote[17] teased that "the rouge of the women and the officers would be enough to turn the Black Sea red!" and Emil Hoppe[18] found

> a gaiety here, however, which one does not get in London or even Paris. The riders are all very gallant and debonair; the ladies sparkle like jewels; languid beauties recline in their cars and survey the scene between half-closed eyelids.

---

[15] *A Roumanian Diary,* 1917.

[16] *Operation Autonomous,* 1992.

[17] *My Wanderings in the Balkans,* 1924.

[18] *In Gypsy Camp and Royal Palace,* 1924.

Newman became rather pompous in Bucharest, bestowing on the Union Hotel the back-handed compliment that "it was quite up to the best Western standards."[19] He went whoring and much to his surprise he met a 'post office girl in a brothel,' married no less. It was not her moonlighting which shocked him but the very idea of a Government employee 'on the game.' The Calea Victoriei, for him, was "one of the naughtiest streets in Europe." And all this from a man who admitted he was unattractive to women, yet was capable of writing:

> there is a dreamy beauty about the Roumanian girl; I had met her in the fields and on the road — a glorious, athletic figure, blouse split down the middle revealing a white bosom, and a face of misty loveliness.

Not to be out done for pomposity, he was pipped by William Curtis:[20]

> Men of experience assert that Bukharest is a wickeder city than Budapest, and that is saying a good deal.

Sir Steven Runciman, later to achieve fame as the author of the definitive study of the Crusades, visited Bucharest as a young man in 1934. He found it perplexing in that:[21]

> It was sometimes hard to remember who was now married to whom. I was, I remember, much impressed to meet a Princess Soutso who, I was told, was aged nineteen and already on her third husband. She had green lacquered toe-nails, such as I had never seen before.

To a classicist like Sitwell, "the character of Bucharest was in its personality, not in its monuments."[22]

My own love of Bucharest is as a pre-war city with its rich store of 1930s architecture. One commentary[23] sums up this era:

> This was the city to which contemporaries gave the endearing name of "Little Paris." That was the biggest, most beautiful, most fashionable, most civilised city in South-Eastern Europe. On seeing it,

---

[19] *The Blue Danube,* 1935.

[20] *Around the Black Sea,* 1911.

[21] *A Traveller's Alphabet,* 1991.

[22] *Roumanian Journey,* 1938.

[23] Aristide Ştefănescu, *Bucharest, the Thirties,* 1995.

Balkan visitors had the feeling they had the privilege of getting in touch with the life in the cities of Western Europe. A visit to Bucharest was, for the fourth decade people, tantamount to a trip to Paris.

My hotel was a small pension, the Casa Victor, in Emanoil Porumbaru Street, just off the Aviatorilor Boulevard. This area was developed in the thirties as a summer suburb with "bourgeois residences of refined taste." The fashion was for three to four-storied houses, each of which had its own design, yet all having the belvedere device of Brâncoveanu. Very little had changed and with their shaded gardens and snow proof eaves, they still stand for gracious and stylish living. From my room, I overlooked a small garden of luxuriant vegetables, which housed two wild rabbits and a rambunctious cockerel.

Bucharest is a city for walking and fifteen minutes from the Casa Victor brought me to the Calea Victoriei, once called the Podul Mogoşoaia which Brâncoveanu had built to link the city with his summer residence. Poduls are the oak beams referred to by Wilkinson used to make roads. Always a favourite for the nobility to build their palaces along, it was in 1878 that the street was renamed in honour of the Russo-Turkish War of Independence and since then has remained the main artery of life in the capital. On either side there are the galleries and offices of state; the Royal Palace of the 1930s and Atheneum Român of 1888 now both restored to their former glory. The Hotel Athenée Palace (1912) is once more the fashionable meeting place of its heyday in the interwar years.

In her eyewitness account of the city in 1940-1941, Countess Waldeck described the Athenée Palace[24] with the eye of a seasoned journalist:

> In this summer of 1940 the Athene Palace was the last cosmopolitan stage on which post-world-war Europe and the new-order Europe made a joint appearance. There was, of course, the Hotel Aviso in Lisbon... but there, the old society, harried and terrified, just waited around for boats to America. There was still the Serbsky Kral in Belgrade... where the two orders mingled, but here the setting as well as the cast lacked glamour. In the Bergues in Geneva or in the Dunapalato in Budapest, there was no play on at all. Only at the Athene Palace, a glamorous setting in the traditional style of European grand Hotels, the cast of post-world-war Europe and the

---

[24] *Athene Palace*, 1943.

> cast of the new order, all-star casts both, still had equal billing and the play itself was full of suspense....
>
> In the lobby of the Atheneé Palace, old post-World War Europe and New Order Europe were acting out their parts in this drama. It was an epic setting, for in the last twenty five years this lobby had been the forum of the Balkans. Here secrets of the alcove, secrets of court, secrets of diplomatic pouches were whispered into ears that miraculously turned into microphones. Here opportunities were made and destroyed; here stories were invented and from here spread like epidemics; here the skeletons of all the Balkan closets were promenaded and laughed at, and gossip sold short the honour of every politician and the virtue of every woman. Nobody minded it, not even the victim.
>
> This summer there were in the Atheneé Palace spies of every Intelligence Service in the world; the diplomats and military attaches of great and little powers; British and French oilmen on their way out, and German and Italian oilmen on their way in; Gestapo agents, Ovra agents, and OGPU agents, or men who were at least said to be agents: amiable Gauleiters and hardheaded economic experts; distinguished Romanian appeasers and the mink-clad German and Austrian beauties who were paid to keep them happy; the mink-clad Romanian beauties who were paid (by the Romanians) to make the Italian and German ministers talk and who were also paid by the German and Italian ministers to make the Romanians talk.

The British contribution to this exotic cast of characters was Mervin Minshall who probably came closest to the fictional stereotype of James Bond. In *Secret Service,*[25] Christopher Andrew recounted Mervin's exploits in Bucharest:

> By his own (never understated) account, Minshall actually exercised his license to kill while travelling on the Orient Express and had his intelligence work frequently interrupted by a succession of demanding women such as the 'dish' who burst naked into his hotel room at Bucharest, claiming to bear a message from the British legation, threw herself full length on the bed, and beckoned in Minshall's direction. It seemed to Minshall 'a funny way of bringing a message from the British Legation. Assuming she was from the Legation.' The enemy was less fortunate. Minshall succeeded in having the

[25] *Secret Service,* 1985.

German naval attaché black-balled from 'the best brothel in Bucharest.' To the understandable alarm of British legation staff, whom Minshall found 'scared stiff' by his adventurous schemes, he was given diplomatic cover as vice-consul in Bucharest and supplied with plastic explosive through the diplomatic bag. His first scheme, to disrupt Danube navigation by bribing 40 of the 50 Iron Gates pilots to leave the country for 500 gold sovereigns each and having the remainder 'unobtrusively bumped off, fell through for lack of sovereigns. Minshall then devised a scheme to sail barges down the Danube with a score of naval ratings improbably disguised as art students and sink the barges to block the Iron Gates. But after German agents had tricked his crews into going on shore leave while they stole their fuel, he concluded that 'at every turn I had been outthought and out-witted by the Nazis.'

Irrespective of Minshall's hair-brained plans, the British secret service did succeed in removing Romania's entire stock of gold: the vaults of the National Bank were emptied twenty-four hours before the Nazi Legions of Europe's New Order arrived.

Bucharest's old hotels have a quaint way of surviving over time. When Samuelson stayed in 1888, his 'top five' hotels were The Grand Hotel du Boulevard, Brofft, Hugues, The Imperial, and Manon. In 1931, the Romanian Tourist Office recommended only six: Athenée Palace, The Boulevard, Grand, Splendid, Stănescu, and Union. Today, post-bombing and post-earthquakes, the Athenée Palace and the Boulevard are still very much in business as are the Majestic and Lido which were, for some reason, excluded from the pre-war list.

Further along the Calea Victoriei, past the neo-French Renaissance Continental Hotel which looked splendid in its new paint, is the Cercle Militaire, an imposing French neo-classical building of 1912, and, opposite it, the Capşa Restaurant of 1868. Founded in the nineteenth century by an entrepreneur who had made a small fortune making rose jam for the army in Bulgaria, it was described in 1930 as "the city's soul, the tympanic membrane of Bucharest, this huge ear."[26] Its clientele boasted Caruso, Sarah Bernhardt and Josephine Baker and Sitwell found its reputation well deserved and 'its confiserie and sweet shop having no equal in Europe."[27] David Walker, a hard-nosed journalist, was more cynical.[28] "At Capşa's,

[26] Paul Morand, 1930.

[27] *Roumanian Journey,* 1938.

[28] *Death at my Heels,* 1942.

the most famous restaurant in south east Europe, you could watch half the crooks in the Balkans, or listen to Roumanian snobs talking French amongst themselves." Harry de Windt certainly knew how to have a good time. This 'Boy's Own' adventurer with his natty moustache and such throwaway lines like "wolves (in Romania) are as common as cats in a London Square," urged his readers[29] to:

> Dine at the Restaurant Capşa (where the cuisine rivals that at Paillard's) in dress-clothes and go on to the opera, or partake of sausages and lager-beer in tweeds at Frascati's, and drop into a music or dancing hall, and you are pretty sure, either way, to be amused.

Today, Capşa is still in business, a bit dowdy, obstinately hanging on to its reputation. But to be fair to Capşa, it is a survivor: where are Cina's, Bucureşti de Altă Dată, Finnochi, and the night clubs — Colorado and Zissu Bar — of yesteryear?

More rewarding to the eye was the Caru cu Bere, just round the corner in Stavropoleus Street. This is one of the best surviving examples of an art nouveau fin-de-siècle restaurant;[30] its entrance flanked by wrought iron dragons suspended from wall brackets, one surmounted by a black cockerel, the other by a hissing cat with back arched in fury. Inside, diners are shown to vaulted 'caves' of church-like dimensions, covered with romantic Slavic murals.

Opposite the Caru is the tiny Stavropoleos Church of 1724. First impressions were of Moorish arches, reminiscent of Granada and Cordoba, which extend into the small cloister to the right of the church. The porch is 'open,' supported by four delicate spiral wooden columns with ornamental scrolling. Its tiled roof has a tiny octagonal tower: there was nothing grandiose about this humble parish church: perhaps its very humility has ensured its survival.

The winter had not yet arrived, allowing me to enjoy balmy late autumn weather. I wasn't complaining although Countess Waldeck's description[31] of the snow sounded alluring:

> Winter becomes Bucharest. Suddenly, overnight, all noises of the city were suspended and there was a new sound: the little bells of

---

[29] *Through Savage Europe,* 1908.

[30] Dismissed as 'a beer and luncheon room' in the 1911 Baedeker.

[31] *Athene Palace,* 1943.

> sleighs. A thick fur of white, the blue and absolute white of pure diamonds, padded everything, lying in luscious cushions on the cupolas of the hundred-odd Byzantine churches. Except on the boulevards, where street cars pushed the snow away by using an inefficient contraption of wood, nobody touched the snow in Bucharest and thus it retained its noble freshness. Most of the time the air was calm; around noontime it was warm, with the sun bursting from a clear blue sky. At times, a severe wind coming from Russia, the crivat, which the Bucharestians say 'has teeth', drew tears from your eyes... On the streets, so silent that one got alarmed at one's own steps crunching on the snow, Gypsy children sold paper flowers, huge red and white roses and daisies, and threw corn at you while shouting that they hoped you would grow old, 'wrinkled like an apple'... The cold made everyone appreciate Romanian food, which really was Russian, Hungarian, Turkish, Greek, Viennese and Polish — only more so. You are ciorba, a sour soup seasoned with lemon, with fowl or game or boiled beef in it, and a dab of sour cream; chopped meats, rolled in vine leaves, served in double cream; warm pates; pilafs of shrimps and chicken livers; immense grillades. You ate parts of animals you never thought of eating, such as cow's udders done in a red wine sauce, or — a special delicacy — the testicles of a ram, which in Romanian are called the pride of the ram, done in a sauce which has everything in it.

Long gone are the shops visited by Ethel Greening Pantazzi. A Canadian married to a Romanian naval officer, Ethel left a wonderful record of life in Bucharest before and during the First World War.[32] She wrote how the shops on the Boulevard Elizabeta and Calea Victoriei had exotic names like the Three Blue Stars, the Parrot and the more prosaic, Bon Gout. Her pastry shop was called The Lion and the Sugar Cone and her local restaurant the Golden Chop — the meat apparently had the same consistency as the metal.

So much of the architecture of Bucharest is late nineteenth century French, that rich, nouveau riche mixture of over-decorated neo-classical, that it is easy to conclude that the city is but a poor copy of Paris. However hard Romanians like Prince Ghika tried in introducing a belvedere into his French designed neo-classical 1897 home on the Calea Victoriei, the effect was stiflingly unoriginal and, after a while, emetic. For me, the real architectural treasures of Bucharest are 'modernist.'

---

[32] *Roumania in Light and Shadow,* 1921.

On the corner of Câmpineanu and Academiei streets are two fine 1930s buildings, the Union Hotel of 1934 and the Negoiu Business Centre, formerly the famous Stănescu Hotel. The difficulties of a corner site are magnificently solved by the Union with its seven stories cascading in terraces down from the roof and a corner façade topped by a square tapering tower. And there, on the fifth floor, is the ubiquitous Belvedere, disguised as the arcaded balcony of the presidential suite.

An American, John I.B. McCulloch admired "the twelve-story Telephone Building in the Calea Victoriei... in the best of modern taste." In his dramatically titled book of 1936, *Drums in the Balkan Night,* McCulloch had an odd slant on the city:

> A great deal has been made of the startling tendency of Rumanian men towards effeminate practices. No journalistic description of this country is complete without mention of foppish officers, corseted and rouged. Betty (Mrs. McCulloch) and I — very much on the alert for such evidence of masculine decadence — found comparatively few.

Parallel to the Calea Victoriei is General Gheorghe Magheru Boulevard, a broad and busy street started in 1894. In the 30s it was the architectural hub of the city with the Lido Hotel completed in June 1930 and the pioneering Mihăescu Garage shortly after. Now called the Ciclop, this seven storied building still has a helicoidal ramp allowing cars access to the upper floors and is a milestone in modernism, certainly the first inner city multi-story car park in this part of the world. The adjacent workshops for servicing Renaults and Nash's is now the site of the Ambassador Hotel.

Nearby, on the same boulevard, is Horia Creangă's ARO cinema block, today the Patria. This huge design incorporated apartments, offices, a cinema/ theatre, and bar as well as shops on the ground floor and in its day was well in advance of its Western counterparts. All of these buildings miraculously survived the earthquake of March 1977. Sadly, the thirteen-story Wilson building, the epitome of 1930s simplicity of style and the wonderful Dunărea, a seven story apartment block of Romanian Gothic design, both collapsed.

No visit to Bucharest is complete without viewing the Cotroceni Palace. Edmund Chishull[33] had gone to look at it when it was just a monastery:

---

[33] *Travels in Turkey and Back,* 1747.

> It is situated on the Dembowitza which washes it on two sides: whilst the other two are adorned with a grove of lovely, close and shady oaks. The neighbouring pastures offered an entertaining prospect whereas the parts nearer to the convent are disposed into orderly vineyards and gardens. The fabric itself is an oblong quadrangle, built of regular and massy stone, divided into cells for about forty monks, with lodgings for the abbot, a common refectory, kitchen and other public appartments.

Originally a seventeenth century monastery and home of the extraordinarily gifted and influential Cantacuzino family who ruled Wallachia from 1678 to 1688, Cotroceni was converted by Prince Cuza in the 1860s as a summer residence for himself, then given to Nando and Marie in 1893 as their home. The French architect, Paul Gottereau, was commissioned to restyle the palace for the young couple and produced a complete mishmash, ranging from a Napoleon III entrance hall (almost a copy of Charles Garnier's space at the Paris Opera), Neo-Baroque, German Renaissance, Henri II, Louis XV, and Louis XVI. The effect is suitably dazzling and royal. One can see the difficulty Gottereau had in reconciling the tastes of both a German prince and an English princess; after passing through two dark, masculine, heavy German rooms, one enters a shimmering white 'Flower Room' with rose-stuccoed walls and feminine Louis XVI chairs, their backs embroidered with flowers. In a corner by the window is a pretty white piano decorated with roses and cherubs. It had started life as a traditional black polished Steinway until, bored with it, Marie summoned her sister Ducky from Hesse and set about redecorating it.

Having discovered the art of Byzantium, Marie created what Carmen Sylva described as "something between an Indian temple and a fairy tale." Anne-Marie Callimachi found it a "cross between a Church and a Turkish bath" and went on:[34]

> Crossing its threshold, one hesitated between horror and laughter, and then I decided to concentrate on the hostess, beautiful in brocaded silks, or floating gauzes, wearing heavy barbaric jewelry designed to fit the setting, which suited her to perfection.

Hannah Pakula[35] writes:

[34] *Yesterday was Mine,* 1952.

[35] *Queen Marie of Romania,* 1984.

> Marie's salon rarely left visitors indifferent. Its colourful walls were nearly obscured by yards of cascading ribbons and hedge roses, carved from wood and gilded. In the middle of the room stood a bronze statue of a girl holding a brightly lit cross. The coverings on the furniture were embroidered with peacock feathers, worked by the Crown Princess herself. Bronze chandeliers hung from the vaulted ceiling, while huge jars of flowers and exotic plants were scattered around the green tile floor. Marie's beloved church bedroom was done in silver, its cathedral ceiling carved with branching trees. The woodwork, painted ivory, was executed by Missy and Ducky themselves. There were silver braziers on the floor filled with lilies; antique silver lamps hung over massive silver-leaf furniture. Marie's bed was a low couch on a platform, backed by a headboard in the shape of a Greek cross; it stood under an elaborate canopy and was covered with fabric shot on silver, purple, and gold. Across from the bed was a fireplace and over the mantle, a picture of white anemones painted by Ducky for her sister and lit by concealed lighting. Beneath the picture there was an inscription: "Once it was always springtime in my heart."

Never one to sit still and admire her handiwork, Marie 'Romanianised" the exterior of Cotroceni between 1913 and 1915 with a 'Brâncoveanu' wing designed by Grigor Cerchez and later, in 1925, he and Karl Liman, Marie's pet architect, redesigned the old dining room into today's white barrel vaulted chambers. In 1929, two years after the death of her husband, Marie redid her bedroom, choosing a Tudor arched oak-beamed ceiling with a floor of purple tiles with dark blue and green scroll motifs. The result is to transport one to a Scottish castle; after all, Marie had started life as the daughter of the Duke and Duchess of Edinburgh. Fortunately, Marie did not change the décor of the little Norwegian room which is set off from her bedroom, a memento of her visit to that country in 1911 when she fell in love with its simple, wooden interiors.

Visitors to Cotroceni were, as in all Marie's homes, spellbound by both her and the surroundings. Runciman took tea with the Queen, enjoying 'China tea and red caviar sandwiches:'[36]

> The palace was redolent with the scent of frangipani and stephanotis; and she herself was dressed in white. She was still beautiful. Her golden hair may have had some help to retain its colour but her complexion was still wonderfully fresh and her eyes

[36] *A Traveller's Alphabet,* 1991.

> deep blue. The [British] minister had told me that if she held out her hand to be kissed, I was not to do so. British gentlemen did not kiss hands, he said. But when she did I could not resist what seemed to be a fitting gesture.

This was nothing new. When William Macmichael was presented to the Wallachian prince in 1816, he noted[37] "to the usual salutations were added the extraordinary one of kissing the palm of the hand of the Hospodar."

This act was performed by both men and women.

Beverley Nichols[38] had the same enjoyable experience. One of the devices which Nichols self-deprecatingly makes use of in his book is a dialogue with an irate reader and when he finds himself bragging about his knowledge of Romania, he allows himself to be interrupted:

> Irate Reader: You know, really I'd rather hear about the palace and all that. I go into very few palaces these days.
>
> Author: What do you want to hear?
>
> Irate Reader: About passing sentries, and being wafted up enormous staircases. You left out all that.
>
> Author: Well, I did pass sentries, and I was wafted up an enormous staircase. And at the top of the staircase was a young ADC., in a comparatively sober uniform. The ADC showed me into a very lofty room, whose walls were covered with gold plaster work, in which the main design was composed of madonna lilies. The design was rather like the early work of William Morris, only better and simpler. There was an enormous table covered with white china animals, rabbits, dogs, and cats predominating There were masses of flowers, arranged with a pleasantly barbaric treatment of colour. It was a fabulous room and though I have made it sound rather awful, it had a real dramatic beauty... [Nichols is shown into another room]. But as the Irate Reader is still jogging at my elbow, asking for more details of this remarkable woman (and quite rightly), let me observe that she was wearing a dress of pale flame colour, and that apart from a superb pearl necklace, she wore no jewels. And that the room was small, delicately lit and of a most individual charm. I have never seen a room in the least like it, any-

---

[37] *Journey from Moscow to Constantinople,* 1819.

[38] *No Place like Home,* 1936.

where. I should say that the inspiration for it was Norwegian. It was very simple. Its main decoration was gained by a number of Byzantine ikons, which proved, on inspection, to be the best I have encountered, in or out of a museum. Let me add that we had tea and caviare sandwiches, and that during tea a very sentimental spaniel dribbled on my knees, arousing immediate problems of etiquette. What do you do when a Queen's spaniel dribbles on your knee? No... surely not that. Stroke it? But that will only intensify the dribble... in fact.[39]

Cotroceni is still unmistakably Queen Marie's home. One can sense everywhere her restless enthusiasm, her disregard for convention, and her love of innovation. There are four portraits of her at the palace which capture her at the key moments of her life. The first, by the Austrian artist, Tini Rupprecht, is of her aged seventeen, a blue-eyed golden-haired bride of astonishing beauty.[40] Seven years later, the same artist portrayed a confident young woman of 26, now a mother of three, wearing the robes of Moldavian national dress. For by now Marie had become a fully-fledged Romanian.

On the wall next to her bed, there is an enchanting pastel drawing of 1910 by Boleslaw von Szankowski of Marie and her youngest daughter, Mărioara, in which mother and daughter share the same electric blue eyes. Marie, her head slightly tilted back, looking every inch the success she had become, holds the artist in her magnetic gaze. The last portrait by Philip de Lazlo was painted in London in 1924 when Marie was at her zenith. I find this a sad picture for all the girlishness and impishness has left her face, eradicated by the weary years of war. She wears the mask of personal tragedy, not that of triumph at Versailles.

One cannot leave Cotroceni without experiencing the disbelief that a Communist government in 1984 ordered the demolition of the church of 1679 which had stood in the courtyard since the time of the first Cantacuzinos. Aghast at this order, the architect Nicolae Vlădescu defied Ceauşescu by carefully dismantling it, stone by stone, so that it could be rebuilt at some point in the future. Today, the reconstruction of the church is a prior-

---

[39] The china animals to which Nicols refers are Copenhagen china and the collection is currently on display at the Museum of National History.

[40] There is an even better pastel portrait of this time by Kaulback in the National History Museum.

ity of the current administration, provided that adequate funding can be arranged.

Of all the other buildings which have vanished through bombing, earthquakes, neglect or redevelopment, the one I would most liked to have seen is the Sturdza Palace, on the site of today's Victoria Square. Built in the second half of the nineteenth century for Prince George Sturdza, the palace

> was a lavishly decorated edifice... with towers at its corners, the strangest structure in Bucharest. Its facades were adorned with decorative elements of the most varied epochs and styles. The exterior decoration, with bossages, ironworks, arcades, plasterwork, and flower belts was completed by roofing made of latticed sheets with profiles and scales. The same diversity was obvious with the building materials and colours used. The palace was also known as the calf palace as the young owner used to carry a calf in his arms during childhood, for sport, and during his mature years, for fun.[41]

An old photograph shows a building that excelled its French cousins in sheer intricate vulgarity. The site is now occupied by a dreary government office, housing the prime minister, probably the most uninspired structure in Bucharest.

When it was time to leave the Casa Victor, all was handled with quiet efficiency and charm in contrast to Philip Thornton's hilarious departure[42] from his hotel in 1939:

> The manager, who had not shown any marked friendliness during my enforced stay, now became peculiarly affable and communicative.
>
> (The two of them discussed the activities of the local branch of the Anglo-Romanian Society.)
>
> "And what do you do at the club social gatherings?" I ventured.
>
> "We practice our English language, yes, and also we reads papers to each other man," he replied, with much satisfaction. "I myself have given several lectures — one you would have enjoyed — yes — very much you would have enjoyed." He paused and looked coy, giving me my obvious cue to inquire with a wealth of enthusiasm: "How nice, and what did you talk about?"

---

[41] Aristide Ştefănescu, *Bucharest: The Thirties,* 1995.

[42] *Ikons and Oxen.*

"My subject, Mr. Thornton, was the 'isory of loff — yes — very nice.'" He proceeded to give me a fantastic resume of his lecture. "I find that there are three sorts of loff — the sort that a mother gives 'er baby — the sort that young mens give to each other, and the sort that young mens buys from women — you know what I mean." He leered knowingly and fumbled with his watch chain. "Tomorrow I shall speak about the loff-life of your poet, William Shakespeare, a very good subject... yes?"

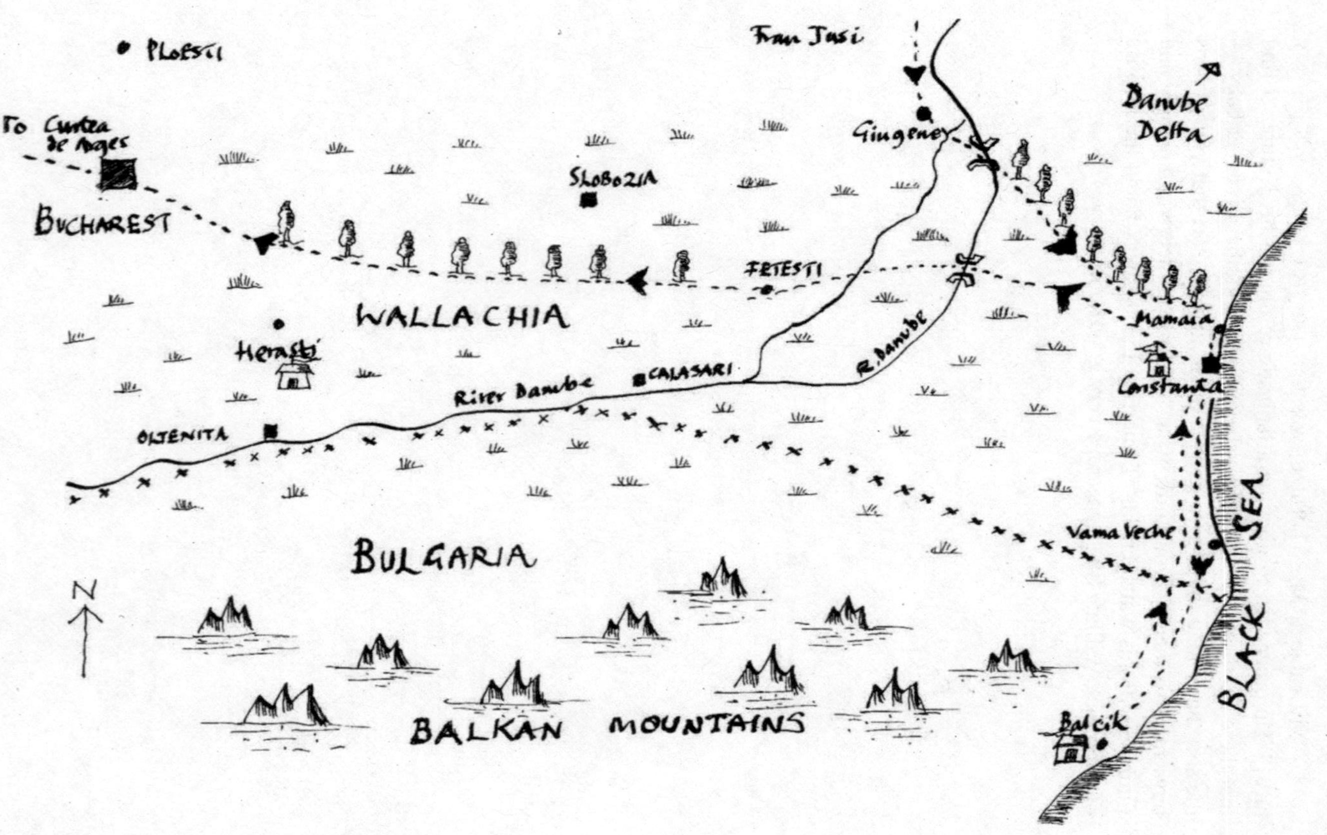
PLOESTI
From Jasi
To Curtea de Arges
BUCHAREST
SLOBOZIA
Gingeney
Danube Delta
FETESTI
WALLACHIA
Herasti
Mamaia
R. Danube
CALASARI
Constanta
River Danube
OLTENITA
Vama Veche
SEA
BULGARIA
N
BLACK
Balcik
BALKAN MOUNTAINS

Chapter Thirteen

Iaşi, Once a Capital, Always a Capital

Driving up to Iaşi from Bucharest, I sensed, in the sheer distance separating the two old capitals, that Iaşi was going to have an entirely different personality to its Wallachian counterpart.

The flat Wallachian plain gave way to a rolling prairie, once covered with forests, that marked the end of the steppes; here the hordes of the Dark Ages had freely roamed, finally peeling off to the north and south, blocked by the steep slopes of the Eastern Carpathians. The Jesuit, Father Avril, on his way to China in 1693 found

> ...one of the finest and pleasantest provinces in Europe. There are great plains watered by divers Moldavia rivers, the chief of which is the Moldavia, which has turnings and windings not unlike the Seine; and seems, through its whole extent, to carry plenty everywhere.[1]

At Târgu Frumos, I turned south and followed a winding avenue of poplars to Miclăuşeni to see the house of the Sturdza family, once rulers of Moldavia and later ministers of Romania. Now a school with a convent in the grounds, it was a monument to bad taste with its pinkish battlements and ivy covered entrance, an uninspiring replica of Regency Britain.

Like Rome, Iaşi is situated on seven hills but that is where the similarity stops. The capital of Moldavia for three centuries and briefly of

---

[1] *Travels in Divers Parts of Europe and Asia,* 1693.

Romania in 1916-1918, Iaşi is not immediately attractive to the eye as a city but it is full of interest. Hector Bolitho's description[2] of Bucharest in 1939 rather suits it: "Bucharest withholds its charm from the casual visitor. It has neither glamour nor great beauty...."

Lord Baltimore[3] reached Iaşi in 1764, after travelling through Bârlad and Gassovi, both "miserable places and the lands uncultivated:

> The streets of Jassi are boarded with deal boards like our floors; the houses are all on one story, low and miserable... they are built of earth except a few belonging to the Spodars; in one of these huts, having put up a small mattress bed to lie down on, just as I was closing my eyes to sleep, a large cow, which was on the outside of my hovel, eat off the straw covering of the roof, run her head through it and through the top of my bed; this, together with the innumerable swarms of vermin all over the place, obliged me to sit up all night.

He retired for the next two days to a monastery where the friars asked to his amazement whether England was in London or London in England.

Twenty years later, nothing much had changed when the Hungarian Baron de Tott[4] arrived here.

> We perceived, however, that we were entering the town, by means of a few scattered lights, and the noise of planks, on which I found the carriage rolling, made me inquire of the secretary the meaning of it. He informed me that these pieces of wood, laid near to each other across the streets, served to bear up the carriages, on account of the miry soil on which Jassi was built. He added that a fire had just reduced the greatest part of the town to ashes....

When Adam Neale[5] crossed into Moldavia from Czernowitz in 1818 and arrived in Iaşi, he stayed with Prince Alexander Moruzzi, nephew of the hospodar. The origin of this term for a ruler was, according to William Wilkinson,[6] due to the Russians who were the first to enter into official

---

[2] *Roumania under King Carol,* 1939.

[3] *Tour to the East,* 1767.

[4] *Memoirs* (1785). De Tott organised the defence of Constantinople against a Russian attack in 1770.

[5] *Travels,* 1818.

[6] *An Account of the Principalities of Wallachia and Moldavia,* 1820.

correspondence with the Greek princes and styled them *hospodars,* from Slavonic *gospodin* or lord.

These princes were the Phanariots who had been installed by the Ottomans at the beginning of the eighteenth century to administer the Principalities in the financial interests of the Porte.[7] They were far from popular but then that was not surprising given that their tenure was at the whim of the sultan and the idea was to make money — quickly. John Cam Hobhouse, the companion of Lord Byron, observed[8] in 1809 that "in no situation does a Greek appear in so unamiable a light as on the throne of Bucharest or Jassy." He told how

> the Princes of the Fanar [Greeks in Constantinople] are, when abroad, to be distinguished from the rest of their nation only by their beards and yellow slippers, and the privilege of riding on horseback.

One day, the Sultan, walking incognito in Constantinople, spotted a man with yellow slippers who, on questioning, turned out to be an imposter. The Sultan gave orders for him to be executed on the spot and then nonchalantly returned to his palace. Such was the insatiable ambition of many Greeks;[9] as one of them put it, "the prevailing God of all the inhabitants of Constantinople is financial self-interest and everything is secondary where this is concerned."[10]

With its population of 10,000 Albanians, Greeks, Russians, Jews, and native Moldavians, Neale found Iaşi in winter a primitive place

> where troops of hungry wolves would pour down during the long winter nights... and carry off domestic animals and sometimes even women and children.[11]

That same year, outside Bârlad, near Iaşi, William Macmichael found himself stranded one night:[12]

> The family of the post-master, consisting of himself, two sons, and a daughter, a very fine girl, who was suckling her child on the floor, consented to allow us to sleep in one corner of their hut; our

---

[7] Translation of Turkish title of central office of Ottoman government.

[8] *Journey through Albania, and other provinces of Turkey,* 1813.

[9] Not all the Phanariot Princes were Greeks: the Ghikas were Albanian, the Ypsilantis from Trebizon and the Callimachis Romanian.

[10] Philip Mansel, *Constantinople,* 1995.

[11] *Travels,* 1818.

[12] *Journey from Moscow to Constantinople,* 1819.

> rest was disturbed in the middle of the night by an alarm occasioned by a wolf... in the morning they lamented... the loss of one of their swine.

Edmund Spencer, on his way back from adventuring in the Caucasus in 1836, stopped at Iaşi and was not impressed:[13]

> The streets, like the roads, are unpaved, except one or two of the principal, and these are merely boarded, a channel for conveying away the filth of the street being formed underneath; but, owing to the slovenliness of the inhabitants, and the entire absence, we presume, of any sanitary police to enforce cleanliness, it is suffered to accumulate for months, thus poisoning the atmosphere and engendering a miasma sufficient to create a pestilence.

In pure Sitwelleese, Spencer concluded that "Jassy offers but little to interest the traveller, with the exception of a glance at its motley inhabitants."

Mrs. Edward, full of missionary zeal, opined in 1847 that

> ...but the people how degraded! The pastor's wife told me that she does not know of one house in Jassy where no scandal has occurred, of course here the word scandal is scarcely known.[14]

She had staying power; having arrived to convert the Jews to Christianity, the mission moved on after seven and a half years with a total bag of 29 converts of "the seed of Israel." Despite the uphill struggle, Mrs. Edward had that essential English sense of humour in her ability to laugh at herself and her colleagues. Writing to her brother, she asks:

> What shall I tell you? That both the missionaries had a good fall in the muddy streets the other day, to the no small amusement of the spectators? Or shall I describe to you the worthy Mr. Wingate marching through the mud, his trowsers tucked up about this Wellington Boots, and clogs over his boots, a huge Hungarian fur cloak on, a Boonda and comforter around his neck, and thus rolled up, coming home with whiskers and even eye-lashes frozen?

My lodgings were at the Hotel Trajan, a solid nineteenth century building in the Piaţa Unirii that had started life off as a concert hall. Designed by Gustav Eiffel, better known for his tower in Paris, there was a hint about its former use as I stood in reception, a curiously cramped area

---

[13] *Travels in the Western Caucasus,* 1838.

[14] *Missionary Life amongst the Jews of Moldavia,* 1867.

for such a large building. Of course, it was once the ticker office, the tall columns with friezes of gold fleur de lys now the last remnants of its theatrical origins.

Behind the hotel is the old town house of Alexander Cuza, the father of modern Romania. This remarkable man engineered the unification of Wallachia and Moldavia in 1859, introduced compulsory schooling for both sexes, and secularised monastic property which then accounted for over 20% of all land. These measures gave him huge popularity across the board but when he emancipated the serfs, he went one step too far with his boyar peer group and they demanded his resignation in 1866. On the night of 23 February a loud knock on the door interrupted Cuza as he made love to Marie Obrenovitch, the King of Serbia's daughter-in-law. Grabbing a robe, he opened the door and was confronted by a squad of soldiers demanding his abdication. Their colonel thrust the letter of resignation at him to which Cuza protested: "Gentlemen, you can see I have no pen to sign." A pen was produced and Cuza again protested: "Gentlemen, I have no desk on which to sign." The colonel went on his hands and knees and proffered his back. Cuza signed.

After the fall of Bucharest in 1916, Cuza's house became the home of Nando and Marie and it was from here that she threw her heart into leading the Romanian people at the nadir of their fortunes in the First World War. Dressed in a starched linen nurses uniform with no regal insignia, a white kerchief around her head, Marie was to witness the terrible plight of the wounded of both sides. So appalling were the conditions in wartime Iaşi, that Captain George Hill remembered:[15]

> One morning I witnessed a driver trying to get one of two buffaloes yoked to a cart to rise from the ground where it had settled from exhaustion. He pulled and tugged, whipped and kicked at the beast who simply refused to stir. Finally he picked up in the road a small handful of wood shavings and after forcing them under the poor beast's tail, set them on fire: in agony, the beast rose.

Occasionally Marie was able to escape to her little house at Coţolăneşti — "it was ecstasy" — and to the Monastery at Moşinoaia, "a profoundly poetical sanctuary hidden away amongst the secular beech trees in the very heart of the forest."[16]

---

[15] *Go Spy the Land,* 1932.
[16] *Story of My Life,* 1934.

The centre of Iaşi is built around a single boulevard called Stephen the Great, and halfway down on the west side, stands the great Metropolitan cathedral, a late nineteenth century[17] church inspired by the Italian Renaissance. Supposedly a copy of the Trinita del Monte in Rome, the neo-classical exterior has a look of London stone about it, almost an influence of Wren. The original design incorporated a dome but the roof collapsed during construction and it was never realised, thus leaving the large rectangular vault, with its four hexagonal capped towers, heavy and lumpy.

Inside, the decoration is of late Victorian style with ornamentation used extensively on columns and cross beams. Little St. Paraschiva lies in her coffin to the right of the iconastasis. This patron saint of Moldavia, households, harvests, traders, and travellers cost Vasile Lupu one and a half times the annual budget of Moldavia when he bought her in 1641.

Mrs. Loughborough[18] in 1939 thought the cathedral was frankly most disappointing, but

> one object in the great church, however, seemed very alive, and strangely enough this life-force came from a corpse. A very small open coffin, containing a figure draped in purple satin pall, and head and face covered with a velvet cloth, had a stand for tiny tapers placed at the head, and here many people came to pray and light a taper.... It seemed so utterly strange that there, unprotected, unadorned, should lie this little body revered as a saint over 1500 years old, with only a little fresco on the pillar above the coffin, of a girl, like hundreds of other frescoes, with white-girded robe and brown eyes, looking placidly down on us and on those who had loved and prayed for her help through all these ages.

Next to the Cathedral is the Church of the Three Hierarchs, namely St. Gregory, St. Basil, and St. John Chrysostom. The glory of this church is its intricately carved stone exterior with no fewer than sixteen horizontal bands of different motives, including rosettes, meanders, chevrons, crowns, and snakes' heads. Originally the entire church was gilded and the effect must have been literally to dazzle the onlooker. Locals will tell you

---

[17] In the late 1950s, the architect Georges Cantacuzino was commissioned by the Bishop to enhance the prospect from the west (main) door, which he achieved through a combination of terracing and framing the view of the far-off monastery with two pavilions. Cantacuzino died in Iaşi in 1960 before his vision was completed, his physique broken by years of unjust imprisonment by the Communist authorities.

[18] *Roumanian Pilgrimage,* 1939.

that the Ottomans stripped all the gilt off but surely any passer-by would have been tempted to take just a tiny piece.

Robert Bargrave[19] was a visitor here in 1650:

> Yash is the Residency seat of Lupulo the new Moldavian Prince or Voivoda, where first we went to see his Particular Chappell, the outside whereof is all of carved stone and the inside adorned from the bottom to the tops with Gold, with Pictures of saints and Apostles.

William Macmichael, arriving in Iaşi, was much impressed by the church:[20]

> The whole of its exterior is covered with stucco, moulded into the most curious and intricate forms, not unlike the irregular patterns sometimes seen on paper or carpets.

He was lucky enough to be invited to the 'nomination ceremony' when the hospodar appointed boyars to the various court posts — in exchange for large sums of money! On his way to the court, he noticed:

> On walking out, the first, and the most striking object that meets the eve of the stranger, is the enormous balloon-shaped Moldavian cap, or calpak, of an appearance so unwieldy, as to seem ready to annihilate the person who has the courage to move under such an oppressive burden.

Inside the have of the Three Hierarchs, on the entrance wall, is a fresco of the donors, Vasile Lupu, his wife, and his daughter Ruxandra. She is depicted in the heavy gold robes of 1639, with a sash of pearls around her waist plus a further six strings around her neck and threc giant sapphire pendants in each earlobe. There is a newness about the interior which can be put down to its restoration by Lecomte de Nouy in 1887. Sitwell raged about this, finding the churches of the Three Hierarchs and that of St. Nicholas "entirely ruined by Lecomte de Nouy, that pupil of Viollet le Duc[21] who was responsible for what can only be termed the massacre in Church at Curtea de Argeş."[22]

---

[19] *Narration of a Journey from Constantinople to Dunkirke,* 1652.

[20] *Journey from Moscow to Constantinople,* 1819.

[21] Best known for the 'restoration' of Carcassonne and the cathedrals of Notre Dame, Lyon and Chartres.

[22] *Roumanian Journey,* 1938.

Situated at the end of" Stephen the Great Boulevard, the Courtly Church of St. Nicholas, the oldest building in Iaşi, dating from 1491, has been entirely rebuilt, using new materials in its entirety. The result is an irrevocable tragedy and Sitwell was right to be angry.[23]

This soured his opinion of contemporary Iaşi:

> We may prefer to think of Jassy in connection with the fur-lined robes and fantastic prodigality of the Boyars. For its modern shops and cinemas are a decline of inheritance from that.

Not everyone was an admirer of ecclesiastical architecture. Thomas Thornton[24] felt strongly that:

> In each (Bucharest and Yassy) the churches and convents are the most conspicuous feature... the walls of the religious houses are covered with grotesque representations of the saints and the history of their miracles. The churches are heavy and inelegant buildings, bedecked, in their inside, with pictures, which, though perhaps they may inspire devotion, certainly tend to vitiate the taste or judgement.

And Robert Bargrave cast a critical eye on secular architecture:

> By favour we had sight of his Palace, a stone building, rather great than goodly, having neither majesty, uniformitte, nor Apt Adornments for a Princes Palace. Only his stables are indeed very observeable for theyr Satelyness and Convenience, but chiefly for the nomber and Qualitie of his horses very much surpassing those of the Duke of Florence or the King of England.

Vasile Lupu certainly needed his horses for he was in dire trouble with both the Cossacks and the Tartars who had joined forces and burnt Iaşi to the ground in 1650. He finessed his way out of it by marrying his daughter to a Cossack general, the same September as Bargrave's visit.

Across the southern aspect of St. Ştefan's looms the Palace of Culture, a vast neo-Gothic design built between 1905 and 1926. Dominated by a central clock tower worthy of mad King Ludwig of Bavaria, the palace boasts 365 rooms, most of them titillated with stained glass and armorial reliefs. On the first floor is the Museum of Modern Art, conveniently divided into general or foreign, Romanian and modern. Sadly, many of the pictures in the general section are badly lit, including a Carravaggio, "Cae-

---

[23] I doubt he realised that King Carol I had personally funded these and other restorations by Lecomte de Nouy.

[24] *Present State of the Turk,* 1809.

sar Regarding the Head of Pompey." There is a charming landscape of Iaşi in 1842 by Ludovic Stavski in which, in the foreground, the artist has included every type of inhabitant, Gypsies, peasants, gentlefolk, musicians and soldiers. There is a pair of lovers sitting holding hands on a primitive wooden fairground wheel, a 'scrânciob'; how clean and cosy an artist's brush has made the city look.

The best pictures are to be found in the Romanian section, where for some reason, the lighting is much better though many of the canvasses are hung far too low. A good collection of Grigorescus is crowned by a major canvas "The Ox Cart," at five foot by eight foot uncharacteristically large for this artist. I could really feel the heat and dust of summer as the carts trundled slowly towards me. Another striking Grigorescu is "the Fortune Teller," a good-sized portrait of a sensual Gypsy girl, her head tilted back in knowing mockery, arms folded over half-exposed large, firm breasts.

Styling himself Commander of the Imperial Order of the Medjidieh and of the Royal Order of the Redeemer, Knight of the Imperial Order of Franz Josef and of the IR Austrian Order of Merit of the First Class with Crown, holder of the Star of Roumania, Crown of Roumania, and Takova of Servia, W. Beatty-Kingston was in Iaşi in 1888 and observed[25] a Jewish likeness to this Gypsy girl on Grigorescu's canvas:

> As we were slowly driving down the Calea Cacu, there came out of a house towards us a great handsome girl of about 18, 5'8" in height, and as broad shouldered as a sergeant in the Guards, with nothing on but one garment hanging completely off her shoulder and half way down to her arm. As she was passing us she bestowed on us a fierce stare. Her coarse black hair floated over her bare brown shoulders, and sturdy legs, of which any Highlander might have been proud. No Congo negress could have displayed a more absolute, barbarous indifference to her semi-nudity that did this comely daughter of Zion, who scowled at us because we were Christians and foreigners, but manifestly did not vouchsafe a thought to the bareness of her superb bosom, or to the fact that, in the bright sunlight, every detail of her statuesque form could be plainly discerned through the slight texture of her loose shift.

The mid-Victorian traveller, like Charles Boner,[26] was taken aback by the bra-less society:

---

[25] *A Wanderer's Notes,* 1888.

[26] *Transylvania: its Products and its People,* 1865.

> What busts you see here, where stays are unknown, and there is nothing to cramp the full development of the figure! The linen covering does not conceal the beautiful outline of the bosom, but rather serves to define it; marking now an oval bud and now a full-rounded form. And the drapery falls over this loveliest feminine feature in a sharp angular line, as though beneath were firmest marble; and marble it is, but glowing with passionate life.

Two smaller Grigorescu paintings I particularly liked were an oil sketch 'Ciobanaşul' or the 'Little Shepherd Boy,' and 'Ţărancă torcând pe plai,' a 'Little Peasant Girl Winding Wool on the Hill.' These are to my mind the artist at his best, capturing the attitudes and moods of country folk with a wonderful combination of light, colour, and line.

Of the other Romanian artists, noteworthy pictures included an interior by Jean Steriadi, some of the Băncilă portraits and Iser's 'Ballerina,' who lies slumped on a green chaise long exhausted from the dance, her red tights and white toutou making for a riotous mass of colour.

I bought tickets for that evening's performance of 'Tosca' at the National Theatre. Built by the Viennese architects Helmer and Fellner[27] between 1894 and 1896, the theatre is pure fin de siècle Roccoco. One enters a hall of pale green walls, its columns and recesses picked out in gold and their tops embroidered with reliefs of lyres and flutes, acathantus leaves everywhere. Once up the dark pink marble staircase and into the auditorium, I was overwhelmed by the lush décor of dark red velvet seats in balconies sumptuously supported by rows of wicked satyr faces in rotund gold frames. The centre ormulu rosette suspends a great chandelier of eight cherubs, arms held aloft supporting three giant lamps. Swooping birds of prey mixed in with either naked or scantily clad maidens in the pose of freefall parachutists descend on one from the ceiling.

Billed as a *spectacol extraordinar,* I was on the alert for a sparkling performance. The Iaşi Opera Orchestra solidly supported a rather wooden cast, saved by George Solovăstru's brilliant Sacristan who cringed, shuffled, and collided with every prop and person on stage. Tosca herself was a blonde which somewhat threw the libretto about her "beautiful black hair." At the end of Act 2, an already dead Scarpia was nearly guillotined in real life by the curtain descending on his neck.

---

[27] They also designed the Franz Josef Theatre in Timişoara.

Chapter Fourteen

A River, a Delta, and a Black Sea

I left Iaşi early on a misty November morning, following a steep winding road through beech forests which were eerily lit by the fading full moon before it disappeared at sunrise. In the darkness, horses and carts trotted by, some already piled high with maize stalks, indicating that work had started in the fields well before 4 a.m. Passing the Princely Court of Iordache Ruset at Pribeşti, one of the few examples of the Brâncoveanu 'open' plan architecture this far north, I drove through a series of gentle valleys whose watercourses eventually flowed into the Bârlad River, south of Vaslui.

James Skene had journeyed to Vaslui in 1853, where he passed a grand country house at Milesci.[1] It had once belonged to Nicholas Kârnul Milescu, who, in 1660, had been a great favourite of Prince Ştefăniţă with whom he played cards. Milescu foolishly entered into correspondence with Constantin Basarab (ex-ruler of Wallachia from 1654-1658) who was living in retirement in Poland. The contents of this correspondence so horrified Constantin for it was mooted that he should raise a force and usurp Ştefăniţă, that he blew the whistle and Milescu ended up with his nose cut off in public, hence *Kârnul* "the noseless."

Not a man to let the loss of a nose get him down, Milescu had a false nose made in Germany, but yet again, he was caught in secret communica-

[1] *The Frontier Lands of the Christian and the Turk,* 1853.

tion, this time with the Swedes who were at war with Brandenberg's ally, Poland. So off he fled to Stockholm and from there to Moscow where Czar Alexis made him an instructor to young Peter. Sent then as Russian ambassador to China, he reputedly received from his hosts a diamond as big as a pigeon's egg. On his return to Russia in 1682 he was promptly seized by the Strelitzes and sent to Siberia. When Peter came to the throne after his long minority he recalled his old tutor, the Noseless, and Milescu spent the rest of his life in 'quiet opulence.' What an astonishing story of survival in high places.

At Tecuci, one hundred miles south of Iaşi, the valley broadened and nearing Galaţi, a fen land of dykes, ditches, and drains replaced the hills which had been mysteriously flattened, leaving no edge to this new world. It was here that I became aware of the presence of the great Danube River, although out of sight as it changed course northwards to the delta. Something broody was out there, its influence all pervading. In ancient times, commodities came up the river from the cast: fine cotton from India according to Herodotus; pearls, diamonds, emeralds, indigo, dragon's blood (red resin) according to Pliny: cinnamon, nutmeg, gingers, and perfumes to impregnate the air in vapour baths.

Galaţi is Romania's main Danube port and has always attracted mixed reviews. Adam Neale had found[2] "Life at Jasi... comfortable" with "Grecian handmaidens entered after every meal to pour rose water on the hands of the company ...novel and amusing" but as his journey progressed through Vaslui and Bârlad to Galaţi where they stayed with the governor, "a ghastly old Turk with a long grey beard, shabbily equipped in a ragged silk pelisse," so did its hardships. He stayed overnight in a monastery where "the window frames, instead of being glazed, were covered with the membranoses or air bladders of the sturgeon taken from the Danube." Actually, this was little different from the inland villages where "in the houses are galleries with close lattices or windows, made with dried hog's-bladders; for glass is very uncommon."[3] He bought five large sturgeons for three shillings from the villagers "an industrious but barbarous and filthy race," descendants of the Bastarnae Peucinae, a horde of Teutonic origin who settled on the Ister and occupied the Danube Delta or peuce.

---

[2] *Travels,* 1818.

[3] Anonymous account in Richard Phillips. *A Collection of modern and Contemporary Voyages and Travels,* 1805.

When he reached Isaaci, with its ruined castle and tower, Neale recognised that he was standing on a major crossroads of history. It was here in 513 B.C. that Darius threw a bridge across the river and passed over into the Scythian deserts at the head of an army of 700, 000 Persians; it was here that the lurks under Osman crossed the Danube to invade Poland; and here, in 1711, that Baltaji-Mehemet rode through with his army of 150,000 to attack Peter the Great of Russia. Hence a simple explanation for its name: *Is,* 'labour' or 'workmanship,' coupled with *axi,* 'power,' or an 'army.'

Neale was a most erudite traveller and developed his own esoteric lines of thought. One fascinating story he told was of a Greek coin he found near Galaţi: on one side of it there was a water bird devouring a tunny fish, on the other, two heads turned in opposite direction, most likely the heads of the Dioscuri, Castor and Pollux, whose constellations were favourable to mariners. Their worship was widely diffused all over Europe wherever the Phoenicians and Milesains had extended their commerce to. He compared this combination of symbols to the Port of St. Andero in Northern Spain, where the local pagan deities were admitted to the Christian Church after receiving new names and being cannonised. Thus Castor and Pollux, the dioscuri of St. Andero, became Honorius and Arcadius who miraculously floated into harbour one afternoon in a stone boat. Their bleeding heads were removed and kept in the cathedral.

Skene called on the governor in 1853[4] and "duly received his formal visit in return: a stupid man, with a clever wife to do his work for him."[5] True to form, Beatty-Kingston found Galaţi in 1874 with "a highly respectable English colony constituting the elite of its society."[6] For little Yvonne Fitzroy,[7] a Scottish nurse in Romania in the First World War:

> Galaţi is big and middling dull... but boasts a very fine cake shop, where we lived most of the day — when we weren't washing — enjoying a very unwarlike diet.

But she said it all about Galaţi in her last entry in her diary: "nothing will make me believe that Aberdeen is not the eighth wonder of the world and the most beautiful city on earth!" Robert Bargrave had the same gas-

[4] Twenty years before the British were nowhere to be seen in Galaţi; of 135 vessels which arrived in 1832, not one was British.

[5] *Frontier Lands of the Christian and the Turk,* 1853.

[6] *A Wanderer's Notes,* 1888.

[7] *Scottish Nurses in Roumania,* 1918.

tronomic experience as Yvonne: “very good beere and excellent Mede.... abounds in Honey, and has the best ordinary bread I remember to have tasted.”[8]

The Vicar of Godalming in Surrey, the Rev. Charles Elliot, late of the Bengal Civil Service, had a problem with his throaţ and found himself “unable to preach.” So he decided to go travelling and arrived in Galaţi in 1839. Elliot,[9] who up until then had spent most of his time on a steamer on the Danube, opined that “the people are divided into two classes; rich and poor; the rich are given up to display indolence and political chicanery; the poor are in a state of abject misery and degradation.” That was the bad news; the good news was that “articles of food are remarkably cheap: a goose in good condition costs 7p, a fat sheep three shillings, and an egg a farthing.”

Another good Christian, Mrs. Edward, found “Galatz... a semi-barborous town” in 1847.

Sitwell found it “dark and endless” and “a portion of Roumania that bears no resemblance to any part of the Western world.” Nonetheless, he was fascinated by Pedracchi, the giant Skoptzi cab driver who came to meet him. This sect, on the run from Russia, castrated themselves after siring a child and believed that Christ had never died. With his love of Gypsy music, Sitwell also noted that “it is said from Galaţi... come many of the Gypsy musicians who lead the restaurant orchestras in all parts of the world.”[10] How lucky all these visitors were to arrive in Galaţi before Ceauşescu earmarked it as a major centre for the production of steel.

Brăila, a sprawling modern town a few miles to the south of Galaţi, was of little interest save it lies on the road to Tulcea, the ancient trading town on the south bank of the Danube as the river heads east into the Black Sea. Early travellers commented on the danger of stray dogs there and the necessity of taking a *Kavasse* or bodyguard with them at night, holding a lantern in one hand and a thick stick in the other.

The Danube River follows three passages: to the north, it meanders along the border of the Republic of Moldova, passing through the towns of Chilia and Valcov, whose “canals could not be more romantic or peculiar” for Sitwell: in the centre, a canal has been engineered which leads to Sulina, where Beatty-Kingston sailed to on the gunboat ‘Cockatrice’ with

[8] *Narration of a Journey from Constantinople to Dunkirke,* 1652.
[9] *Travels in the Three Great Empires,* 1838.
[10] *Roumanian Journey,* 1938.

"mosquitoes as large as quails and as bloodthirsty as tigers," only to find that "Sulina impressed me as being at the end of the world;" and to the south, the channel twists and turns until reaching Sfântu Gheorghe on the shores of the Black Sea.

Sulina is, indeed, a desolate spot. Thomas Forester[11] in 1857 observed the island of Leuce, 24 miles northeast of Sulina. Called the White Island[12] because of its white pelicans, it was the site of the Temple of Achilles, the island having been given to him by Thetis. Forester reported that

> these birds alone have care of the shrine. Every morning they repair to the sea, and, dipping their wings in the waves, sprinkle the temple, and afterwards sweep with their plumage its sacred pavement.

My route to Constanţa took me along a low escarpment set on a desolate, featureless plain. In this lonely landscape, the villages were compact, huddled like cold children with arms folded and knees tucked up into their chins, with little stalls along their skinny streets offering plump green and white cabbages, red peppers and crispy cauliflowers to passersby. Thomas Thornton had also noticed these cabbages:[13]

> In virgin land, of which from the neglect of culture there is much in both provinces, they plant cabbages the first year, which grow to a prodigious size, or cucumbers which succeed equally well.

Then, quite suddenly, the roadside was full of young men dangling fishes of all shapes and sizes before me: the moment had come to cross the Danube at Giurgeni. Its girth massive by now — Bargrave found it "about the breadth of the Thames above the bridge" — the Danube moved like an obese old man, its waters stained brown with mud. Gone were the youthful torrents of the Alps, the rippling currents of Linz and Vienna; from here, it oozed like thick, viscous oil into the Black Sea.

There was plenty of water unlike in 1834 when Michael Quin recorded[14] that his steamer, "for want of water in the Danube," kept running aground. This necessitated having to unload all the passengers, luggage, and cargo laboriously onto small boats and then wait for the ship to refloat itself.

---

[11] *The Danube and the Black Sea,* 1857.

[12] The modern name is Fido-nisi or Serpent Island.

[13] *The Present State of Turkey,* 1809.

[14] *A Steam Voyage Down the Danube*, 1835.

A seventy mile long, straight road, flanked with poplars, limes, and almond trees, brought me to Constanţa, the old Roman town of Tomis, most famous as Ovid's place of exile and death. There is no record of why he was banished here in 8 AD but most likely it was for writing the *Art of Love.* Thomas Churchyarde in his translation of Ovid supported this view:[15]

> Of Ovidius Naso his banishment, divers occasions be supported but the common opinion and the most likely is that Augustus Caesar, reading his bookes of the art of love, misliked them so much that he condemned Ovid to exile.

There was also talk of 'an error,' probably in connection with the Emperor's profligrate daughter, Julia. Poor Ovid, how he hated it here, just as Seneca loathed Corsica and, nearly 2,000 years later, how Turgenev exiled by the Czar for inappropriate writing, despised Paris. Ovid was fifty-one and at the height of his popularity, one minute right in the midst of glittering Roman society and then, like a thunderbolt, whilst on holiday in Elba, the Emperor's edict was promulgated and it was all over. He arrived at Constanţa after a terrible voyage where he continued to write but in a melancholic vein, finishing four books of *Epistulae Ex Ponto* and *Tristia,* his poems of sadness which painted the worst possible picture of his surroundings.

> The town is protected in summer by the Danube stream; but when winter comes all is frost and deep snow, which the sun has scarcely power to thaw. Nay, sometimes it lies throughout the whole year, and one year's new is piled upon the snow of another. So violent is the north-wind that it often levels towers and carries roofs away... the shaggy hair of the inhabitants rattles as they move with hanging icicles: the beard is white and glistening. The very wine freezes, and the Danube itself becomes a firm mass of ice, The barbarian enemy avails himself of the opportunity to cross the river, and with his mounted archers overruns the whole countryside. Cattle and waggons and all the farmer's poor possessions fall a prey to him: many are led into captivity; many die in torments, wounded by the poisoned arrows. What they cannot carry away they burn. Even in time of peace the constant fear of war blanches every cheek. All industry is at a standstill. Here there is no corn crop, no vineyard, no orchard, nothing but the desolate expanse of bare and treeless fields.

---

[15] *The First Bookes of Ovid's De Tristibus,* 1572.

Not surprisingly, Ovid was accused by some commentators of "an excess of dolorous lamentation which betrays a want of manly endurance."[17] He died at age 61, bitter and saddened by the cruel fate he felt himself victim of Thomas Forrester[18] summed up Ovid's predicament:

> As to these Roman exiles, the fact is, that to them existence was insufferable out of brilliant Rome and the sunshine of the imperial smiles; the re-admission to which they implored by the most abject flattery.

I had come to Constanţa to visit Carmen Sylva's house about which Queen Marie rather disparagingly wrote: "Aunty had a queer little house built on a pier overlooking Constantsa." Carmen herself referred to it as "a beautiful kiosk." Situated at Eforie-Sud, just to the south of Constanţa, it is now a hospital and not open for visitors. I had to be content with Saligny's Casino of 1904, still standing on the edge of the harbour, and now used as a disco, casino, and restaurant. The enormous art nouveau fan window over the entrance and its elegant white classical façade on the seaward side are magnificent and utterly outdo the competition in Biarritz for sheer elegant grandeur.

Carmen loved it here and

> like a ghost, all clad in white, she haunted the terraces of her wave-bound abode, a figure become dear to those who watched beneath the stars: and she used a megaphone, through which she would call messages to the departing ships, blessing their way in those many words which came so easily to her tongue.[19]

The house looks out onto one of the largest shipbuilding yards of the Black Sea, yet somehow it survives this terrible prospect and retains much of the old magic it once undoubtedly had.

It was here on 13 June 1914 that the Russian royal family arrived on their yacht to visit Nando and Marie. The hidden agenda was to introduce Grand Duchess Olga, the Tsar's eldest daughter, to Prince Carol. Hannah Pakula[20] takes up the story:

---

[16] Ovid, *Tristia iii,* translated by Sydney Owen.

[17] Lord Macaulay.

[18] Who was commissioned by the important sounding "Danube and Black Sea Railway and Kustendjie Harbour Company Ltd," to write a book about the region.

[19] Elizabeth Burgoyne, *Carmen Sylva,* 1941.

[20] *Queen of Romania,* 1985.

It was a standard Royal visit. After the usual Te Deum and a public drive through Constanţa, there was a military review led by the King past the Tsar. "Family lunch" was followed by a rest period based on the ill health of the seventy-five year old King of Roumania and the forty-two year old Tsarina. Tea was served on the Imperial yacht, and at the end of the day there was a gala banquet in a hall built specially for the occasion. Nicholas was placed between Queen Elizabeth and Crown Princess Marie in the centre of a long narrow table of eighty-four guests. The Queen of Roumania had forgotten to put on her orders. The Tsarina removed hers. Marie did not. Grand Duchess Olga was seated next to Prince Carol; his attentions towards her were half-hearted, and her replies to his questions unenthusiastic.

The next day Olga and her family returned to Russia. Two weeks later the heir to the Austro-Hungarian Empire was assassinated at Sarajevo, and within four years Olga would meet a dreadful end in Ekaterinberg.

There is another version about the visit which suggests that Queen Elizabeth, looking like a 'priestess of Ancient Egypt' with her white hair and flowing white robes, had been deliberately kept out of events until:[21]

> she came into her own with a gala dinner at her pavilion, fireworks, dramatic readings and allegorical tableaux thrown in. When the final tableau — little girls with angel wings — proved too much for the set and the children collapsed in a tangle of scenery and broken limbs, the audience agreed that it could not be helped.

As well as being Romania's major Black Sea port, Constanţa is a large beach resort with a clutch of 'satellite' villages named after planets — Neptune, Jupiter, Venus, Saturn — to its south. My destination was Mamaia, just north of the town, where I hoped to find the famous pre-war Rex Hotel. Incredibly, there, in the midst of a forest of architectural eyesores of the 1960s and 1970s, stood this jewel of the thirties. Originally, when it was completed in August 1936, the hotel had the beach to itself and the architect, Prince Georges M. Cantacuzino, used this freedom to position his building between the sky and the sea, using the empty space on either side as balance.[22]

---

[21] Leslie Gardiner: *Curtain Calls,* 1976.

[22] In the Romania National Tourist Office magazine of September 1937 there is a photograph of the hotel which illustrates this point and shows how perfectly Cantacuzino judged the height of the hotel.

For lovers of pre-war luxury, the Rex is a must, from the blue and white mosaics of swimmers on the walls either side of the reception desk to the wide corridors and spacious rooms. This is an architectural triumph of balance, functionality, and sheer good looks, especially the pool area overlooking the Black Sea. Whilst I was enthusing with the hotel staff about this miracle of conservation, there was talk about redecoration but I was assured it was only the lower floor at sea-level.

In the dining room, the thirties furniture has gone, replaced by tasteless white bedroom chairs with embroidered scenes of eighteenth century lovers. But the ten giant marble square columns remain, giving a feel of tremendous strength and space. The service was delightfully attentive and old-fashioned in its discreteness. After dinner, as I walked along the beach, thin slivers of silver ribbon caught the moonlight on the breaking waves, born and buried in a muffled instance.

From Constanţa, I headed south into southern Dobrogea, part of Bulgaria since 1940, to the town of Balcic, the site of Queen Marie's last architectural fling. The border crossing proved difficult for fate had placed me behind ten buses full of Turks to whom the Romanian authorities wished to talk — individually. So I back-tracked to the small, deserted beach at Vama Veche, where the only noise was that of the waves, aimlessly breaking over a rusting hulk, and the only life a pair of friendly, stray dogs, surprised and delighted at my unexpected company There was the same sense of mystery here, as I stared out to sea, as at Cape Byron in Australia or Cabo Finnistra in Spain. It was the knowing, the sensing that what lay beyond the horizon was so utterly different. Here Europe ended; here, on this sandy beach, was the fine line which separated Christianity from the Eastern religions. When I returned to the border the queue had fortuitously evaporated and I reached Balcic that evening.

Hannah Pakula[23] explains how in 1925, on her return from England, Marie started on the last of her retreats here. Introduced to Balcic by a group of painters who had founded an artists' colony there, she bought an old mill house and called it Tenya-Yuvah, Turkish for 'solitary nest.' She designed it entirely à la turque with heavy white walls and relatively few rooms. Upstairs she built an octagonal bedroom with two wide windows overlooking the sea. The bed, a couch covered with cushions and coverlets, was placed in a raised recess opposite the windows. Low carved and

[23] *Queen of Romania,* 1985.

painted doorways opened into a dressing room, a miniature Turkish steam bath, and a porch, for she often slept outside.

As always, the garden was all important to Marie. Her flowerbeds were terraces cut out of the hillside and ornamented with huge Greek amphorae, old stone benches, and decapitated columns culled from her travels. Here she could indulge her passion for lilies and roses, delphiniums and hollyhocks.

Mrs. Martineau, who had helped Marie redesign the gardens at Cotroceni, came to stay at Balcic in 1927:[24]

> Always fond of the sea, the Queen of Roumania has recently acquired a small property at Balcic, on the Black Sea, originally an old Turkish fort, and she has converted it with inimitable skill into a delightful dwelling overhanging the sea — turquoise as the Mediterranean. Four old Turkish mills have been bought there, and set up as dependences for the servants. The garden has been literally carved out of the rock in terraces, a separate garden to every terrace, and each is named after one of her children — Mircea, Ileana, Nicky, Mignon, Elisabeta, and Carol.
>
> Every bit of work was done under the Queen's own direction, and it is entirely her own creation. The rocks will soon be covered with roses and climbers, and in every little crack possible the miniature iris, found at Balcic, is planted.

Balcic appealed to the romantic in Marie. Here she was neither English nor Roumanian but just herself. It is more Turkish than European and Marie would have shared Lady Mary Wortley Montagu's enthusiasm when she discovered the key to a Turkish love letter in 1714.[25]

Gift	**Meaning**
Pearl	Fairest of the young
Clove	You are as slender as this clove
Rose	You are an unblown rose; I have long loved you
Jonquil	Have pity on my passion
Paper	I faint every hour
Pear	Give me some hope
Soap	I am sick with love
Coal	May I die and all my years be yours

[24] *Roumania and Her Rulers,* 1927.

[25] *Letters,* 1763.

A rose	May you be pleased and your sorrows mine
A straw	Suffer me to be your slave
Cloth	Your price is not to be found
Cinnamon	But my fortune is yours
Match	I burn! I burn! My flame consumes me
Golden thread	Don't turn away your face
Hair	Crown of my head
Grape	My eyes!
Gold wire	I die — come quickly
Pepper	Send me an answer

One imagines these symbols could be sent either individually or en masse but the order of opening would very much determine the message. If a jonquil, piece of soap, scrap of paper, and a strip of gold wire didn't do the trick, what more could one do?

When she died on 18 July 1938, Marie's last wish was for her heart to be buried, at Balcic. Her heart was placed in a silver box, similar to a Georgian tea caddy, which was then inserted into a larger box, about eight inches high, of silver covered with gold. On each corner, there was a figurine of a child and on the main panel, the initial 'M' encrusted with diamonds. The casket arrived at Constanţa where it was taken on board a two-masted white brigantine, aptly named 'Mircea' after her youngest child who had predeceased her by nearly twenty-two years. The little brig with its billowing jibs and staysails tacked slowly to Balcic and there, in the last of her architectural creations, Marie's heart was laid to rest in the Stella Maris Chapel.

Two years later Romania was faced with demands to return southern Dobrogea to Bulgaria. Countess Waldeck in her eyewitness account of those days reported:[26]

> The passion which surrounded the issue of Romanian revisionism was chiefly centred around Transylvania. Nobody got very excited about the Southern Dobrogea, which Romania has annexed after the Balkan War in 1913 for chiefly strategic reasons. Carol could have ceded it — 2,983 square miles with a population of 380, 000
>
> without much loss of face, had it not been for Queen Marie's heart, which was buried in her castle at Balcic, in Southern Dobro-

[26] *Athene Palace,* 1943.

gea. The Queen had been charmed with this country, where the tombs of the Scythians formed little round hills surmounting the wide bare plains, where the minarets still rose in the villages and Tartar women in wide trousers veiled their mouths in Islamic modesty.. But this was not the only reason why the Queen wished her heart to be buried here. The beautiful Queen, who in spite of her weaknesses took a deep and ambitious interest in Greater Romania, had a knack for symbolic gestures. This one was meant as a reminder and an obligation for her heirs never to give up this province. In 1938, when she died, the Queen could not imagine that by 1940 fear, weakness, and defeatism would black out her country so that her people would not think of fighting for the soil to which she had given her heart, but would only argue where to move it.

In 1940 General Zwiedinek was despatched to Balcic and moved the casket to the Castle of Bran;[27] subsequently, it was taken to Bucharest where it now rests. Even today, Marie retains an extraordinary degree of affection with Romanians of all classes and of all ages. She was in many ways the first 'media' royal of the twentieth century. She loved publicity, indeed overplayed it on her tour to America. She was eminently photogenic with her beauty and sense of the dramatic in her dress. She was mildly scandalous with her love affairs and rebellious in her behaviour, like smoking cigarettes in public. The love that still surrounds her memory stems from the fact that she was a giver; she gave her life to the Romanian people; she lived and breathed Romania until her dying day.

Of all the words written of her, I find Beverley Nichols's succinct pen-portrait the most compassionate and deeply moving:[28]

> Queen Marie of Rumania is not a woman about whom you can have two opinions. You either hate her or you adore her. I am to be found, unashamedly, in the ranks of the adorers.
>
> The people who hate her are either those who know nothing whatever about her, or those who feel it is their duty to hate every woman who dares to be both beautiful and intelligent. Very few women of that class are ever without enemies. Be beautiful and dumb, by all means. Or even better, be brilliant and hideous. But just you try to be beautiful and brilliant, and a queen, and see what happens!

---

[27] In 1941 Marie's daughter, Ileana, obtained permission to move Mircea's body from Cotroçeni and place it with his mother's heart in the chapel at Bran.

[28] *No Place like Home,* 1936.

The cumulative effect of them (my notes) gives me a picture of a woman who would have been an outstanding figure into whatever rank of life she had been born. A woman who has lived fully and loved deeply, who has braved the crowd, and commanded it. And though life has brought her many days in which her crown lay heavily upon her, she has worn it always with grace.

Marie's last words to her people were touching:

I was barely seventeen when I came to you. I was young and ignorant, but very proud of my native country, and even now I am proud to have been born an Englishwoman... but I bless you, dear Romania, country of my joy and my grief, the beautiful country which has lived in my heart.

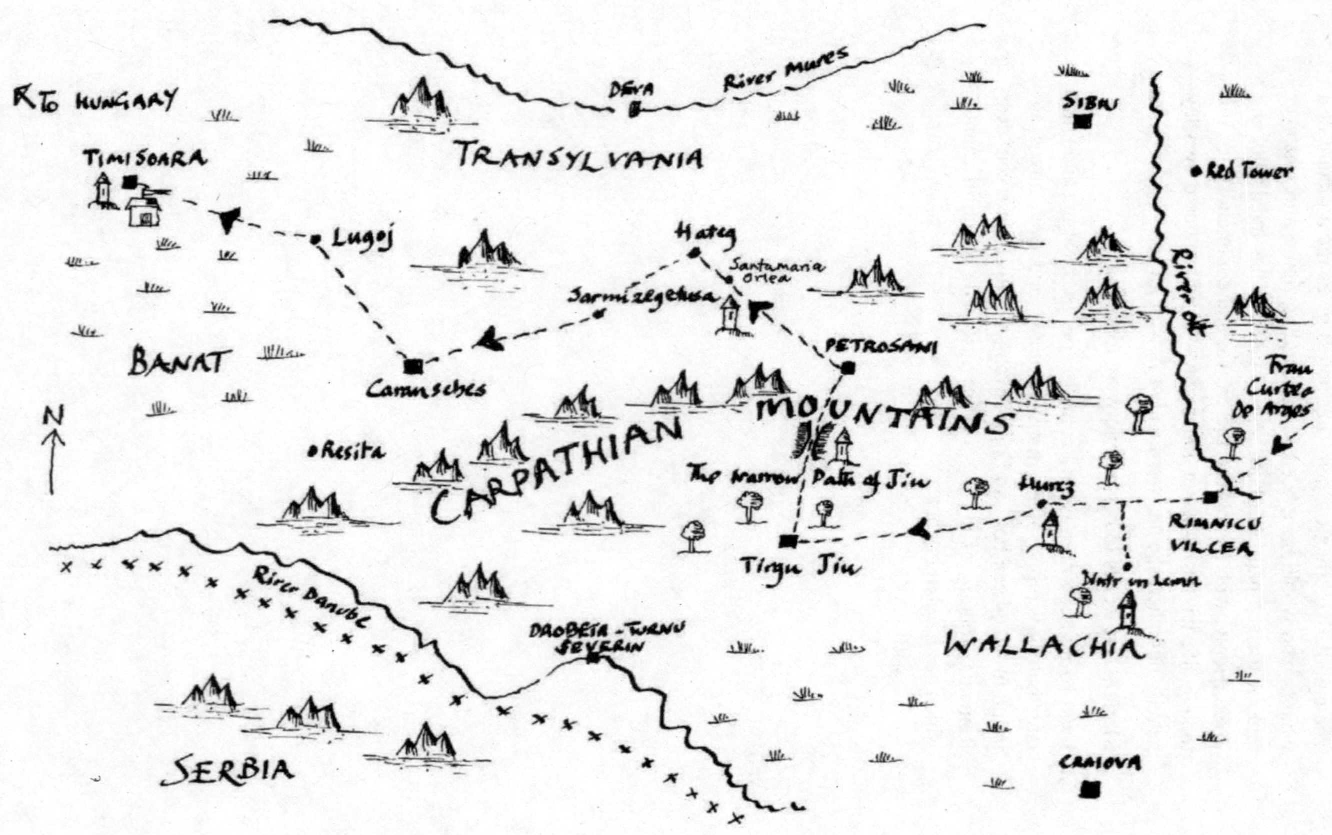

To HUNGARY
TIMISOARA
TRANSYLVANIA
DEVA
River Mures
SIBIU
Red Tower
River Olt
Lugoj
Hateg
Santamaria Orlea
Sarmizegetusa
PETROSANI
BANAT
Caransebes
N
Resita
CARPATHIAN
MOUNTAINS
The Narrow Path of Jiu
Hurez
From Curtea De Arges
RIMNICU VILCEA
Tirgu Jiu
River Danube
DROBETA-TURNU SEVERIN
WALLACHIA
SERBIA
CRAIOVA

Chapter Fifteen

Oltenia: Heavens above, Rugs below

One of Romania's eminent ecclesiastical historians, the Archimandrite Bartolomew, recalls[1] how he arrived at Curtea de Argeş as a young monk just after the Second World War:

> It must be more than forty years since I left Polovragi in Gorj county, together with Father Iaşim, determined to go to Argeş monastery on foot. It took us three or four days to get there. At Râmnicu Vâlcea we were put up by a cousin of mine, Costică Abagiu, who worked with the forestry inspectorate. As he knew all the thickets and clearings of the forest, he drew for us a map of all the paths and shortcuts across the hills. It was getting dark when we crossed the last hill and climbed down into the Argeş valley, but there we found the sky darkened by clouds forecasting a storm. We hurried up, darkness enveloped us, it somehow seemed to us that we had arrived at the monastery gate, we were far from sure about it, but at that moment the sky was split by a gigantic flash of lightning, revealing to me, all of a sudden and right in front of me, Manole's church like an apparition detaching itself from the dark.

My own arrival at Curtea de Argeş was distinctly pedestrian compared to this, having driven up from Bucharest on a sunny late autumn morning. Yet Manole's church, whatever time of day or year, makes a dramatic impression on the visitor. Started in 1517 by Basarab the Great,

[1] Valeriu Ananiu, *The Heavens of the Olt*, 1990.

founder of the dynasty that ruled Wallachia for three centuries, the building was continued by his son, Nicholas, and finally finished by his successor, Vlaicu. High on the banks of the Argeş River, this episcopal church is the most important building of the sixteenth century in Wallachia. Standing like a stone island in the grounds of the monastery, the church is 'crowned' with four corner towers. The two front ones, spiralling upwards, have an immediate impact on the eye — did the builder see the church as a princess in the position of an *Orante,* a praying woman, standing on tiptoes, her arms outstretched, imploring God's mercy? For the steeples are twisted from outside inwards, just like human arms.

Inside, the magnificent pro-nave is supported by eight free-standing columns with a further two supporting a semi-circular arch into the knave. On either side of the pro-nave are the simple, stone slabs of the tombs of Carol I and Elizabeth,[2] and of Ferdinand and Marie. The rather poorly executed frescoes of the former King and Queen by the entrance prompted Sitwell[3] to give vent to his feelings of being cheated:

> As for the episcopal church, this is, in all respects, the worst thing in Roumania. It is hard to believe it ever had any quality, so completely has it been ruined by Lecomte de Nouy, the pupil of Viollet-le-Duc. But this church at Curtea de Argeş is, in reality; a florid and sugary example of the Armenian style; the religious architecture of the old Armenian or Georgian Kingdom, as witnessed by the ruins of Ani, had a strong influence on the Roumanian brand of Byzantine architecture, especially in Moldavia... It is as an Armenian building that this vaunted wonder should be considered.

I agree with Sitwell's verdict about the restoration work by de Nouy; he effectively repainted the interior of the church as opposed to restoring it, as well as grafting Venetian mosaics and Parisian woodwork onto the outside. But I find his classification of it as "Armenian" unfair. No one knows the name of the architect or his origin. We do know he was familiar with Armenian-Georgian, Athonite, Constantinopolitan, and Western art and, of course, with the Romanian traditions. It was entirely in keeping with the architecture of those days that all these influences would have combined to create something new to that part of the world. As the traditions of Christianity had remained unbroken in Georgia, it was not surprising that its influence should predominate. Indeed, the monastery of

---

[2] And her little five year old daughter.

[3] *Roumanian Journey,* 1938.

XLIX. Bucharest: The Old Union Hotel

L. Bucharest: The Ciclop Building

LI. Bucharest: Atheneul Român

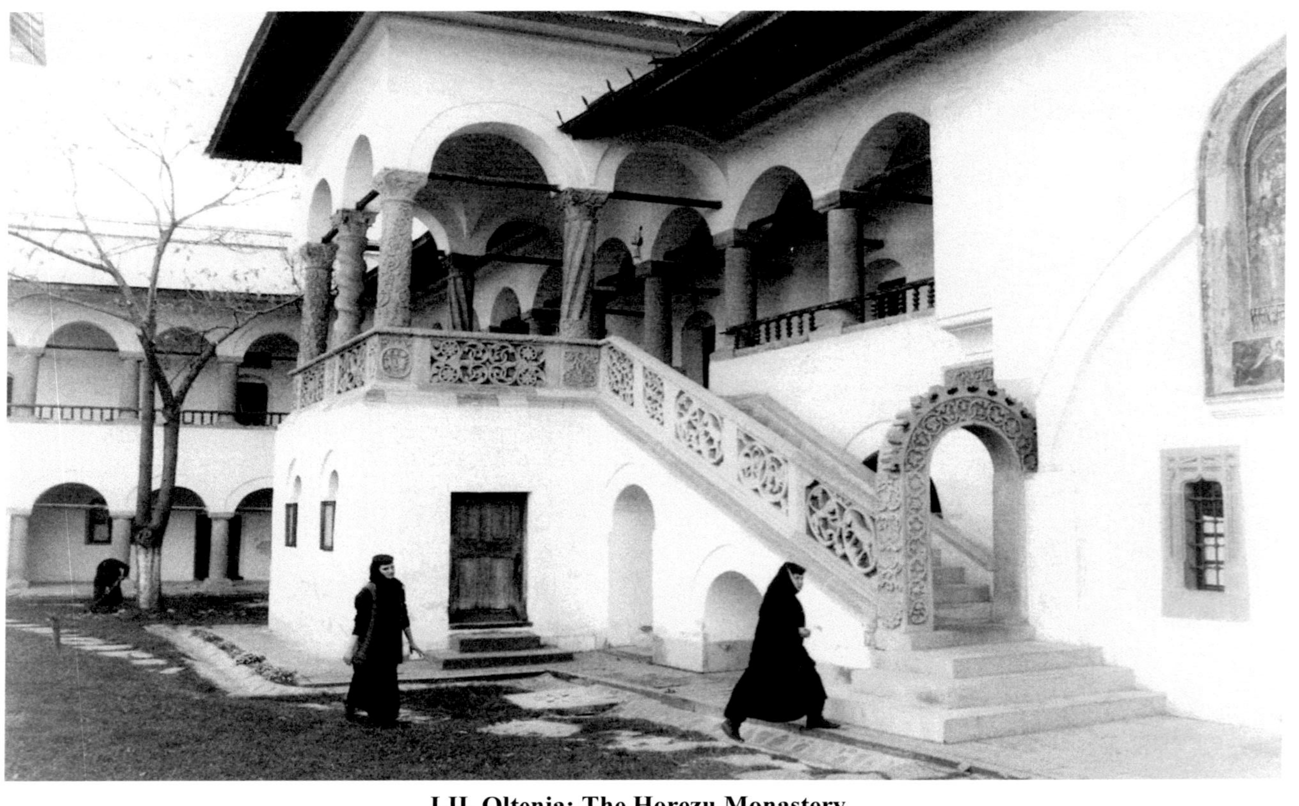

LII. Oltenia: The Horezu Monastery

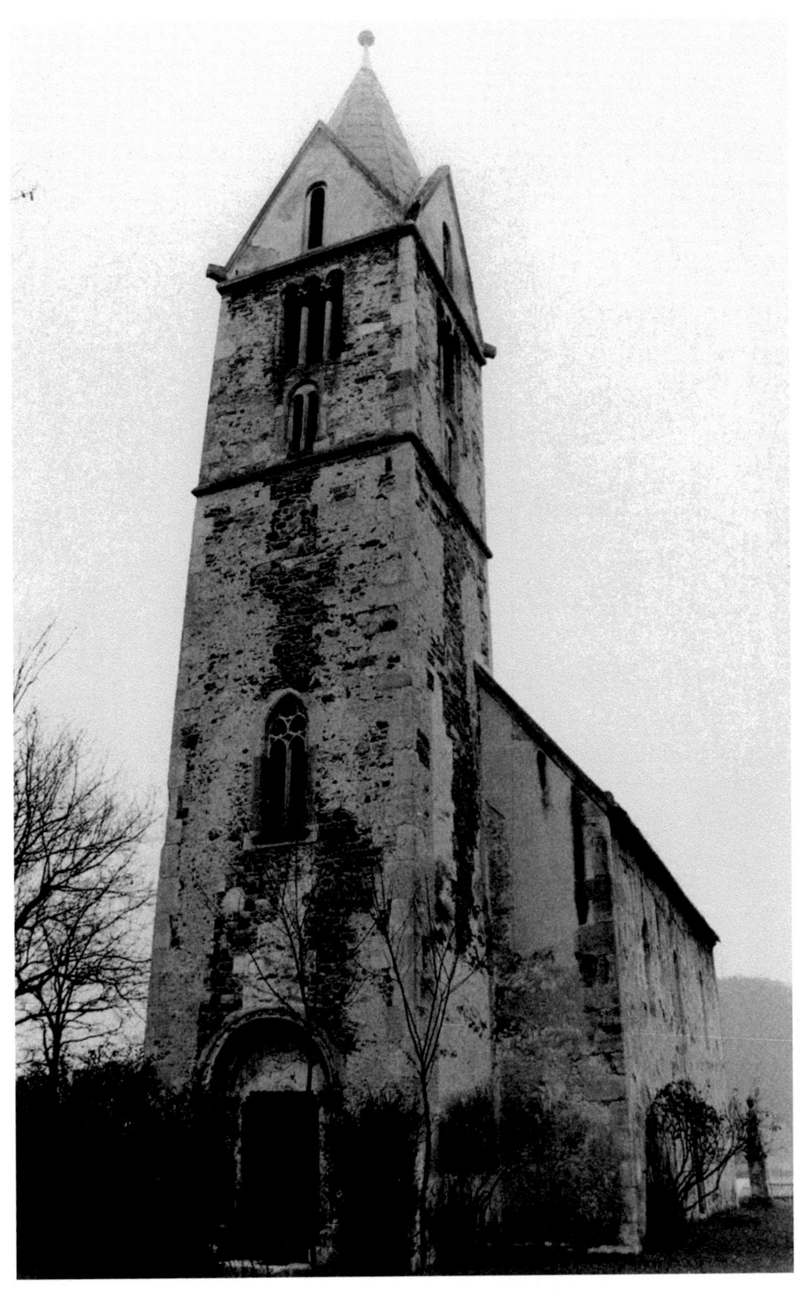

LIII. Sântămăria-Orlea: The Cândea Church

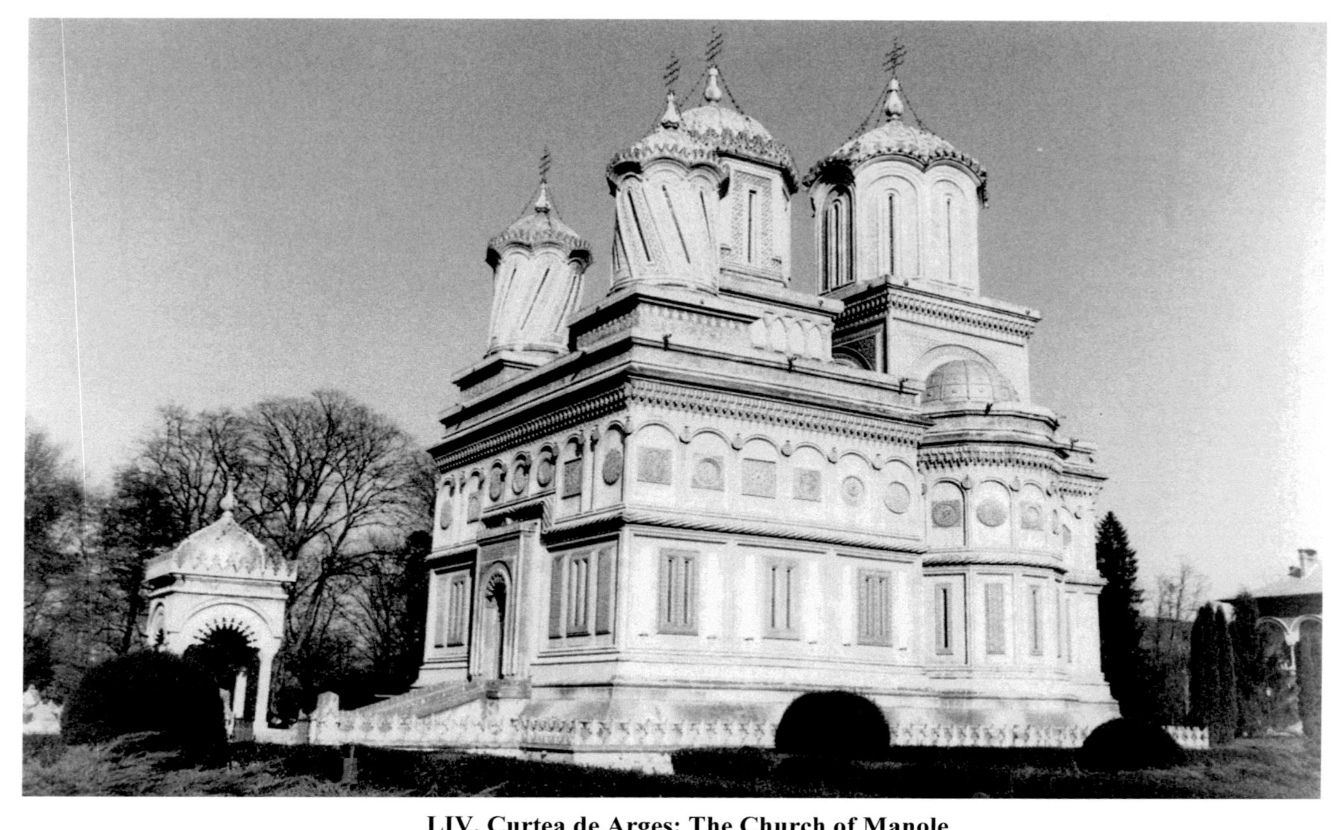

LIV. Curtea de Argeş: The Church of Manole

LV. Timişoara: (l) Banca de Scont; (r) The Serbian Bishops' Palace

LVI. Timişoara: The Serbian Bishops' Palace

Batchovo near Plovdiv in Bulgaria is so Georgian in style that it prompted the visiting President of Georgia recently to exclaim: "I am home!"

The legend of the foundation of Curtea de Argeş is told by Archimandrite Bartholomew.

> Negru Vodă — the Black Prince — accompanied by master builder Manole and his nine masons were walking down the Argeş Valley, looking for *A Place/ Where to build a shrine/ A cloister divine.*[1] He however was not interested in finding the most sheltered place with abundant streams, fertile lands or charming surroundings, but wished to arrive at *An old wall all rotten/ Unfinished; a vestige forgotten,* which had to be somewhere in that area, but nobody knew exactly where. The initiated one proved to be *a Handsome little swain/ On a sweet pipe playing,* who guided the Prince towards the place he was seeking, where they actually found the wall and the monastery was eventually erected.

So the church may well have been erected on the site of an earlier Christian church which had not been completed for one reason or another, or else possibly on the remains of a pagan temple.

Taking the road to the west, through beech woods and valleys draped in a fine web of fruit trees, I arrived at the little monastery of Dintr' un Lemn in the Otasaului valley, near the town of Franceşti. When Sitwell was here, he found:

> There are monasteries or nunneries in so many of the mountain valleys. A particularly charming example is the convent of Dintr' un Lemn, a curious name which repeats the legend attached to it. According to this, a miraculous icon was discovered, wedged, or embedded into the trunk of a tree. No strength could remove it, and the tree had to be carried away bodily and the church built round it.

Actually, the legend is somewhat different, indeed there are two versions. The first was told by Paul of Aleppo and Macarius of Antioch[2] during their journey of 1653-1658. It follows the same story as Sitwell but ends with the church being built out of the single oak tree — *Dintr' un Lemn* means 'from one piece of wood.' The second variant, recounted by

---

[1] From an old poem

[2] Sitwell used his book extensively. "This book, which is among the minor curiosities of literature owing to its half language, is an account, written by his secretary, Paul of Aleppo, of the journey of the Syrian Archbishop of Antioch to Moscow, in the years 1652-1660"

another bishop in 1745, features a shepherd called Radu who dreamt of an icon and a voice from heaven directed him to an oak tree in which he found it.

Why was the monk or Radu told to build a church from just one oak as opposed to several? Archimandrite Bartholomew suggests:

> First, the monastery was built on godly commandments: secondly, the oak tree in which an icon was found was not an ordinary tree but a sacred one whose roots marked a sacred place. It was a divine pole. Do you remember the archaic mentality? The first act performed by the head of a family was to stick a pole in the ground, thus marking the centre around which the household was to be set up. With one end pointing towards the sky and the other towards the heart of the earth, the pole became an *axis mundi,* the symbol not only of stability but also of the uranic-telluric/divine-human bipolarity. The significance of the oak-tree is even more powerful. For the wood of the sacred tree was turned into a ship sailing to the eschaton, a ship not only consecrated but holy by itself, homogeneous, unitary, undivided and unsevered, having at its helm Jesus Christ who is always in the centre, wherever He may go.

The little church, made from the single tree, is on a hill above the monastery, fittingly surrounded by a ring of tall oaks. Although an eighteenth century replica, it retains the mystique of the original, berthed in the field like a small ark. Further down the slope is the larger monastery church, built in 1630 by Matei Basarab and his nephew, Preda Brâncoveanu. Deceptively large on the outside with an open porch and twin rotundas, the tiny interior with its beautiful seventeenth and eighteenth century frescoes is dark to the point of gloomy, and presumably rather cramped for its community of over fifty nuns.

As I was wandering around the church, I noticed a middle-aged couple in earnest conversation with a nun. Aida was sent to eavesdrop and returned, scarcely able to contain her laughter. She explained that the couple's problem was that their daughter couldn't find a husband and such was the family's distress that they had driven for over six hours to the monastery to enlist God's help.

"And how can He help?" I asked outloud, not expecting Aida to answer on behalf of Him.

"Well, the nun has written down her name and it will be read out at prayers — along with a list of others."

"Will that work?"

"I doubt it but at least they will be able to blame God and not their daughter from then on."

A terrible scene was enacted here in 1714. Princess Păuna, the ambitious and scheming wife of Ştefan Cantacuzino, went to the monastery with her maid for the Feast of the Dormition. Păuna and her maid were offered a room with a nun called Olimpiada. The next day, 15 August, the Princess threw a sudden lit during the liturgy — she moaned, shouted, screamed, took all her clothes off, and finally passed out. When she came round, she explained that she had seen a vision in the face of the icon of the Holy Mother of God, of Constantin Brâncoveanu and his four sons being beheaded in Constantinople. Her husband acted quickly He tried and hung the maid for witchcraft and walled up the nun, alive. Why?

The answer lay to the north, down a poplar-lined avenue, at the monastery of Horezu. This, the greatest monastery in Romania, was a court of Constantin Brâncoveanu. Set on the side of a beech-wrapped hill amidst open pastures, its white walls and graceful towers represent Brâncoveanu's greatest architectural achievement. In the centre stands a large church, almost a cathedral, in which all the styles which Brâncoveanu adopted come together. From neighbouring Argeş, come the large narthex and stone walled foundation; from Moldavia, Baroque window frames; from Italy, the loggias and sculptured columns and from the Orient, the high stone portal of the church. This was an experiment to mould a princely court with a major religious foundation and it worked brilliantly. Today, Brâncoveanu's apartments form the museum. Under their airy stone vaulted halls with their massive Byzantine columns is a wonderful collection of seventeenth and eighteenth century icons.

Little has changed since Sitwell's visit:

> In one corner of the courtyard, trestle tables were set up and the peasant women and children were at their dinner. Great cauldrons of soup were carried up, huge hunks of bread and bunches of white grapes. It was the scene of a thousand years ago: the monks, or nuns, and their serfs lived in this manner in any great Byzantine convent of the tenth century.
>
> As for the nuns of Horezu.... their dark habits culminate in a little round black hat, inimitably smart and attractive, but of a date it is difficult to determine. These are the hats of the young popinjays in Carpaccio's paintings; hats which can still be seen worn in Dalmatia, the native land of Carpaccio.

> It is with a heavy heart that one leaves Horezu; for it is the living relic of a world in which, once upon a time, all visual things were beautiful. The life of meditation had its rewards in this environment. Poverty was not poverty; riches not riches. Now, it is only in a few remote places that the shadow, or ghost, of those days is still to be found.[3]

And, here, in the pro-nave of the church is the key to Princess Paula's terrible secret. Facing one, to the right of the two great silver chandeliers which Constantin brought from Venice and Vienna, is the fresco of the votives, Constantin, his wife Marica, and their eleven children. As I looked at the likeness of the great man, surrounded by his handsome family, it was as if the events of his life had happened only yesterday.

He was only a year old when mercenary troops mutinied in Bucharest and the Brâncoveanus found themselves surrounded by blood-thirsty soldiers. The rioters stormed into the family house, killing Constantin's father in the gateway, and demanded the body of his son. According to eyewitnesses of the time, the servants came forward with a small boy wrenched from the arms of its Gypsy mother. The rioters promptly slashed the child to pieces and went away, their bloodlust satiated. Such was the violent start to life for Constantin; his end was worse.

Behind, on either side of the back wall, are paintings of Constantin's parental families; on the left, his father's and on the right, his mother's. It is the latter one must study carefully, for all heads are turned towards Constantin except two:[4] Stolnic[5] Constantin Cantacuzino, father of Ştefan, and Spătar[6] Toma. These were the Judases who, together with Ştefan, betrayed Constantin to the Turks. The charges which resulted in his arrest on Good Friday 1714 had the fingerprints of the conspirators all over them:

> seeing that Preda Brancovano has had a secret understanding with Austria, Russia, Poland, and Venice; that he has accepted from the Emperor the title of Prince of the Holy Empire, and from the Czar the Grand Cross of St. Andrew;[7] seeing that he has forwarded his treasures to Vienna, and has only rebuilt the palace at Târgovişte that he might the more easily be able to flee; seeing that he pos-

---

[3] *Roumanian Journey,* 1938.

[4] This 'affectation' may well have been added by a later artist to make a political point.

[5] High steward.

[6] Army commander.

[7] Hence Marthe Bibesco's remark to the Russians at Mogoşoaia.

> sesses property and castles in Ardialia, and that he has agents in Vienna and Venice; seeing that the desertion of Thomas Cantacuzene is only the fruit of his counsels; seeing that he has made cymbals of silver and has struck coinage bearing his effigy, the Sultan Achmet condemns him and all his family to be beheaded.[8]

Brâncoveanu was philosophical about this turn of events. "Such will always be the fate of those who serve tyrants" were his last words. Archimandrite Bartholomew describes Constantin's last days:

> On that terrible 15th August 1714, Constantin Brâncoveanu turned sixty in the prison of Istanbul, while Princess Marica, in prison as well, remembered it was her name day. That was the day chosen by the sultan for beheading Brâncoveanu and his four sons after having them devilishly tortured for four months, day after day, sometimes under the unfortunate Princess's eyes of a wife and mother. Barefoot and dressed only in shirts, the convicts were taken to the scaffold in Ialikiosk market and aligned, like cattle to be slaughtered, before the whole of Europe, whose ambassadors had been invited to the bloody performance. In keeping with the Sultan's order, the first to fall was the head of the eldest son, Constantin. Ştefan was beheaded next. Then the axe cut off Radu's head. Deeply shaken, the youngest son, Matei, aged barely eleven, threw himself at the Sultan's feet promising he would become a Muslim if his life was spared. His request was neither accidental, nor hopeless. Already while they were tortured the mufti had promised their pardon provided they agreed to turn Muslim — an offer rejected by the prisoners. Matei was begging for it now, in front of the block splashed with his brothers' blood, under the executioner's arm awaiting the Sultan's decisions. After having learnt of his request through an interpreter, the sultan asked Brâncoveanu if he agreed. The son's life was now in the father's hands. It would have meant the certitude that Brâncoveanu's descent continued. How harrowing must have been that moment's split in the old man's soul! If he had given Matei his life, as the latter wished, this would have shattered the perfection of the work of 'an old boyar and Christian prince,' tragically rounded off by fate. Perfection cannot be conceived other than round. The unfortunate father did not have time to voice his thoughts. He motioned to his son: redeem your soul, not your life! Matei put his head on the block and the axe fell like lightning! Some people think that Brâncoveanu's beautiful

[8] Ottoman archives.

head (he went next) remained attached to his body by a strip of flesh. I, however, see it tumbling to the ground and stopping near Matei's, cheek to cheek, in godlike tenderness.

After the execution, the victims heads were displayed on the walls of the Seraglio[9] and their bodies thrown in to the streets below to be eaten by dogs. However, fearing a revolt by the city's Christians, the Sultan's servants recovered the corpses and dumped them in the Bosphorus where they were fished out by the Patriarch's men and buried on Halki Island off Constantinople. Princess Marica finally managed to arrange for her husband's remains to be secretly brought to Bucharest in 1720, where they remained undiscovered in the Church of St. George until early this century. The tomb Constantin had prepared for himself at Horezu remains empty.

So Paula's vision had been true. Her husband, Ștefan, whether as an act of atonement or not, restored Dintr' un Lemn, commissioning new frescoes for the nave. It was not enough to spare him from his treachery: he and his father[10] were strangled by the Turks in the very same cell where Constantin has spent his last days. Their executioners would probably have been the Sultan's gardeners but may have been the Sultan's fearsome black dwarfs, dressed in hooded black habits, who shuffled silently around the palace in soft slippers, grasping their gruesome garottes.

On the outside of the porch of Horezu Church, there is a huge panorama of hell and all its attendant torments. Bartholomew contrasts this with the quiet tones of Paradise on the opposite wall, concluding that "suffering has more shapes and steps than happiness, like a game of vicious mirrors." Under the panorama, there are five most unusual monochromatic drawings, entitled Tartar, Teeth Gritting, Sleepless Worms, Darkness, and The Devil's Dam. They depict a mass of naked bodies, mostly with their hands tied behind their backs, packed together like cattle. No one is being tortured; the symbolism suggests a fare of depersonalised nothingness, punishment by anonymity. The modern parallel of life under a totalitarian regime is inescapable.

It was beginning to get dark, so I went in search of the Mother Superior or *Stareță* to beg a bed off her. I found her in the refectory, a perfectly

[9] In London, traitor's heads were usually exhibited on a bridge or gate of the city; in Constantinople, 'senior' heads were on white marble pillars in the first courtyard of the palace, 'lesser' heads in niches on either side of the imperial gate. Only 'senior' heads were stuffed with straw.

[10] Together with eight other members of their family.

proportioned room that managed to scat her flock of sixty around a U-shaped table, under the gaze of a beautiful Mother of God in the dome above. After cursorily inspecting me, she approved my request and I was shown to the old guest wing at the top of Brâncoveanu's spectacular staircase, the Dionesus. My high-ceiling room, with a tile stove pumping out heat in one corner, was draped in colourful Oltenian rugs on the floor and walls. The two windows looked south across the valley, down the almond-lined cobbled road which led under the gatehouse towards the Olt River which tumbled into the Danube at Turnu Severin. In the cold and peaceful night air of the cloister, a black-clad nun flitted in and out of the arcades, drumming on her toacă. A peel of bells rang out and like bats disturbed in a cave, the nuns flocked to the church for vespers.

At breakfast the next day, Stareţa Ileana joined me, standing propped up against the back of a chair. She had a mischievous face, so I recounted Mrs. Martineau's story[11] about Queen Marie to her:

> We ended up at the beautiful convent of Horezu, where the old staritsa (abbess), who adores the Queen with a love that is pathetic, was waiting for us. This old lady is very advanced in years, but no walk is too long and no climb too hard if she is only allowed to be in the company of her beloved Regina. The architecture was very Spanish in appearance, the convent running round the courtyard on all four sides, and with an ancient church in the middle with a tall fir-tree on each side of the door as is usual in Romania. The Queen had told me much of the glories of this place seen by moonlight. It is situated high on a hillside, and has a superb view over the river and plain below. Our dinner had been sent from the (Royal) train and was served to us in a loggia open on three sides to the moonlight at a great height — a really wonderful experience in the cool pine-scented air. The next morning we drove to the convent in order to distribute the Queen's annual gift of sugar, clothing etc. Sugar is very expensive in Roumania, and a whisper had reached the Queen that the old Staritsa had been in the habit of trading with the sugar given to her for the nuns, in order that she might buy useful clothing, flour etc. for them. The nuns, who had, collectively, a very sweet tooth, resented bitterly being deprived of their sugar. The Queen was far too tactful to tell the Stareţă that the sugar was for the nuns only, so she very sweetly said: "I have thought the work of weighing the sugar too heavy for you, and so I

[11] *Roumania and Her Rulers,* 1927.

have brought Monsieur the Chief of Police, who has kindly agreed to weigh out the portions."

When I had finished, the Staritsa looked at me quizzically as if I was trying to infer something suspicious about her 'management.' After a pause, she roared with laughter and said: "We had King Michael here this summer. He didn't bring any sugar — he brought his daughter (Margareta), who is just as sweet." The visitor's book was then produced and she solicitously looked on as I experienced a severe case of writer's cramp. After an embarrassing delay, I found some words which Aida translated as the ink was drying. The Stareţă beamed at me, clucking soothingly, and departed for church. No exam was ever passed with such relief.

Chapter Sixteen

Timişoara: The Long Arm of Vienna

It is impossible to leave Horezu willingly such is its beauty and repose. It was time that wrenched me away and I began to drive westward along the foothills of the Carpathians, through small unspoilt villages until I reached Novaci, a stylish, tree-lined little town. In this part of Romania, the architecture changes: wood is "out," brick and red tiled roofs are "in." The influence of the Brâncoveanu style percolated down to the humblest dwelling.

At Bumbeşti, a new design appeared. The two-storied houses originally were built with a three-sided verandah on the top floor; at some stage, this space was enclosed with windows, giving the impression of a house wrapped in glass, similar to the seafront buildings of Corunna. I stopped to photograph a particularly good example when a ruddy faced lady in deep discussion with her neighbours along the street, noticed me.

"What's going on?," she exclaimed breathlessly as she ran towards me.

"Madame, I assure you nothing. I am merely admiring your windows."

"My windows? My grandparents installed them, all very well, but scant thought was given to their cleaning. Give me the open verandah of the old days any day of the week!"

So much for the fashion of gracious living when it confronts the practicality of a hard-working housewife.

Bumbeşti is situated at the southern entrance of 'the Narrow Path of Jiu,' the great pass linking Oltenia to Transylvania. From here, I followed the Jiu River upstream through some of the most rugged and spectacular scenery in all Romania, past the little fifteenth century monastery of Lainici hidden in the depths of a gorge. These hills, the Retezat and Parâng Munţi, are honeycombed with mines, hence the dark brown inky colour of the river never changed, however much I willed it to.

At the northern exit of the pass is Petroşani, a mining and industrial town of indescribable ghastliness. I pitied the poor people of Petroşani, engulfed in a bilious blanket of poisoned air. Were their mines and factories making profits or merely being kept operating to mitigate unemployment? Whatever the reason for the pollution at Petroşani, there can be no justification for it to continue unchecked. Coughing and spluttering, I emerged into breathable air near Haţeg. There, in the middle of nowhere, utterly alone, was the small village of Sântămăria-Orlea.

The home of the old princely family of Cândea, Sântămăria has an exceptionally fine thirteenth century Gothic church, an astonishing sight for while commonplace in England and France, it is unique in Romania. The church has a high tower surmounted with a small steeple with three Romanesque arched windows for the bells. As usual the gate was locked but my frantic rattling was heard by a charming middle-aged lady who was thrilled to show me around. The interior was very plain and simple, with a whitewashed gallery overlooking a single nave and apse. The frescos were dreadfully faded so it was hard to date them. The very Englishness of this little church was quite extraordinary.

From Haţeg to Caransebeş, past Decebalus's old capital at Sarmizegetusa, I drove towards Timişoara which aptly rhymed with Tipperary — it was certainly "a long way." This part of Romania was called the Banat and was the only area actually occupied by the Ottomans. There was little evidence today of their stay, unlike in Bulgaria where many of the villages still keep their mosque and minarets. One explanation of this is that when the Turks arrived in 1552 most people simply moved away, effectively de-populating the countryside and thereby turning it into an unproductive asset for the Porte.

The Hapsburgs set out to recover it at the beginning of the eighteenth century. Mercenaries were much in demand then for standing armies were the exception, not the rule. 'Wild as a goat in the highlands,' the young Earl of Crawford from Scotland fought with both the Russian and Imperial armies against the Turks, earning the praise of George I for "hunting in the fields of glory, while others were rioting in the lap of luxury." This brilliant soldier fought at Timişoara and Belgrade before having his thigh shattered by a Turkish musket ball at the battle of Krotzka in July 1739. He continued to soldier, joining George II at the battle of Dettingen in 1745, before dying of his old wound in 1748, aged just 46.[1]

The Banat was handed over to Prince Eugene of Savoy on 13 October 1716 and the Hapsburgs set about reconstructing it on a massive scale, stamping the architectural authority of Vienna on the two main cities, Timişoara and Arad. I reached the former on a rain-drenched, cold evening but even the awful weather could not dampen my enthusiasm for Union Square. Here is a superb Hapsburg cobbled open space, constructed between 1720 and 1760, with wonderful facades of eighteenth century elegant townhouses. The building of the square was overseen by Count Andrew Hamilton, a fellow countryman of Crawford, who was president and commander-in-chief in the Banat between 1734 and 1738. A large Roman Catholic cathedral of 1754 is the 'important' building in the square, yet such is the size of the open space that it doesn't dominate it. The cathedral took sixteen years to complete as the first attempt to erect it ended with the building sunk without trace in the marshy ground!

Peace was relatively long-lived for this part of the world and strife only returned after the rebellion of 1848. When Andrew Paton arrived here in 1851, the town was in ruins:[2]

> As I approached the town itself, I in vain looked for the noble alleys of trees that used to be the delight and ornament of the place; all had been hewn down by the grim axe of war, the fortifications covered with the marks of cannon-balls, and the roofs of the houses within battered to the bare rafters, or altogether roofless.

The corner, diagonally opposite the cathedral was of great interest to me. Here on the junction of Vasile Alecsandri and Gheorghe Lazăr streets are two most peculiar buildings. The first is the light-green palace of the Serbian Orthodox bishops. Designed in 1905, its Moorish windows and pepper-potted towers almost suggest that it is an Islamic institution of some sort; the little towers could be dwarf minarets.

Across the road from the bishop's palace is an extraordinary Art Nouveau building of bulbous, protruding facades. It looks like an elephant has been plastered into the walls, which are studded with electric blue

---

[1] *Memoirs of the Life of the Late Rt. Hon John, 20th Earl of Craufurd,* 1769.

[2] *The Goth and the Hun,* 1851.

enamels like small light bulbs. The windows on the first floor have identical surrounds with similar motifs, this time like giant blue pearls. I was intrigued by this design and Aida went inside to discover more. Nobody seemed to know anything about its history — she returned with vague news that maybe it had once been a private house belonging to a Serbian family. I found the answer later. Two Hungarian architects, Komor and Jakob, had designed it in 1906 as a bank, "Banca de Scont." The ceramic decorations were inspired by Hungarian folklore but as to which tale, I never discovered.

There are two other squares in Timişoara, the small Liberation Square of non-descript Austro-Hungarian architecture in the centre of the city, and the much larger Victory Square. It was here that the crowds gathered in 1989, finally exasperated by the antics of Ceauşescu and it was here that his troops opened fire, killing several hundred of their fellow countrymen, almost a repeat of the bloody peasants revolt of 1540. Victory Square, like Wenceslas Square in Prague, is a long oblong space, with the modern 1923 façade of its theatre and opera house at one end and the imposing 1926 Orthodox cathedral at the other. The interest is in the facades of the large houses which connect the two, all built between 1910 and 1913. The Palace Weiss, Palace Lloyd and Palace Loftier are fine examples of fin-de-siècle offices and apartments, though much in need of a clean these days.

Offset to one side of the square is the old Hapsburg palace, 'Huniade Castle.' Although started in the fourteenth century, the palace was rebuilt in 1856 and today houses the Museum of Banat History. Apart from the inner courtyard, which had been given an attractive coat of yellow paint, the palace was disappointing. The Museum of History, like so many of its ilk in Romania, was poorly laid out, seemingly with the intention of persuading the visitor that Romania has been the cradle of civilization since the first day when man swung down from the trees.

Timişoara, with its Hapsburg legacy, was the perfect place for me to leave Romania, for it is an example of the many strands of history that make up this fascinating country. For English travellers over the ages, Romania has had a mesmerising mystique; Elisa Craven found the people dressed as Turks who weren't Turks. It has had a glamour; male travellers, to a man, were enamoured by the beauty of its women. It has had a flamboyant charm; Queen Marie soon discovered this and adopted this as her own. It has had an eccentricity which provoked and sometimes infuriated; witness William Wilkinson and his frustrations.

This 'composite' reputation stems from the rich mix of Romanian history. It is a melange of Hapsburg, Magyar, Polish, Saxon, Ottoman, Russian, Wallachian, Serbian, Greek, and Moldavian influences and consequently Romania is hard to define; it is quite unlike any other country. Despite attempts to eradicate most of these engaging traits over the last fifty years by clumsy efforts to re-write history, Romania has managed to preserve its curious identity. It succeeds in infuriating those who don't know her, beguiling those who do. For the traveller who seeks to enquire, she awaits with open arms; for those who seek the obvious, she remains an impenetrable enigma.

Most travellers when they leave Romania try to summarise their experiences of this extraordinary country

In what can only be politely described as schoolgirl poetry; Isabel Trumper dedicated 'A Sunny Land (Roumania)' to Queen Marie in 1924:

There's a charming and sun-kissed region I know,
Where purple and sweet-scented violets blow:
The forests are hallow'd by lilies snow-white
And th' valleys with blossom rouse keenest delight.

The supple acacias are laden with flowers,
While lime trees in majesty perfume the bowers:
The mountains are clothed with strawberries sweet
And raspberries tempt the brown bears them to eat.

Their pearly teeth peeping through coppery skin,
Coy Gypsies so broad, and yet lissom and thin:
With long raven tresses (but merry and gay)
Mix magical potions, then curtsey and play.

Merrily sledges glide swiftly along,
Filling the air with their joy fullest song!
Blue are the skies, and yet much bluer still
When snow lieth deep on valley and hill.

Wide surging plains, waving green or bright gold,
Allure and bewitch one with joys yet untold!
Soft spreading hills in the morning all shine
With th' glistening leaves of the far-flinging vine.

Gracefully peasants in close-kerchief'd head,
Move amid all with their firm, silent tread:
Soft voices there — above — below —
Voices that none other land can bestow.

Whatever her poetic limitations may have been, Isabel captured[3] the populist ideal of Romania that had been gaining ground since the late nineteenth century.

Sitwell was uncharacteristically lengthy, possibly under pressure to flatter the government of King Carol which had contributed £500 towards the cost of the publication of his book.[4]

> In writing this book, which must be forgiven for a certain superficiality after only four weeks spent in the country, there has been a stress or over-emphasis upon the picturesque elements of the land. These may be the first things that strike a stranger; but, also, may I say to Roumanian readers that it is some of these first impressions that endure. When all is said and done, the integrity of the peasant population, the popular music of which I became so fond, the country fairs, the picturesque Laetzi, the lovely landscapes of Oltenia or of the Delta, these, after all, are Roumania. It is delightful that there should be good roads and an excellent train service; but these things are concomitant and a proof of wise government. What is more important, both to Roumania and to the world, is the preservation of its true character. For Roumania is still unspoilt. Perhaps there is no other country in Europe of which this is true to the same extent. More than this, under good rule, it has limitless possibilities from its unfired human stock, who have come safely through the nineteenth century in their pristine state. Let us hope there will never be a town in Roumania with a million inhabitants. Bucharest must be getting near that mark. For there is always misery in very large towns; and the good fortune of Roumania lies in its mountains and its plains. And this must bring us back, once more, to our general contention. What is permanent and unforgettable in Roumania is the great plain of Transylvania, the woods of Oltenia, the swamps of the Danube Delta, the valleys of the Neamţ, painted Suceviţa and Voroneţ, and the wooden houses and gay costumes seen upon its roads. That is the permanent Roumania; while the modern Roumania of factories and model flats is only its amelioration into twentieth century conditions of civilisation. We prefer the old. And it is that which will last, tempered by the new.

---

[3] *A Song of Roumania and Other Short Poems,* 1924.

[4] He was not alone in benefiting from King Carol's PR campaign of the 1930s; Hielscher was also commissioned by the government. By today's standards, they did nothing amiss for neither claimed political objectivity as their forte.

By his own admission, Sitwell's judgements were based on what he saw, often from the window of a car or train. When I asked old Marie in Maramureş what she could remember about life before the war, she answered with only one word: "Hunger." Life in Sitwell's Arcadia may have been picturesque but it was far from easy.

When she left Bucharest in January 1941, Countess Waldeck's summary of her experiences was altogether more insightful:[5]

> The wind from Russia blew sharply the day I drove to the Bucharest station and a new layer of snow covered the ground, very white and pure. It was early in the morning and, as I glanced back at the Athene Palace from the square, I saw the crack that criss-crossed its white façade, a reminder of the earthquake, showing as clearly as does a scar on a face asleep. This scar had done no damage to the structure of the Athene Palace but had only marred the whiteness, and thus seemed to fit in with what was my strongest impression of Romania in these seven months: the indestructible quality of this flexible, realistic, fatalistic people whom destiny had established on the frontier between Orient and Occident. Two thousand years of severe foreign masters, barbarian invasions, rapacious conquerors, wicked princes, cholera, and earthquakes have given Romanians a superb sense of the temporary and transitory quality of everything.
>
> Here nobody complained about the 'end of civilisation' just because Hitler tried to set up a mere one thousand-year Empire. A people that saw the Roman Empire come and go and saw all sorts of barbarians invade their country, and still survived, does not believe that there is a definite end to anything. Such people are instinctively wise in the strange ways of history, which invariably seems to run into compromise, and so they are less afraid than many great nations of the West. The Romanians possess to the highest degree the capacity of 'receiving the blows of destiny while relaxed. They fall artfully, soft and loose in every joint and muscle as only those trained in falling can be. The secret of the art of falling is, of course, not to be afraid of falling and the Romanians are not afraid, as Western people are. Long experience is survival has taught them that each fall may result in unforeseen opportunities and that somehow they always get on their feet again.

---

[5] *Athene Palace,* 1943.

In April 1939, as Hector Bolitho[6] left Roumania on the train to Salzburg, he watched the landscape pass by. As he looked out of the carriage window, he caught sight of

> a village within a fold between the hills. The square white cottages cluster near to the spire of the church, like a brood of ducklings, aware of the gathering darkness. The village seems small, lost in the vast blue scene: but it is the symbol of life in Roumania. It is a stronghold: it stands for poverty with courage and for the continuity of freedom. A village of people who believe, with their contemporaries in my own village in England, that they were born to be free and to use the fruitfulness of the earth for their happiness.

And Donald Hall, after a year of living and working in the villages of Romania, summarised his experience[7] as:

> In the happiness of these people lay their strength. Because in the West we have made a world which is hard on us if we are not continuously busy, we have made work a standard of morality and affect contempt for what we call idleness. Even in our leisure time we must always be doing "something." These people have no such fetish; they worked to eat, no more. They were not lazy. It was only that they had not forgotten the meaning of composure.

All three travellers identify the essence of Romania as its countryside. In many ways, this was my own conclusion too, for nobody can pass through such an Elysian landscape without being deeply affected by its beauty and by the integrity of the relationship which the villagers have with the land. Yet, in the cities, however ugly the architectural legacy of Communism, the urban Romanian holds his own, looking at the world, slightly tongue in check, accepting tragedy and grief, embracing happiness for its fleeting nature and, above all, finding something to laugh about most days. But it would be wrong to conclude that Romanians are fatalistic; everyone I met had a goal they aspired to and were determined to achieve it. However, the Romanians don't confuse success with ambition, possibly at a financial cost, but never at the expense of what Hall aptly termed 'composure.'

---

[6] *Roumania under King Carol,* 1939.

[7] *Roumanian Furrow,* 1934.

A Brief Summary of Romanian History

82-44 BC	Dacian kingdom under King Burebista
105 AD	Rome conquers Dacia (Romania)
271	Rome pulls out
2nd-9th C	The great migrations from the East
10th-13th C	Hungarians conquer Transylvania
1054	The Great Schism; Romania goes with the Orthodox Church
1310	Wallachia founded by Basarab the First
1359	Moldavia founded by Voievod Bogdan
1415	Wallachia recognises Ottoman suzerainty
1456	Moldavia recognises Ottoman suzerainty
1541	Ottoman suzerainty over Transylvania
1600	Michael the Brave unities all three principalities
1686	Transylvania accepts the protection of the Hapsburgs
1711	The Ottomans install the Phanariots in Moldavia
1716	The Phanariots installed in Wallachia
1775	Bucovina annexed by Hapsburgs
1802	Bucharest flattened by earthquake
1812	Bessarabia annexed by Russians
1822	Phanariots sacked; native princes take over
1859	Union of Wallachia and Moldavia
1864	Full autonomy from the Porte
1867	Hapsburgs create dual monarchy; Transylvania annexed by Hungary

1877	Romania cooperates with Russia against the Ottomans
1880	Germany, France, and Britain recognise independent Romania
1881	Carol the First crowned King
1914	Ferdinand proclaimed King
1916	Romania declares war on Austria-Hungary
1916	Germans capture Bucharest
1918	Union of Transylvania, Bucovina, and Bessarabia with Romania
1927	Ferdinand dies; Michael, aged 6, becomes King and a Regency is established.
1930	Prince Carol's rights restored; he becomes King
1938-1940	Royal dictatorship; Romania declares neutrality
1940	Romania joins with Germany Northern Bucovina and Bessarabia seized by Soviets Carol II abdicates; Michael again becomes King
1944	Romania joins with Allies
1947	Michael abdicates; People's Republic proclaimed
1965	Ceauşescu becomes Party Secretary
1977	Earthquake hits Bucharest
1989	Overthrow of Communist Rule; Ceauşescus executed
1990	Democracy returns

Bibliography

Introduction

In researching previous accounts by English travellers of their journeys in Romania, my primary source was the British Library in London. Initially, it was a simple question of 'how long is a piece of string?' but, as time went by, the piece of string began to look like a multi-coloured telephone cable, with loose ends all over the place. To make sense of all these leads. I have classified them as follows:

The adventurers and mercenaries of the seventeenth and eighteenth centuries, e.g. Captain John Smith, William Lithgow, and the Earl of Crawford. I put Elisa Craven in this bracket since she was in reality an adventuress with a good address book! Their accounts are full of daring, living for the moment and never deterred by adversity.

The 'passers through' en route to or from Constantinople or Moscow, often with an embassy party like Chishull. The majority of eighteenth century and early nineteenth century travellers fall into this category, e.g. Bargrave, Father Avril, Jackson (from India), Neale, Macmichael, de Tott, Spencer (from the Caucasus). By the time they all returned to England, Romania had become a memory of just another 'odd' place and their recollections bizarre and wonderfully entertaining.

The first tourists who came purely to see Romania in the nineteenth century, e.g. James Ozanne, John Paget, Andrew Crosse, Mary Walker, motivated by a sense of adventure. This group were made of hardy stuff; travelling for the sake of adventure and curiosity was no picnic in those days, e.g. Mrs. Walker's ordeal of capsizing on a raft on the Bistriţa River. I see them as the pioneers of modern travel writing.

The 'codifiers' of the nineteenth century, a curious hybrid between travellers and information compilers, e.g. Thomas Thornton, James Skene,

Andrew Paton, Charles Boner, James Noyes, James Samuelson, William Curtis. Their accounts are admirably comprehensive, their reportage of journalistic standard.

Diplomats, soldiers, and their wives, e.g. William Wilkinson, Lady Mary Wortley Montagu, Emily Gerard, Dorothy Kennard, Ivor Porter. The 'Ladies' excel here with their keen observations and wit. They had the advantage of being on the inside track, moving in high circles and hence were able to get under the skin of their environment.

The journalists 'in country' like Rosie Waldeck and David Walker. Relatively late comers to Romania, their eyewitness writing skills really do get to the heart of what most see as inexplicable. *Athene Palace* is, for me, in a class of its own.

And with the advent of the motor car came the photographers, the 'royal watchers,' and travellers-in-comfort — De Windt, Hoppe, Hielscher, Heathcote, Baerlein, Newman, Martineau, Dagget, Patmore, and Sitwell. All these accounts are pacey and amusing, some rather superficial, e.g. Heathcote and Patmore. Queen Marie was undoubtedly the first royal media megastar, well ahead of her cousins in Britain, and she had quite a following. Her PR was exemplary! Sitwell, although party to this, produced a superb account of Romania which remains a benchmark for today's travellers.

Finally, I had to come up with a special category for Konrad Bercovici, Donald Hall, Patrick Leigh Fermor and Walter Starkie — so I call them the Romantics. They were all very different as personalities and so were their motivations. Yet they all shared an emotional commitment to Romania and its people. Some criticise them for looking at life through rose-tinted glasses. I disagree with this viewpoint of social reality, ' simply because in reading their work, one is aware of their straightforward and uncomplicated love for Romania and if love is not just a little bit blind, then it is not love.

Fiction writers were excluded although avidly read, e.g. Thomas Hope and Olivia Manning. *Smaranda* was too autobiographical to be fiction — maybe Lord Thomson could claim to have invented fiction!

The general bibliography, arranged alphabetically by author, includes texts on history, art, and biography. I have also included in it the post-1941 travel writers who have collectively so marvellously described today's Romania. At the end I have included some Constantinople-only titles that provide first-hand accounts of that city which exercised such an influence over Romania during her formative centuries.

On the Trail:[1]

The Gentlemen

Captain John Smith. *The True Travels and Adventures of Captain John Smith, 1593-1629.* London: T. Slater, 1630.

William Lithgow. *Rare Adventures and Painefull Peregrinations (1632).* Edited B.I. Lawrence. London: Jonathan Cape, 1928.

Robert Bargrave. *Narration of a Journey from Constantinople to Dunkirke.* London, 1652.

Father Avril. *Travels in Divers Parts of Europe and Asia... to discover a New Way by Land into China.* London: Tim. Goodwin, 1693.

Richard Pococke. *A Description of the East.* London, 1743.*

Edmund Chishull. *Travels in Turkey and Back 1698-1703.* London: W. Bowyer, 1747.

Lord Baltimore. *A Tour to the East in the Years 1763 and 1764.* London: W. Richardson and S. Clark, 1767.

John Lindsay. *Memoirs of the Life of the Late Rt. Hon. John, 20th Earl of Craufurd etc.* London: T. Becket, 1769 (Compiled by Richard Bolt 1753).

Socivizca. *The Life and Extraordinary Adventures of Captain Socivizca.* London: John Law, 1778.

Elias Habesci. *The Present State of the Ottoman Empire.* London, 1784.

Baron Francois De Tott. *Memoirs*. London: Jarvis, 1785.

Robert Townson. *Travels in Hungary in 1793.* London, 1797.

John Jackson. *Journey from India towards England in 1797.* London: T. Cadell, 1799.

Richard Phillips. *A Collection of Modern and Contemporary Voyages and Travels.* London, 1805.

Thomas Thornton. *Present State of the Turk.* London: Joseph Mawman, 1809

---

[1] The travel accounts are arranged chronologically.

* Indicates background on relations with Constantinople.

C.R. Cockerell. *Travels in Southern Europe and the Levant 1810-17.* London: Longmans, Green, & Co., 1903.*

Edward Clarke. *Travels in Various Countries.* London: T. Cadell & W. Davies, 1810-23.

John Hobhouse. *A Journey through Albania and Other Provinces of Turkey.* London: J. Cawthorn, 1813.

Adam Neale. *Travels through Some Parts of Germany, Poland, Moldavia, and Turkey.* London, 1818.

James Morier. *A Second Journey through Persia, Armenia, and Asia Minor to Constantinople.* London: Longman, Hurst, Rees, Orme and Brown, 1818.*

William Macmichael. *Journey from Moscow to Constantinople.* London: John Murray, 1819.

William Wilkinson. *Account of the Principalities of Wallachia and Moldavia.* London, 1820.

Sir Robert Ker Porter. *Travels in Georgia, etc.* London: Longman, Hurst, Rees, Orme and Brown, 1822.

Michael Quin. *A Steam Voyage down the Danube.* London, 1835.

Major Sir Grenville Temple. *Travels in Greece and Turkey.* London: Saunders & Oltley, 1836.*

Rev. Nathaniel Burton. *Pedestrian Journey from Constantinople etc.* Dublin: John Yates, 1838.

Edmund Spencer. *Travels in the Western Caucasus.* London, 1838.

Charles Elliott. *Travels in the Three Great Empires.* London, 1838.

John Paget. *Hungary and Transylvania.* London: John Murray, 1839.

Andrew Paton. *The Goth and the Hun.* London, 1851.

Anatoly Demidov. *Travels in Southern Russia and the Crimea in 1837.* London: John Mitchell, 1853.

James Skene. *The Frontier Lands of the Christian and the Turk.* London: Richard Bentley, 1853.

Lord de Ros. *Tour in the Crimea, etc.* London: John Parker, 1855.

Thomas Forester. *The Danube and the Black Sea.* London, 1857.

James O. Noyes. *Roumania, the Border Lands of the Christian and the Turk.* New York, 1858.

David Ansted. *A Short Trip to Hungary and Transylvania in the Spring of 1862.* London: W.H. Allen & Co, 1862.

Charles Boner. *Transylvania: its Products and its People.* London: Longmans & Co., 1865.

James Ozanne. *Three Years in Roumania.* London, 1878.

Andrew F. Crosse. *Round about the Carpathians.* Edinburgh and London: William Blackwood & Son, 1878.

Andrew Chalmers. *Transylvanian Recollections.* London: Smart & Allen, 1880.

James Samuelson. *Roumania, Past and Present.* London: Longman & Co., 1882.

A British Resident. *The Danubian Principalities.* London: Richard Bentley, 1884.

William James Tucker. *Life and Society in Eastern Europe.* London: Sampson. Low, Marston, Searle, and Rivington, 1886.

William Beatty-Kingston. *A Wanderer's Notes.* London: Chapman & Hall, 1888.

William Miller. *The Balkans (Story of the Nations).* London: T. Fisher Unwin, 1896.

Harry de Windt. *Through Savage Europe.* London: T. Fisher Unwin, 1907.

William Eleroy Curtis. *Around the Black Sea.* London and New York: Hodder & Stoughton, 1911.

William Le Queux. *The Balkan Trouble.* London: Eveleigh Nash, 1912.

G. Matarollo. *Letters from Roumania and Constantinople.* London: A.H. Stockwell, 1915.

John Reed. *The War in Eastern Europe.* New York: Charles Scribner's Sons, 1916. Chapter on Romania reprinted in John Reed, *Romania during World War I: Observations of an American Journalist,* Center for Romanian Studies, 2018.

Konrad Bercovici. *Love and the Gypsy.* London: E. Nash & Grayson, 1923.

Konrad Bercovici. *Singing Winds.* London: Jonathan Cape, 1927.

Konrad Bercovici. *The Story of the Gypsy.* New York: Cosmopolitan Book Corp., 1928.

Konrad Bercovici. *The Incredible Balkans.* New York: G.P. Putnam's Sons, 1932.

Emil Hoppe. *In Gipsy Camp and Royal Palace.* London: Methuen & Co., 1924.

Edward Herbert. *Roumania as I Found It: United Roumanian Jews of America.* New York, 1924.

Frank Rattigan. *Diversions of a Diplomat.* London: Chapman and Hall, 1924.

John Buchan. *Bulgaria and Romania.* London: The Waverley Book Co., 1925

Dudley Heathcote. *My Wanderings in the Balkans.* London: Hutchinson & Co., 1925.

Lord Thomson. *Smaranda.* London: Jonathan Cape, 1926.

Charles Upson Clark. *Bessarabia.* New York: Dodd, Mead & Co., 1927.

Hans Carossa. *A Roumanian Diary.* London: Martin Seeker, 1929.

Henry Baerlein. *And then to Transylvania.* London: Harold Shaylor, 1931.

Henry Baerlein. *Bessarabia and Beyond.* London: Methuen & Co., 1935.

Henry Baerlein. *In Old Romania.* London and Melbourne: Hutchinson & Co., Ltd., 1940

Henry Baerlein. *All Roads Lead to People.* London: Stanley Paul & Co., 1952.

George Hill. *Go Spy the Land.* London: Cassell & Co., 1932.

Walter Starkie. *Raggle Taggle.* London: John Murray, 1933.

Walter Starkie. *Scholars and Gypsies.* London: John Murray, 1963.

Kurt Hielscher. *Roumanie.* Leipzig, 1933.

Donald Hall. *Romanian Furrow.* London: Methuen & Co., 1933.

H.H. McWilliams. *The Diabolical.* London: Duckworth, 1934.

William Wegdwood Benn. *Beckoning Horizon.* London: Cassell & Co., 1935.

Bernard Newman. *The Blue Danube.* London: Herbert Jenkins, 1935.

David Footman. *Balkan Holiday.* London and Toronto: William Heinemann, 1935.

Beverley Nichols. *No Place like Home.* London: Jonathan Cape, 1936.

John McCulloch. *Drums in the Balkan Night.* New York: G.P. Putnam's Sons, 1936.

General Sir Tom Bridges. *Alarms and Excursions.* London: Longman, Green & Co., 1936.

Philip Thornton. *Dead Puppets Dance.* London: Collins, 1937.

Philip Thornton. *Ikons and Oxen.* London: Collins, 1939.

Sacherverell Sitwell. *Roumanian Journey.* London: B.T. Batsford, 1938.

R.H. Bruce Lockhart. *Guns of Butter.* London: Putman & Co., 1938.

Derek Patmore. *An Invitation to Roumania.* London: Macmillan & Co., 1939.

Hector Bolitho. *Roumania under King Carol.* London: Eyre & Spottiswoode, 1939.

Beverley Baxter, MP. *Men, Martyrs, and Mountebanks.* London: Hutchinson & Co., 1940.

Cedric Salter. *Flight from Poland.* London: Faber, 1940.

David Walker. *Death at My Heels.* London: Chapman & Hall, 1942.

Bickham Sweet Escolt. *Baker Street Irregular.* London: Methuen & Co., 1965.

Patrick Leigh Fermor. *Between the Woods and the Water.* London: John Murray, 1986.

Ivor Porter. *Operation Autonomous.* London: Chatto & Windus, 1988.

Gregor von Rezzori. *The Snows of Yesteryear.* London: Chatto & Windus, 1990.

Sir Stephen Runciman. *The Traveller's Alphabet.* London: Thames and Hudson, 1991.

The Ladies

Lady Mary Wortley Montagu. *Letters.* Dublin: P. Wilson, 1763.

Lady Craven. *A Journey through the Crimea to Constantinople.* London: G.G.J. and J. Robinson, 1789. (Broadley and Melville. *The Beautiful Lady Craven.* London: John Lane, 1914).

Georgina MacKenzie. *Across the Carpathians.* Cambridge and London: Macmillan & Co., 1862.

Mrs. Edward. *Missionary Life among the Jews of Moldavia, Galicia, and Silesia.* London: Hamilton, Adams & Co., 1867.

Mary Walker. *Untrodden Paths in Roumania.* London: Chapman & Hall, 1888.

Emily Gerard. *The Land beyond the Forests.* Edinburgh and London: W. Blackwood & Sons, 1888.

Carmen Sylva. *Legends from River and Mountain.* London: G. Allen, 1896.

Mary Durham. *Through the Lands of the Serb.* London: Edward Arnold, 1904.

Mrs. Lion Phillimore. *In the Carpathians.* London: Constable & Co., 1912.

Dorothy Kirke. *Domestic Life in Roumania.* London and New York: John Lane, 1916.

Dorothy Katherine Kennard. *A Roumanian Diary.* London: William Heinemann, 1917.

Winifred Gordon. *Roumania, Yesterday and Today.* London and New York: John Lane, 1918.

Yvonne Fitzroy. *With the Scottish Nurses in Roumania.* London: John Murray, 1918.

Ethel Greening Pantazzi. *Roumania in Light and Shadow.* London: T. Fisher Unwin, 1921.

Maude Parkinson. *Twenty Years in Roumania.* London: G. Allen & Unwin, 1921.

Rosamund Boultree. *Pilgrimages and Personalities.* London: Hutchinson & Co., 1924.

Mabel Daggett. *Marie of Roumania.* London: Brentano's, 1927.

Mrs. Philip (Lady Alice) Martineau. *Roumania and Her Rulers.* London: Stanley Paul & Co., 1927.

Gertrude Mendl. *Roumania Calling.* London: Lincoln Williams, 1933.

Elizabeth Kyle. *Mirrors of Versailles.* London: Constable & Co., 1939.

Margaret Loughborough. *Roumanian Pilgrimage.* London: SPCK, 1939.

Clare Hollingworth. *There's a German Just Behind Me.* London: Seeker and Warburg, 1942.

Countess Rosie G. Waldeck. *Athene Palace.* London: Constable, 1943. Second edition: Iaşi: The Center for Romanian Studies, 1998.

General Bibliography

Alcock, John & Antonia Young. *Black Lambs and Grey Falcons.* University of Bradford, 1991 (including Jennifer Finder's essay "Women Travellers in the Balkans 1991").

Anania, Valeriu *The Heavens of the Olt.* The Bishopric of Râmnic and Argeş, 1990.

Andrew, Christopher. *Secret Service.* London: William Heinemann, 1985.

Ascherson, Neal. *Black Sea.* London: Jonathan Cape, 1995.

Baedeker Guide to Austria and Hungary. Leipzig, 1911.

Baerlein, Henry, ed. *The Romanian Scene: Anthology on Romania and Her People by Writers in English.* London: Frederick Muller, 1945.

Baerlein, Henry, ed. *Romanian Oasis: A Further Anthology on Romania and Her People by Writers in English.* London: Frederick Muller, 1948.

Barca, Ana. *The Wooden Architecture of Maramureş.* Bucharest: Humanitas, 1997.

Baron, Petre. *Romania.* Bucharest: Editura Royal Company, 1998.

Benger, G. *Romania in 1900.* London: Asher & Co., 1900.

Bennett, Henry. *The Pastons and Their England.* Cambridge: University Press, 1922.

Beza, Marcu. *Roumanian Proverbs.* London: A.M. Philpot, 1921.

Beza, Marcu. *Paganism in Romanian Folklore.* London and Toronto: J.M. Dent & Sons, 1928.

Bibesco, Marthe, *Isvor, Land of Willows.* London: William Heinemann, 1924.

Bielz, Julius. *The Craft of Saxon Goldsmiths of Transylvania.* Bucharest: Foreign Languages Publishing House, 1957.

Blanche, Lesley. *Under a Lilac-Bleeding Star.* London: John Murray, 1963.

Brătuleanu, Anca. *Romanian Princely and Nobiliary Courts.* Bucharest: Simetria, 1997.

Burgoyne, Elizabeth. *Carmen Sylva.* London: Eyre & Spottiswoode, 1941.

Callimachi, Anne-Marie. *Yesterday was Mine.* London: Falcon Press, 1952.

Chappell, Jennie. *Women of Worth.* London: S.W. Partridge & Co., 1900.

Churchyarde, Thomas. *The First Bookes of Ovid's De Tristibus.* London: Thomas Marshe, 1572.

Cornish, Louis. *Transylvania, the Land beyond the Forest.* Philadelphia: Darrance & Co., 1947.

Cutara, Alexandru. *Timişoara.* Timişoara: Amarcord, 1998.

Dawson, Thresher. *The New Roumania.* London: Philip Reid, 1927.

Deichman, Baroness. *The Life of Carmen Sylva.* London: Kegan Paul, Trench, Trubner & Co., 1890.

Drysdale, Helena. *Looking for Gheorghe.* London: Sinclair-Stevenson, 1995.

Dumitriu, Petru. *The Prodigals.* London: Collins, 1962.

Dumitra, Petru. *Incognito.* London: Collins, 1964

Elsberry, Terence. *Marie of Romania.* London: Cassell, 1973.

Florescu, Radu R. *Essays on Romanian History. Iaşi*, Oxford, Portland: The Center for Romanian Studies, 1999.

Forbes, Rosita. *Gypsy in the Sun.* London: Cassell & Co., 1944.

Forter and Rostovsky. *The Roumanian Handbook.* London: Simpkin Marshall, 1931.

Fotescu, Diana, ed. *Americans and Queen Marie of Romania. Iaşi*: The Center for Romanian Studies, 1998.

Gardiner, Leslie. *Curtain Calls.* London: Duckworth, 1976.

Goldsworthy, Vesna. *Inventing Ruritania.* New Haven and London: Yale University, 1998.

Gorelik, Mikhael. *Warriors of Eurasia.* Stockport: Montvert Publications, 1995.

Hagemeister, Julius de. *Report on the Commerce of the Ports of New Russia, Moldavia, and Wallachia.* London: Effingham Wilson, 1836.

Hall, Brian. *Stealing from a Deep Place.* London: William Heinemann, 1988.

Hildinger, Erik. *Warriors of the Steppe.* Staplehurst: Spellmount, 1997.

Hoffman, Eva. *Exit into History.* London: William Heinemann, 1993.

Hope, Thomas. *Anastasius or Memoirs of a Greek.* London: John Murray, 1820.

Ileana, Princess of Romania. *I Live Again.* London: Victor Gollanz Ltd., 1952.

Iorga, Nicolae. *Roumania: Land, People, Civilisation.* London: T. Fisher Unwin, 1925.

Jones, Liane. *A Quiet Courage.* London: Bantam, 1990.

Kaplan, Robert D. *Balkan Ghosts.* New York: St. Martin's Press, 1993.

Kligman, Gail. *The Wedding of the Dead.* Berkeley, London: UCLA Press, 1988.

Latham, Ernest H., Jr. "Not all Happiness: Henry Baerlein and Bessarabia," pp. 115-133 in *American -Romanian Academy Journal: Journal of the American-Romanian Academy of Arts and Sciences* (19), 1994.

Lizst. Franz. *The Gypsy in Music.* Translated by E. Evans, 1926.

Maclean, Rory. *Stalin's Nose.* London: Harper Collins, 1992.

Magris, Claudio. *Danube: A Sentimental Journey from the Source to the Black Sea.* London: Collins Harvill, 1989.

De Makoldy. *Pictures of Transylvania.* Budapest: Victor Hornyanszky, 1920. '

Malcomson, Scott. *Empire's Edge.* London: Faber and Faber, 1994.

Mansel, Philip. *Constantinople.* London: John Murray, 1995.

Marie, Queen of Romania. *The Story of My Life.* London: Cassell & Co., 1934.

Massie, Robert. *Nicholas and Alexandra.* London: Victor Gollanez, 1968.

McNally, Raymond and Radu R. Florescu. *In Search of Dracula.* London: New English Library, 1975.

Munţii Carpaţi. Sibiu: Editura Thausib, 1997.

Murphy, Dervla. *Transylvania and Beyond.* London: John Murray, 1992.

Nicolle, David *Hungary and the Fall of Eastern Europe 1000-1568.* London: Osprey, 1988.

Norwich, John Julius. *A Short History of Byzantium.* London: Viking, 1997.

O'Conner, Peter. *Walking Good.* London: Weidenfeld and Nicolson, 1971.

Onasch and Schnieper. *Icons, the Fascination and the Reality.* 1995.

Oprescu, George. *N. Grigoresco.* Bucharest, 1961.

Owen, Sydney. *Ovid's Tristia.* Oxford: Clarendon Press Series, 1885-1893.

Pakula, Hannah. *Queen of Roumania.* New York: Simon and Schuster, 1984.

Pope-Henessy, James. *Queen Mary.* London: George Allen & Unwin, 1959.

Ramm, Agatha. *Europe in the Twentieth Century.* London: Longman Group, 1984.

Ramos-Poqui, Guillem. *Techniques of Icon Painting.* Kent: Search Press, 1990.

Rothschild, Joseph. *East Central Europe between the Two World Wars.* Seattle and London: University of Washington Press, 1974.

St. John, Robert. *Foreign Correspondent.* London: Hutchinson, 1960

Seton-Watson, Robert W. *History of the Roumanians.* Cambridge: University Press, 1934.

Simpkins, Michael. *The Roman Army from Caesar to Trajan.* London: Osprey, 1984.

Smith, William Bradford. *Captain John Smith, His Life and Legend.* Philadelphia: Lippincott Co., 1953.

Stanley, The Hon. Henry. *Rouman Anthology.* Hertford: Stephen Austin, 1856.

Ştefănescu, Aristide. *Bucharest: 'The Thirties.* Bucharest: NOI Publishers, 1995.

Stratilesco, Tereza. *From Carpathian to Pindus, Pictures of Roumanian Country Life.* London: T. Fisher Unwin, 1906.

Sugar, Peter. *Southeastern Europe under Ottoman Rule, 1354-1804.* Seattle and London: University of Washington Press, 1977.

Sutherland, Christina. *Enchantress.* London: John Murray, 1996.

Swain, Geoffrey. *Eastern Europe since 1945.* London: The Macmillan Press, 1993.

Talbot-Rice, Tamara. *Icons, Art and Devotion.* London: Random House, 1993.

Temple, Richard. *Icons and the Mystical Origins of Christianity.* Shaftsbury: Element, 1990.

Theodorescu, Răzvan. *Bucovina.* Bucharest: UNESCO/Athena Publishing, 1994.

Treptow, Kurt W. *A History of Romania. Iaşi*: The Center for Romanian Studies, 1997.

Treptow, Kurt W. *Vlad III Dracula: The Life and Times of the Historical Dracula.* Second edition. Las Vegas: Center for Romanian Studies, 2020. First edition. Iaşi, Oxford, Portland: The Center for Romanian Studies, 2000.

Trumper, Isabel. *A Song of Roumania and Other Short Poems.* London: H. & W. Brown, 1924.

Wheatcroft, Andrew. *The Ottomans.* London: Viking, 1993.

Wilcox, Peter. *Rome's Enemies.* London: Osprey, 1982.

Zderciuc, Boris. *The Hand-Woven Rugs of Maramureş.* Bucharest, 1963.

Note on the Pronunciation of Romanian Words

This note is intended to give readers who are unfamiliar with the Romanian language some idea of the proper pronunciation of the Romanian works which appear in this book. Romanian orthography is almost entirely phonetical, a letter representing one and the same sound, in all positions, with few exception. Here are the letters of the Romanian alphabet and their pronunciation.

a — as a in *half* but shorter.

ă — as er in *father.*

â — similar to e in *morsel* or u in *sullen.*

b — as b in *baseball.*

c — before consonants, the vowels a, ă, â, î, o, u and at the end of the words, as c in *cat.* Before e and i, as ch in *cherry.*

d — as d in *dog.*

e — as *e* in *pen.*

f— as f in *fire.*

g — before consonants, the vowels a, ă, â, î, o, u and at the end of the words, as g in *got.* Before e and i, as g in *general.*

h — as h in *behind.* In groups che, chi, ghe, ghi, it is mute, showing that c and g preserve their hard sound.

i — as ee in *see.*

î — similar to e in *morsel* or u in *sullen.* Same as â.

j — as s in *measure.*

k — as k in *kite*

l — as l in *like.*

m — as m in *mother.*

n — as n in *neither.*

o — as o in *comb.*

p — as p in *police.*

r — similar to a rolled Scottish r.

s — as s in *sand.*

ş — as sh in *ship.*

t — as t in *toil.*

ţ — as ts in *cats.*

u — as u in *glue.*

v — as v in *valley.*

x — as x in *excellent.*

z. — as z in *zebra.*

Index

D

E

I

J

K

N

T

X

Y

Z